Heideggerian Marxism

Heideggerian Marxism

Herbert Marcuse

Edited by
Richard Wolin and John Abromeit

UNIVERSITY OF NEBRASKA PRESS
LINCOLN AND LONDON

The essays of Herbert Marcuse contained in this volume
are reprinted with the permission of the Literary Estate of Herbert Marcuse
Peter Marcuse, executor.
Supplementary material from previously unpublished work of Herbert Marcuse,
much now in the archives of the Johann Wolfgang Goethe University
Frankfurt am Main,
is being published by Routledge in a six-volume series edited by Douglas Kellner.
All rights to further publication of this material are retained by the estate.

"Heidegger's Politics: An Interview with Herbert Marcuse" is reprinted
with the permission of the *Graduate Faculty Philosophy Journal*.

Set in Garamond.
Designed by R. W. Boeche.

Library of Congress Cataloging-in-Publication Data
Marcuse, Herbert, 1898–
Heideggerian Marxism / Herbert Marcuse ;
edited by Richard Wolin and John Abromeit.
p. cm. – (European horizons)
Includes bibliographical references and (p.) index.
ISBN-13: 978-0-8032-8312-1 (pbk. : alk. paper)
ISBN-10: 0-8032-8312-1 (pbk. : alk. paper)
1. Heidegger, Martin, 1889–1976. 2. Historical materialism.
3. Dialectical materialism. 4. Socialism. 5. Communism.
I. Wolin, Richard. II. Abromeit, John, 1970– III. Title. IV. Series.
B3279.H49M2732 2005
191–dc22
2005012975

For Martin Jay
In honor of his sixtieth birthday

Contents

Preface

The idea for this volume evolved from a remarkable 1998 conference held at the University of California, Berkeley, and organized by John Abromeit and W. Mark Cobb in honor of Herbert Marcuse's centennial.

For the 1960s generation, Marcuse was a towering figure—living proof that the so-called generation gap was, in large measure, a mass media fabrication. Unlike his Frankfurter School *compagnons de route*, Max Horkheimer and Theodor Adorno, Marcuse remained remarkably open and receptive to contemporary political developments. Horkheimer and Adorno's skepticism vis-à-vis the student movement resulted from their critical assessment of Bolshevism as a potent and insidious form of political domination. Their assessment was consistent with the criticisms of the so-called left communists such as Anton Pannekoek, Hermann Görter, and Rosa Luxemburg. But their views were also conditioned by Germany's vulnerable geopolitical position on the front lines of the cold war. Marcuse, conversely, had witnessed firsthand the political evils of McCarthyism, followed by America's grotesque military build-up in Vietnam, in which the horrors of modern war—napalm and massive, indiscriminate aerial bombardment—seemingly knew no bounds.

At the Berkeley conference, it was clear that John Abromeit and I shared a profound interest in German philosophy of the 1920s, whose high points were undoubtedly Georg Lukács's *History and Class Consciousness* (1923) and Martin Heidegger's *Being and Time* (1927). What made Marcuse's intellectual itinerary so unique was that, at a remarkably young age, he attempted a landmark synthesis of both traditions: Hegelian Marxism and existential ontology. Moreover, both John and I felt strongly that Marcuse's contributions were not of merely "historical" value. Instead, we believed that his efforts to combine these two orientations helped to shed important light on problems of the philosophical-political present.

The volume took longer than anticipated to bring to completion. During the late 1920s and 1930s, Marcuse adopted a hybrid, existential Marxist idiom that places peculiar demands on English-speaking readers. Consequently, we felt that our primary responsibility was to ensure that the texts in question appeared in a lucid and accessible English, while at the same time preserving the conceptual rigor of Marcuse's philosophical and theoretical arguments.

Publication of *Heideggerian Marxism* would not have been possible were it not for the solidarity and assistance of a number of individuals. Above all, we would like to thank Herbert Marcuse's son, Peter, for his willingness to grant rights and permissions in his capacity as executor of his father's literary estate. We would also like to publicly acknowledge the efforts of the translators: Ron Haas, Eric Oberle, Matthew Erlin, and John Abromeit. Without their dedication and tenacity, the volume would never have come to fruition. We would also like to thank our editor at the University of Nebraska Press, M. J. Devaney for her keen editorial discernment and consistent enthusiasm for the project.

Allow me to conclude on a personal note. During the 1970s, I had the good fortune to meet Herbert Marcuse on several occasions—in San Diego, Toronto, and Berkeley. No one who met him could fail to be impressed by his humanity, his playfulness, and his generosity of spirit. In so many respects, he was a modern embodiment of the proverbial Aristotelian "great-souled individual." Our conversations—though they were few—remain permanently etched in my memory. Publishing this collection of his early philosophical writings is a modest way of acknowledging an intellectual and personal debt that I could never hope to repay in full.

Lastly, John Abromeit and I would like to dedicate this volume to the man who has perhaps done more than anyone else to promote international interest in the Frankfurt School legacy: Martin Jay. To me, Marty has been a mentor, friend, confidante, and critic. His generosity and open-mindedness are matchless. We have known each other now for nearly twenty-five years. May our friendship last at least another twenty-five.

Richard Wolin
New York

Introduction

What Is Heideggerian Marxism?

Richard Wolin

The relatively late and then very rapid reception of Marcuse's work has allowed a historically inaccurate image of him to emerge: the older strata of his development remain unrecognizable. Marcuse's 1932 book, Hegel's Ontology, *remains essentially unknown. I suppose that one would find few among Marcuse's contemporary readers who would not be completely surprised by the Introduction's concluding sentence:* "Any contribution this work may make to the development and clarification of problems is indebted to the philosophical work of Martin Heidegger." *I don't know what Marcuse thinks about this sentence today; we have never spoken about it. But I think that phase of his development was not simply a whim. Indeed, I believe that it is impossible to correctly understand the Marcuse of today without reference to this earlier Marcuse. Whoever fails to detect the persistence of categories from* Being and Time *in the concepts of Freudian drive theory out of which Marcuse [in* Eros and Civilization*] develops a Marxian historical construct runs the risk of serious misunderstandings.*

Jürgen Habermas (1968)

Since Habermas first wrote these words some thirty-five years ago, more information concerning Marcuse's youthful Heideggerian allegiances has come to light. But confusions and misunderstandings persist. By collecting the philosopher's early, proto-Heideggerian writings in one volume, we hope to shed additional light on what remains a fascinating and underresearched chapter of twentieth-century intellectual life: an encounter between two schools of thought—philosophical Marxism and fundamental ontology—that soon proceeded in opposite directions.

In retrospect it is clear that Marcuse's political worldview was shaped by the key events of his youth: the traumas of world war and, above all, the failure of the German Revolution of 1918–19. At the age of twenty Marcuse was elected as a Social Democratic deputy to one of the Soldier's and Worker's Councils that mushroomed throughout Germany during the climax of World War I. He resigned, he later claimed, when he noticed that former officers were being elected to the same bodies. He bid an unsentimental farewell to Social Democratic politics following the vicious murders of Spartakus Bund leaders Rosa Luxemburg and Karl Liebknecht by Freikorps troops acting at the behest of the newly installed Social Democratic government in January 1919.[1]

During the early years of the Weimar Republic Marcuse underwent a type of self-imposed "inner emigration." After completing a dissertation in 1922 on the German artist novel, which was heavily influenced by the early aesthetics of Georg Lukács, he returned to his native Berlin to work in an antiquarian book-shop.[2] During this time, he compiled a detailed Schiller bibliography, steeped himself in the early Marx, and read two classic texts of Hegelian Marxism that would have a profound influence on his future philosophical develop-ment: Lukács's *History and Class Consciousness* and Karl Korsch's *Marxism and Philosophy*, both of which had appeared in 1923.

Later in the decade there occurred a publication "event" that lured Marcuse back to the university: the 1927 appearance of Heidegger's *Being and Time*. At the time Germany's philosophy seminars were still dominated by staid and fa-miliar prewar approaches: neo-Kantianism, neo-Hegelianism, and positivism. For the younger generation, however, the horrors of World War I represented a point of no return: the worldviews and perspectives that had predominated prior to 1914 seemed entirely delegitimated. As Marcuse noted time and again, Heidegger's thought seemed to offer something that the conventional academic "school philosophies" lacked: a "philosophy of the *concrete*." Reflecting some fifty years later on the excitement generated by the publication of *Being and Time*, Marcuse observed "To me and my friends, Heidegger's work appeared as a new beginning: we experienced his book [*Being and Time*] (and his lectures, whose transcripts we obtained) as, at long last, a *concrete* philosophy: here there was talk of existence [*Existenz*], of *our* existence, of fear and care and boredom, and so forth. We also experienced an 'academic' emancipation: Heidegger's interpretation of Greek philosophy and German idealism, which offered us new insights into antiquated, fossilized texts."[3]

Marcuse's testimony concerning Heidegger's pedagogical prowess conforms with that of the philosopher's other prominent students during the 1920s: Hannah Arendt, Hans-Georg Gadamer, Hans Jonas, and Karl Löwith.[4] All five affirmed that what they found unique in Heidegger's approach was his capacity to revivify antiquated philosophical texts in light of present historical needs and concerns. The leitmotif of Heidegger's courses seemed to be Augustine's *mea res agitur*: "my life is at stake"; in them, doing philosophy ceased to be an exercise in disembodied, scholarly exegesis. At issue was a momentous, hermeneutical encounter between the historical past and the contemporary being-in-the-world. By proceeding thusly, Heidegger was only being self-consistent: he was merely applying the principles of his own philosophy of *Existenz* to the subject matter of his lectures and seminars. Two of the central categories of *Being and Time*'s "existential analytic" were "temporality" and "historicity." Both notions addressed the way that we situate ourselves in time and history. In Heidegger's view, one of the hallmarks of "authentic" being-in-the-world was a capacity to *actualize* the past in light of essential future possibilities. Conversely, inauthentic Dasein (*das Man*) displayed a conformist willingness to adapt passively to circumstances—an existential lassitude that bore marked resemblances to the inert being of "things." Heidegger's ability to fuse the discourse of "everydayness" with the demands of "rigorous science" he had imbibed during his youthful apprenticeship with the founder of the phenomenological movement, Edmund Husserl, distinguished his thinking from the *Lebensphilosophie* or "philosophy of life" that flourished among popular writers (e.g., Oswald Spengler and Ludwig Klages) at the time. Thus, in view of the conservative approaches to scholarship that predominated among the German mandarin professorate during the 1920s, one can readily imagine the genuine excitement Heidegger's philosophical radicalism must have generated, especially among the "lost generation" of the postwar period.[5]

In a colorful 1929 letter, Marcuse described his initial impressions of Heidegger (whom he recalled from his previous stay in Freiburg as a PhD student in the early 1920s) as follows:

> Concerning Heidegger: it is hard to imagine a greater difference between the shy and obstinate *Privatdozent* who eight years ago spoke from the window of a small lecture hall and the successor to Husserl who lectures in an overflowing auditorium with at least six hundred listeners (mostly women) in brilliant lectures with unshakeable certainty, talking with that pleasant tremor in his voice which so excites the women, dressed in a sports outfit that almost looks like a chauffeur's uniform, darkly tanned, with the pathos of a teacher who feels himself completely to be an educator, a prophet and pathfinder and whom one indeed believes to be so. The ethical tendencies found in

Being and Time—which aim at philosophy becoming practical—really seem
to achieve a breakthrough in Heidegger himself, although, to be sure, in a way
that is somewhat alienating. He is all in all too rhetorical, too preachy, too
primitive. . . . In the large lecture on German idealism and the philosophical
problems of the present he has so far treated the dominant tendencies of
contemporary philosophy as anthropological tendencies and metaphysics.[6]

Part of Marcuse's attraction to Heidegger's brand of *Existenzphilosophie* was
spurred by the so-called "crisis of Marxism." For Marcuse's generation hopes
for a radical regeneration of the existing political order—one which seemed
responsible for so much pointless social suffering and injustice—were rudely
dashed with the collapse of the short-lived Council Republics (*Räterepublik*) in
Bavaria and Hungary following World War I. In his eyes, by brutally crushing
the German Revolution, social democracy had merely compounded its sins
of August 1914, when, by voting for war credits, it had forsaken the ideals of
international socialism in favor of jingoistic militarism. Moreover, it is safe
to assume that the Bolshevik Revolution of 1917 harbored few attractions for
him. Marcuse undoubtedly accepted Rosa Luxemburg's trenchant critique of
the authoritarian implications of Lenin's vanguardism.[7] In fact, most European
socialists viewed Lenin's voluntarism as inappropriate for Western and Central
Europe, where a more advanced and experienced proletariat existed.

Yet, concomitant with the *political* crisis of Marxism, there existed an *epis-temological* crisis; in Marcuse's view, the two were necessarily linked. For under
the tutelage of Engels and Karl Kautsky, the Second International had espoused
a resolutely antiphilosophical, mechanistic interpretation of Marxism. This ap-proach was predicated on an unreflective scientism (see Engels's *The Dialectics
of Nature*) as well as an antiquated theory of capitalism's automatic collapse.[8]
Correspondingly, its leading theoreticians displayed a willful indifference to
the "subjective" factor of working-class consciousness. Conversely, it was a
willingness to address such questions directly and unapologetically that made
Lukács's *History and Class Consciousness* seem so refreshing—it stood as a beacon
of illumination in the midst of a bleak intellectual and political landscape.

Thus, Marcuse believed that Heidegger's *Being and Time* represented a po-tentially valuable ally in the struggle against the reified social continuum of
advanced industrial society. He conjectured that Heidegger's philosophy of
existence possessed the conceptual means required to counteract an inverted
social world in which, according to Marx, "social relations between men as-sume . . . *the fantastic form of a relation between things.*"[9] In part, Marcuse

read Heidegger's philosophy as an ontologically veiled *critique of reification*: an indictment of the way in which oppressive social circumstances militate against the possibility human self-realization. It seemed that, like the critical Marxists Lukács and Korsch, Heidegger strove to surmount the fetishization of appearances that characterized the shadow-world of bourgeois immediacy. Like Lukács and Korsch, in *Being and Time* Heidegger strove concertedly to break with the deterministic worldview of bourgeois science, in which human being or Dasein was degraded to the status of a "thing among things." After all, this was the main point behind Heidegger's critique of *Vorhandenheit* or being present-at-hand as a mode of inauthenticity.[10] In Marcuse's view, the critique of "everydayness" in *Being and Time*, division 1, in which Heidegger delivers a powerful indictment of inauthentic being-in-the-world via recourse to concepts such as "falling," "idle talk," "publicness," and "the they," represents a welcome ontological complement to the discussions of reification in *Capital* and *History and Class Consciousness*. As Marcuse formulates this insight in "On Concrete Philosophy":

> The world in which this Dasein lives is also evolving to an ever greater degree into "business" [*Betrieb*]. The things encountered in it are viewed from the outset as "goods," as things that one must use, but not in the sense of using them to meet the needs of Dasein. Instead, they are used to occupy or to fill an otherwise aimless existence, until they actually do become "necessities." In this way more and more existences are consumed simply in order to keep the "business" operational. The form of existence of all classes had to hollow itself out in such a way that it has become necessary to place existence itself on a new foundation.[11]

By proceeding positivistically, contemporary social science fetishized the standpoint of the "object" or "things." Methodologically speaking, it treated "persons" like "things"—as objects of administrative manipulation and control. The breakthrough achieved by Heidegger's philosophy of existence was that, proceeding from the standpoint of Dasein, it placed human reality rather than "objectivity" or "thinghood" at the center of its phenomenological perspective. It was this practice that provided it with the conceptual leverage to overcome the reifying orientation of traditional science.[12] As Marcuse explains:

> The ontological historicity of Dasein must . . . assume decisive significance for the methodology of the "social sciences." Social arrangements, economic orders, and political formations together constitute the happening of Dasein and must be viewed from the perspective of this existence [*Existenz*]. If they

are investigated from the outset as "things," with an eye toward their structure, their relationships, and the laws of their development, the observations (most likely undertaken with the model of the natural sciences as their mistaken ideal) that result will be such that the meaning of these constructs cannot even appear. ("On Concrete Philosophy," 39)

In the "Theses on Feuerbach" (1845) Marx had praised Hegel for having developed the "active side" of the dialectic, a dimension unknown both to the materialism of the high Enlightenment as well as nineteenth-century positivism. "The chief defect of all hitherto existing materialism—that of Feuerbach included—is that the thing, reality, sensuousness, is conceived only in the form of the object or of *contemplation*, but not as human sensuous activity, practice, not subjectively. Hence it happened that the active side, in contradistinction to materialism, was developed by idealism (but only abstractly, since, of course, idealism does not know real, sensuous activity as such)."[13] That Heidegger, whose existential ontology seemed to be motivated by an analogous antiscientific animus, could be enlisted as fellow traveler in the Hegelian Marxist cause was the wager that Marcuse laid in 1928 when, as a twenty-nine-year-old, he followed Heidegger to Freiburg. At the time, Marcuse optimistically described the potential of Heidegger's 1927 masterwork as follows: "*Being and Time . . .* seems to represent a *turning point in the history of philosophy*: the point at which bourgeois philosophy unmakes itself from the inside and clears the way for a new and 'concrete' science."[14]

Marcuse was also favorably impressed by the Freiburg sage's efforts to break with the paradigm of German idealism. The "transcendence of German idealism": here was a project that seemed to unite Heidegger's existentialism and Marxism in a common cause. In keeping with the spirit of the age, thinkers in the second half of the nineteenth century transformed neo-Kantianism into an epistemological vindication of philosophy of science or positivism.[15] The noumenal dimension of Kant's ethics—for example, the regulative idea of humanity as a "kingdom of ends"—had been banished as an atavistic, metaphysical excrescence. From the standpoint of a young philosopher in the 1920s, it seemed impossible to redeem Kant as a genuine critic of the historical present. A similar fate of terminal irrelevance had apparently befallen Hegel's system. For it seemed that, with the exception of Dilthey's work, Hegel scholarship had degenerated into a type of neoscholasticism—an incessant, abstract clarification of the Master's impressive conceptual edifice as propounded in the *Science of Logic* and other works.[16] Since a critical thematization of "lived experience" played such a prominent role in Heidegger's fundamental ontology, at the time Marcuse surmised that it might provide the philosophical stimulus necessary to revivify an orthodox Marxist discourse that had lapsed into advanced senescence.

Marxism tried to diagnose the "objective," economic preconditions of capitalism's collapse, but it seemed to neglect the "subjective" side of the equation, working-class consciousness. Conversely, whereas Heidegger's philosophy excelled at describing the phenomenological structure of being-in-the-world, its weakness lay in its incapacity to address those aspects of the contemporary crisis that were *social* and *historical* as opposed to *timeless* and *ontological*. A careful perusal of Marcuse's writings from 1928–32 shows that his major reservation about Heidegger's thought concerned its capacity to descend from the rarefied heights of fundamental ontology in order to address matters of contemporary social and historical relevance. In other words: did the *Existenzialien* or basic concepts of *Being and Time* facilitate the tasks of concrete social analysis or were they, conversely, an ontological subterfuge?

In the "Theses on Feuerbach" Marx famously observed: "The question whether objective truth can be attributed to human thinking is not a question of theory but is a *practical* question. Man must prove the truth, that is, the reality and power, the this-sidedness of his thinking in practice. The dispute over the reality or non-reality of thinking which is isolated from practice is a purely *scholastic* question" (144). In a parallel vein, *Being and Time*'s existential analytic commenced with Dasein immersed in a series of practical involvements: everydayness, tools, concern, moods, being-with-others and, lastly, historicity. At the time Marcuse imagined, far from implausibly, that the two methodological approaches, both of which sought to transcend the ethereal claims of German idealism in a worldly and practical direction, could be viewed as mutual complements. In his 1929 essay, "On Concrete Philosophy," Marcuse makes it quite clear why he believed *Existenzphilosophie* was uniquely relevant to the practical crises confronting humanity:

> If the meaning of philosophizing is the making visible of truth, and if this truth has a fundamentally existential character, then not only is philosophizing a mode of human existing, but philosophy itself is, according to its very meaning, existential. . . . Authentic philosophizing refuses to remain at the stage of knowledge; rather, in driving this knowledge on to truth it strives for the concrete appropriation of that truth through human Dasein. Care [*Sorge*]

for human existence and its truth makes philosophy a "practical science" in the deepest sense, and it also leads philosophy—and this is the crucial point—into the concrete distress [*Bedrängnis*] of human existence. (36)

In Marcuse's eyes, Heidegger's orientational breakthrough derived from the fact that in his thought, "philosophy is once again seen from the standpoint of concrete human existence and is interrogated with concrete human existence as its end" (37).

Part of Marcuse's attraction to Heidegger stemmed from his frustrations with the limitations of bourgeois "inwardness" (*Innerlichkeit*)—so pronounced in the tradition of German idealism—and his corresponding sympathies for the concepts of "action" and "life" that were so current during the 1920s. He therefore harbored a certain admiration for the "activist" components of existential ontology, in which "decisiveness" or "resolve" (*Entschlossenheit*) was one of the hallmarks of authenticity.

Similarly, in the 1930 habilitation study (or second dissertation) that Marcuse wrote under Heidegger's supervision, published two years later as *Hegel's Ontology and the Theory of Historicity*, the concept of "life" plays a key role. "Life" refers to the dimension of practical-experiential immediacy that, as a rule, is shunned by the contemplative and intellectualized orientation of bourgeois thought.[17] As Marcuse observes: "The 'we-like' process of Life, the confrontation through which reciprocal 'recognition' is actualized, is thus characterized by an 'act' [*Tun*]. Life fulfills its ontological meaning as well as its universal substantiality, that is, the bringing-to-truth and letting-be of all beings, only through the accomplishment of an *act*, through the concrete actual confrontation with itself and the world."[18] Undoubtedly, Marcuse felt that an infusion of "actionist" sentiment might awaken the proletariat from its narcoleptic torpor. Hence, in the passages from these early texts in which Marxian and existentialist notions are most intimately fused, Marcuse treats the proletariat both as the answer to the inequities of capitalism as well as the solution to the (Heideggerian) problem of "authenticity":

Knowledge of one's own historicity and consciously historical existence becomes possible at the moment when existence breaks through reification. . . . Reified objectivities are things that historically come to be in that they have been objects of provisioning by a Dasein living among them. . . . Bourgeois philosophy must, according to its rootedness in being in bourgeois society, insist on the Dasein—independent objectivity of the environment—or alternatively, in those cases where it did maintain that the world is constituted in Dasein, it needed to contain this constitution within the immanence of consciousness. . . . [But] there is a Dasein whose thrownness consists precisely in the overcoming of its thrownness. *The historical act is only possible today as the act of the proletariat because it is the only Dasein within whose existence the act is necessarily given.*[19] ("Contributions," 32; emphasis added)

But undoubtedly the Heideggerian concept that most appealed to Marcuse during the late 1920s was "historicity." As Marcuse observes in "Contributions to a Phenomenology of Historical Materialism": "It is precisely knowledge of historicity that leads to the most momentous decision: the decision either to struggle for the recognized necessity, even against Dasein's own inherited existence" (23). In division 2 of *Being and Time*, Heidegger abruptly shifted from adopting the standpoint of a highly individualized, Kierkegaardian Dasein, reminiscent of *Fear and Trembling*'s Knight of Faith, to adopting the perspective of a *historical collectivity*. Under Dilthey's influence, the categorical framework of division 1 was drastically altered through the employment of concepts such as "destiny," "community," "generation," and "the historical life of a people" (*Volk*).[20] In Marcuse's view it seemed clear that "historicity" represented the essential link between existentialism and historical materialism.

In *The Formation of the Historical World in the Human Sciences*, Dilthey had stressed the importance of *Erlebnis*—"lived experience"—as a response to the "crisis of historicism": the nineteenth-century understanding of history qua positive science. For if in the guise of historicism history writing strove to capture the past "the way it really was" (Ranke), it remained incapable of providing orientation or directives for the historical present. According to Dilthey, "historicity" meant not only that all life was historically determined, but that it was in essence "meaningfully" structured in a way that facilitated hermeneutic understanding across generations. Thus, history qua "historicity" represented a reservoir of interpretive meaning that transcended the soulless, positivist accumulation of data by traditional history writing (*Historie*).

But it was left to Heidegger in *Being and Time* to take the final step in the development of the concept. Whereas Dilthey stressed the fact that life, qua historicity, was *in* history, Heidegger emphasized that *existence was itself historical*: the past yielded traditions on which peoples and individuals could *act* in view of future possibilities. As such "futurity" (*Zukunftigkeit*) became historicity's distinguishing feature. In this way, Heidegger imparted an *activist* component to historicity—historicity as a mode of authentic collective becoming—that remained occluded in Dilthey's formulations. As Heidegger remarks, "history as *Geschichte* signifies a happening [*Geschehen*] that we ourselves are, where we are there present. . . . We are history, that is, our own past. Our future lives out of its past."[21] Thus, in Heidegger's optic, historicity ceased to be a category of contemplative, scholarly understanding. Instead, it became a virtual call to arms, a summons to authentic ontological engagement.

At the same time it is clear that Marcuse never identified with *Existenzphiloso-phie* uncritically or naively. In the essays that follow, time and again, he openly ponders whether Heidegger's ontological standpoint can be reconciled with the genuinely historical concerns of critical Marxism. As he demonstratively opines in "Contributions to a Phenomenology of Historical Materialism": "We therefore demand . . . that the phenomenology of human Dasein initiated by Heidegger forge onward, coming to completion in a phenomenology of concrete Dasein and the concrete historical action demanded by history in each historical situation" (20). In the back of his mind there seemed constantly to lurk a troubling question: were Heidegger's efforts to produce a "philosophy of the concrete" genuine or did they merely culminate in an alluring yet deceptive "pseudo-concreteness"? For if the state of "alienation" (or "inauthentic Dasein") described by existential ontology were perceived as a timeless and unalterable *condition humaine*, there would be no real incentive to practically redress it. Instead, it would represent an inevitable destiny we would be powerless to emend. As Marcuse observes:

> Now in order to even be able to approach Dasein, in order to be able to take hold of it in its existence, concrete philosophy must *become historical*, it must insert itself into the concrete historical situation. The becoming historical of philosophy means, firstly, that concrete philosophy has to investigate contemporaneous Dasein in its historical situation, with an eye toward which possibilities for the appropriation of truths are available. . . .
>
> Concrete philosophy can thus only approach existence if it seeks out Dasein in the sphere in which its existence is based: as it *acts* in its world in accordance with its historical situation. ("On Concrete Philosophy," 44, 47)

Marcuse's early essays make it unmistakably clear that *capitalism*—imperialism, finance capital, monopolies, cartels, and so forth—was the social formation that determined the nature of contemporary politics and society. In his view, in order to become "concrete," philosophy at some point would need to address these problems and themes. After a prolonged philosophical apprenticeship under Heidegger's tutelage (1928–32), during which time he completed the aforementioned habilitation study, Marcuse concludecd that Heidegger's approach was incapable of making the transition from the "ontological" to the "ontic" (or historical) plane of analysis. In other words, fundamental ontology's original existential promise remained unfilled: it provided only a "pseudo-concreteness." In a 1974 interview, Marcuse reflects on the reasons underlying his ultimate disillusionment with Heideggerianism:

> I first, like all the others, believed there could be some combination between existentialism and Marxism, precisely because of their insistence on concrete analysis of the actual human existence, human beings, and their world. But I soon realized that Heidegger's concreteness was to a great extent a phony, a false concreteness, and that in fact his philosophy was just as abstract and just as removed from reality, even avoiding reality, as the philosophies which at that time had dominated German universities, namely a rather dry brand of neo-Kantianism, neo-Hegelianism, neo-idealism, but also positivism. [22]

One aspect of Heidegger's philosophy that, early on, raised suspicions in Marcuse's mind was the metaphysical orientation his thought assumed following the appearance of *Being and Time*. In Heidegger's subsequent writings— "What is Metaphysics?" *Kant and the Problem of Metaphysics*, and *The Essence of Reasons*—it seemed that instead of turning toward problems of lived experience, his thought became increasingly ethereal and unworldly. What differentiated his thought from the traditional contemplative ideal of *philosophia perennis* became difficult to specify. Indeed, circa 1930, with the celebrated "Turn" (*Kehre*) in his thinking, Heidegger's philosophy seemed to abandon the existential concerns that had occupied center stage in *Being and Time*. He increasingly gravitated toward a more hermetic, self-referential, ontological focus in which the "history of being" (*Seinsgeschichte*) took precedence over the paltry pursuits of Dasein. Ironically, as his philosophy became more attuned to the primordial "sendings of being" (*Seinsgeschick*), Heidegger personally became embroiled in a series of compromising political involvements on behalf of the twentieth century's most murderous political dictatorship: Hitler's Third Reich. [23]

The circumstances surrounding Marcuse's failure to habilitate under Heidegger with his study of *Hegel's Ontology* are still ambiguous. Moreover, it seems that, later on, Marcuse himself provided conflicting accounts of what actually transpired. To some, he claimed that Heidegger had never read the work; to others, he maintained that Heidegger had refused to accept it. [24] The most likely scenario that suggests itself is that on finishing the work in the fall of 1930, Marcuse, apprised of the fact that Heidegger would not accept it, refrained from submitting it in order to avoid the ignominy of having it formally rejected. During the 1980s Frankfurt School historian Rolf Wiggershaus found a 1932 letter from Edmund Husserl to University of Frankfurt Rector Kurt Riezler confirming that, for reasons that are still unclear, Heidegger "blocked" Marcuse's attempt to habilitate.[25] The ill-starred habilitation study was published in 1932. A year earlier, Marcuse had apparently felt no qualms about asking Heidegger for a letter of recommendation to the eventual publisher, Klostermann Verlag.[26]

Despite his failure to habilitate in 1930, Marcuse's fascination with the prospects of a Heidegger-Marx synthesis remained keen, as one can discern from a close reading of his important 1933 essay, "On the Philosophical Foundations of the Concept of Labor in Economics." Like his earlier forays, this text, too, tries to enrich the traditional Marxist understanding of labor by recourse to an analysis of labor's main ontological features.

But one of the most surprising aspects of the 1933 essay is Marcuse's distinctly un-Marxian denigration of labor. In the Paris Manuscripts Marx had opposed the predominant Lockean-Puritan understanding of labor ("the sweat of our brow, the blood of our hands"), which is integrally tied to the notion of original sin, by viewing labor as an essential manifestation of human self-fulfillment. Under the influence of romantic doctrines of self-cultivation (*Bildung*), Marx argues that, via labor, humanity simultaneously humanizes the natural world and realizes its own innate potential. Conversely, in "On the Philosophical Foundations of the Concept of Labor," Marcuse's operative idea is the "burdensome character of labor" (*Lastcharakter der Arbeit*). Contra Marx, he suggests that one is never free when one labors insofar as praxis remains subordinate to the contours and dictates of the "object" or "thing." As Marcuse contends:

> Whether explicitly or not, willingly or not, labor is always concerned with *the thing itself* [*die Sache selbst*]. In laboring, the laborer is always "with the thing": whether one stands by a machine, draws technical plans, is concerned with organizational measures, researches scientific problems, instructs people, etc. In this doing he allows himself to be directed by the thing, subjects himself and binds himself to its laws, even when he masters his object, handles it, guides it, and lets it go. In each case he is not "with himself," does not let his own Dasein happen.[27] (emphasis added)

The philosophical sources for Marcuse's skepticism about the emancipatory potential of labor are various. In part, he relies on the Aristotelian (and Scholastic) concept of *scholē* or "leisure" as a sphere existing beyond the realm of material necessity. He also seems to embrace the Hegelian-German idealist elevation of "subjective spirit" (philosophy, culture, religion) over "objective spirit" (politics, economics, social institutions). Lastly, he seems to have been influenced by Marx's claim in *Capital*, volume 3, that the "realm of freedom" exists "beyond the realm of necessity"—that is, beyond the sphere of labor.

The other notable feature of "On the Philosophical Foundations of the Concept of Labor" is Marcuse's enthusiastic endorsement of Schiller's notion of the "play impulse" as a salutary contrast to the drudgery and toil of labor. (After completing his dissertation on the German artist novel in 1922, one of the tasks to which Marcuse turned his energies was the compilation of a comprehensive Schiller bibliography, which he completed in 1925.)[28] In *Letters on the Aesthetic Education of Man* (1795), Schiller defined the "play impulse" as the activity capable of reconciling the "rational" and "sensuous" dimensions of human nature, which, in the modern age seem irreconcilably opposed. In letter 15, Schiller set forth his radical proposition: "Man plays only when he is in the full sense of the word a man, and *he is only wholly Man when he is playing*."[29] In "On the Philosophical Foundation of the Concept of Labor," Marcuse emphatically agrees with Schiller, remarking that when one plays, one no longer gives oneself body and soul to "objects" or "things." Instead, "For once, one does entirely as one pleases with objects; one places oneself above them and becomes 'free' from them." "In a single toss of a ball," Marcuse continues, "the player achieves an infinitely greater triumph of human freedom over the objective world than in the most massive accomplishment of technical labor" (128).

As Marcuse admits in a later interview, he had abandoned his dream of becoming a university professor as of 1932 owing to Germany's deteriorating political climate.[30] Via the mediation of Husserl and Riezler, he established contact with the Frankfurt-based Institute for Social Research, whose director, Max Horkheimer, had already made plans to transfer the Institute's administrative facilities to Geneva. Marcuse oversaw operations of the Geneva branch during 1933, before emigrating, along with other institute members, to New York the following year.

But in 1932 a publishing event occurred that functioned as a watershed in Marcuse's intellectual development: the publication of Marx's *Ökonomisch-*

philosophische Manuskripte vom Jahre 1844 (*Economic and Philosophical Manuscripts of 1844*) in volume 3 of the *Marx-Engels Gesamtausgabe* (MEGA). Marcuse wrote a long review essay that appeared in the Social Democratic journal, *Die Gesellschaft*, in which he hailed the manuscripts' appearance as "a crucial event in the history of Marxist studies."[31] It would only be a slight exaggeration to say that, suddenly, what for four years Marcuse had been seeking in Heidegger he found in Marx: a philosophical grounding for historical materialism. As Marcuse observes in retrospect: in 1932 "the *Economic and Philosophical Manuscripts of 1844* appeared. That was probably the turning point. This was, in a certain sense, a new practical and theoretical Marxism. After that, Heidegger versus Marx was no longer a problem for me" ("Theory and Politics," 125). In this way, Marcuse brought to completion a philosophical odyssey that led "from Heidegger to Horkheimer."[32]

In Marcuse's eyes, the 1844 Manuscripts confirmed his suspicions (based on close readings of early texts such as *The Holy Family*, *The German Ideology*, and the "Theses on Feuerbach," as read through the prism of Lukács) that Marx's project had been formulated in dialogue with classical German philosophy. Moreover, it became increasingly clear that Marxism's philosophical origins, far from being a youthful excrescence, were absolutely central to its status as a program of social and political transformation. As Marcuse remarks, "A rough formula that could be used as a starting point would be that the revolutionary critique of political economy itself has a philosophical foundation, just as, conversely, the philosophy underlying it already contains revolutionary praxis" ("New Sources," 87).

The Paris Manuscripts meant that the Second International's scientific understanding of Marxism qua "socialist economics" was based on a potentially fatal interpretive misunderstanding. Instead, Marxism was centrally concerned with problems of human self-realization—with humanity's "species being" (*Gattungswesen*)—that had preoccupied German idealism, albeit, with an important methodological difference: Marx was interested in solving these problems "practically" rather than merely "theoretically." Moreover, in poring over the manuscripts, Marcuse discovered that the "existential" concerns that, four years earlier, had attracted him to Heidegger were fundamentally shared by Marx. For their leitmotif was "alienation." Thus, they confirmed the reading of Marx that Marcuse had heretofore found most persuasive—Lukács's understanding of Marxism as a critique of "reification," the unwarranted transformation of human society into a world dominated by economic categories or "things." Moreover, Marx's discussion was tied to a vivid, quasiphenomeno-logical, socio-historical portrayal of alienation's genesis and development—yielding precisely the dimension of "concreteness" that Marcuse found lacking in Heidegger's ontological account.

Marcuse's momentous encounter with the early Marx is also fascinating for historical reasons. It foreshadows the rediscovery of the "philosophical Marx" by the Central European dissident movement during the 1960s (Leszek Kolakowski in Poland, Karel Kosik in Czechoslovakia, Agnes Heller in Hungary, and the Belgrade Praxis circle), which provided impetus for the reforms embodied in the slogan, "socialism with a human face" (of course, these hopes for internal reform were brutally crushed by the 1968 Soviet invasion of Prague).[33] Moreover, it anticipates the "phenomenological Marxist" vogue of the 1950s and 1960s, whose leading representatives were Jean-Paul Sartre, Maurice Merleau-Ponty, Tran Duc Thao, Kosik, and Enzo Paci.[34] Like Marcuse, the phenomeno-logical Marxists (who often borrowed as much from Husserl's philosophy as they did from Heidegger) believed that phenomenology represented an impor-tant philosophical counterweight to the positivist domination of the human sciences—and thus a potential methodological stimulus toward the creation of a humane social world.

Shortly after Marcuse joined the Institute for Social Research, Germany's polit-ical landscape underwent a radical transformation: on January 30, 1933, Hitler was named chancellor. The end of the Weimar Republic was a foregone con-clusion. On March 23, following the Reichstag fire a month earlier, German legislators (minus the Communists) voted emergency powers that facilitated dictatorial rule. Weeks earlier the Gestapo commandeered the institute's facili-ties in Frankfurt, confiscating its library. On April 7, the Nazis implemented the anti-Semitic Law for the Restoration of the Professional Civil Service, which effectively banned Jews from university life.

It was under these circumstances that, on May 1, with great fanfare, Hei-degger officially joined the Nazi Party. A few weeks earlier, he had been elected rector of Freiburg University by an academic senate that had already been purged of Jews and political undesirables. In his new position of authority, Heidegger oversaw changes in the university system that accorded with the Nazis' *Führerprinzip*. In June he sent an urgent telegram to Hitler recommend-ing that an upcoming conference of German university rectors be postponed until *Gleichschaltung*—the Nazi euphemism for the elimination of political opposition—could be completed. In the fall, he went on the stump on behalf of the Nazi referendum on Germany's withdrawal from the League of Nations, claiming "Let not ideas and doctrines be your guide. The Führer is Germany's only reality and its law."

One of the most troubling aspects of Heidegger's political conversion was the facility with which he was able to legitimate his Nazi allegiances via concepts seamlessly culled from *Being and Time*. For example, he invoked the notion of existential "decisiveness" (*Entschlossenheit*) as a justification for collective engagement on behalf of the National Socialist *Volksgemeinschaft*. In a stroke, Heidegger reconfigured the ontological framework of *Being and Time*, division 2, which stressed concepts such as "destiny," "historicity," "*Volk*," and "choosing one's hero," to provide philosophical window-dressing for Germany's "National Revolution." As Karl Löwith remarked perceptively: "One need only . . . apply authentic 'existence' [in *Being and Time*] . . . to specifically German existence and its historical destiny in order thereby . . . to proceed from 'destruction' [*Destruktion*] now on the terrain of politics."[35] Marcuse claimed that, although at the time he and his fellow students never suspected Heidegger's right-radical political allegiances, in retrospect, the philosopher's engagement on behalf of National Socialism made sense:

> If you look at his view of the human existence, of being-in-the-world, you will find a highly repressive, highly oppressive interpretation . . . : "idle talk, curiosity, ambiguity, falling and being-thrown-into, concern, being-toward-death, anxiety, dread, boredom," and so on. Now this gives a picture which plays well on the fears and frustrations of men and women in a repressive society—a joyless existence: overshadowed by death and anxiety; human material for the authoritarian personality. ("Heidegger's Politics," 169–70)

To the shock of Heidegger's students and disciples, many of whom happened to be Jewish, it seemed that the philosopher had "chosen" Hitler as his "hero." It turned out to be a fateful decision that would dog Heidegger's reputation until the end of his life. Marcuse, for his part, having recently joined the Institute for Social Research—a milieu that was extremely unsympathetic to Heidegger's thought—had already distanced himself from the Master's framework and influence.[36] In his eyes, the philosopher's Nazism represented a point of no return.

As time progressed, Marcuse seemed able to separate Heidegger's philosophical genius from his ill-fated political alliance with Nazism. In "German

Philosophy in the Twentieth Century," written in 1940, he avowed that during the 1920s, "What Heidegger proposed as a concrete analysis of human existence and its modes of being constitutes one of the most fertile avenues of modern philosophy."[37] With the war's end, Marcuse returned to Germany in his capacity as oss operative and met with Heidegger. By his own admission, the encounter was unproductive. There followed an impassioned exchange of letters, in which Marcuse implored his mentor to distance himself publicly from the evils of the regime he had briefly served.[38] Philosophers are allowed to err, remarked Marcuse. But in this case, the "error"—which involved unqualified allegiance to a fundamentally racist and genocidal regime—signified the negation of the Western tradition and all it represented. True to form, Heidegger remained unrepentant. In his eyes, the Allies had committed atrocities equal to those perpetrated by the Nazis. And certain Nazi goals—for example, a deliverance of the West from the ills of communism—in his view remained admirable. At this point, there seemed little more to say, and communication between them broke off.

Marcuse's renown during the 1960s was totally unexpected. As much as any other works of postwar cultural criticism, his *Eros and Civilization* and *One-Dimensional Man* anticipated the decade's libidinal-political strivings. Like Tocqueville a century earlier, Marcuse's political influence spread rapidly across two continents. He counseled both the American and German New Lefts that, at best, their actions could serve as a catalyst to heighten awareness about the injustices of imperialism and social inequality. However, should the students delude themselves into behaving as bona fide revolutionary actors, they were destined to run aground.[39]

One of the challenging interpretive questions that has beset Marcuse scholarship concerns the extent to which Heideggerian themes play a role in his later writings. Did Marcuse, in some meaningful sense, remain a *Left Heideggerian?* Did he in fact apply a "diagnosis of the age" (*Zeitdiagnose*) formulated by Heidegger and others during the interwar period to the advanced industrial societies of the postwar era? As we have already seen, for a time Marcuse was highly intrigued by the prospects for a "concrete philosophy" presented by Heidegger's existential interpretive framework. Did the later Marcuse then attempt to refit the withering critique of mass society contained in Heidegger's treatment of "everydayness" for the ends of the political left?

In order to answer these questions properly, one must take into account the historical situation with which Marcuse found himself confronted during the postwar period. Fascism had been defeated. Yet, monopoly capitalism—the economic system responsible for its original triumph—remained firmly entrenched. The cold war era, dominated by the apocalyptical prospect of nuclear annihilation, exuded a sinister atmosphere of international stalemate in which radical political demands could find no outlet. Moreover, unprecedented economic affluence lent Western societies a distinctly Huxleyan quality—as though the West had responded to *1984* by creating its own *Brave New World.* A ceaseless proliferation of superfluous commodities seemed to obliterate the distinction between true and false needs. Prodded by Madison Avenue, a narcissistic libidinal cathexis developed between consumers and their commodities: they seemed to be literally in love with their own affluence. In *One-Dimensional Man*, Marcuse proffered a memorable analysis of this strange social psychological conjuncture in his discussion of "repressive desublimation." Whereas for Freud, sublimation bespoke the rechanneling of libidinal impulses into higher creative pursuits, the ethos of postwar capitalism, conversely, demanded a diversion of Eros toward the regressive ends of "consumption for consumption's sake." The entire system, lamented Marcuse, seemed impervious to rational critique. Its implicit rationality—its flawless capacity to "deliver the goods"—masked a greater irrationality: the fact that life's higher purposes were sacrificed to a never-ending cycle of "production for production's sake." Under these circumstances the later Heidegger's quasiphobic concern about "technology" qua "enframing"—the thoughtless expenditure of being under the sign of "standing reserve"—seemed fundamentally confirmed. At a strategic juncture of *One-Dimensional Man*, Marcuse quotes Heidegger's argument in "The Question Concerning Technology" to drive home his point: "Modern man takes the entirety of Being as raw material for production and subjects the entirety of the object-world to the sweep and order of production. . . . The use of machinery and the production of machines is not technics itself but merely an adequate instrument for the realization . . . of the essence of technics in its objective raw material." [40]

In "Some Social Implications of Modern Technology," written during the late 1940s, Marcuse hewed to the Marxist view that technology was socially neutral. [41] Its employment under a given set of social relations determined whether its effects would be emancipatory or reactionary. However, by the mid-1950s, Marcuse came to believe that qualitatively new forms of domination had been introduced by late capitalism. Instead, given the seductive blandishments of a new form of socially administered hedonism that classical Marxism had never anticipated, science and technology now appeared as *autonomous sources of domination*. In *Capital*, Marx, basing his views on a theory of social immiseration, foresaw the collapse of capitalism. But the "New Industrial State" (J. K. Galbraith) of late capitalism had forced critical Marxists to confront an unforeseen situation in which the basic needs of the working classes had been satisfied within the confines of the existing system. In essence, the consumer society had succeeded in rendering the emancipatory aims of social revolution superfluous.

Given the system's unprecedented capacity to sublimate and defuse social conflict, Marcuse began to search for heretofore untapped repositories of contestation. One well-known source was the "Great Refusal" of modern poetry and literature, whose foremost representative was surrealism. Marcuse perceived the surrealists' love of scandal and provocation—their open renunciation of the predominant universe of social signification—as a direct challenge to the reigning social order's raison d'etre. But just as in *Being and Time* Heidegger had explored the ontological bases of social being, during the 1950s Marcuse began investigating whether new incentives to social rebellion could be discovered in Freud's theory of the instincts. Thus, in *Eros and Civilization*, departing from Freud's notion of the pleasure principle, Marcuse postulated a biological drive toward uninhibited libidinal gratification that had been blocked by the "performance principle" of late capitalism. Could there exist, mused Marcuse, an *instinctual basis for socialism*, one capable of undermining from within the contemporary continuum of domination? Certainly these late reflections on matters of philosophical anthropology bore a distinct resemblance to the mode of ontological questioning Heidegger had developed in *Being and Time*. As Marcuse speculates in *"An Essay on Liberation"*:

> Prior to all ethical behavior in accordance with specific social standards, prior to all ideological expression, *morality is a disposition of the organism*, perhaps rooted in the erotic drive to counter aggressiveness, to create and preserve "ever greater unities of life." We would then have, this side of all "values," *an instinctual foundation for solidarity among human beings*—a solidarity which has been effectively repressed in line with the requirements of a class society but which now appears as a precondition for liberation. [42]

From these remarks, one can readily discern the extent to which German thought of the 1920s remained a determinate influence on Marcuse's later worldview. Without much effort, one can trace his powerful critique of social technocracy in *One-Dimensional Man* and other later works to the intellectual framework he developed under Heidegger's tutelage in the late 1920s and early 1930s. For it was under the Freiburg sage's influence that Marcuse first cultivated a sensitivity to the manifestations of societal reification, phenomena that, in *Being and Time*, Heidegger treated under the rubric of "inauthenticity."

If Marcuse's writings still speak to us today—and on this score there can be little doubt—it is because of his talents as an *unorthodox* Marxist. For in an era during which official Marxism had degenerated into a repressive "science of legitimation" (Oskar Negt), the Frankfurt School philosopher proceeded to reinvigorate dialectical thought by drawing freely on a plethora of complementary critical approaches: Hegelianism, psychoanalysis, and the aesthetic dimension. In retrospect, however, it is clear that during the late 1920s he took an important first step in the spirit of left-wing heterodoxy when he experimented with the iconoclastic idea of fusing Heidegger with Marx. It is one of the true ironies of twentieth-century intellectual history that during the 1930s Marcuse went on to refine this paradigm under the auspices of the Institute for Social Research, where matters Heideggerian were viewed as heresy and anathema.

Heideggerian Marxism

Contributions to a
Phenomenology of Historical Materialism

1. Introduction

The object of the investigation must first be provisionally determined according to its givenness. Marxism, in whose epistemological context historical materialism enters into history, does not appear in the form of a scientific theory—as a system of truths whose meaning rests wholly in its accuracy as knowledge [*Erkenntnisse*][1]—but rather in the form of a theory of social action, of the historical act [*Tat*].[2] Marxism is both the theory of the proletarian revolution and a revolutionary critique of bourgeois society; it is a science[3] insofar as the revolutionary action that it wishes to set free and to stabilize requires insight into its own historical necessity—into the truth of its being. It lives in the inseparable unity of theory and praxis, of science and action; and every Marxian investigation must maintain this unity as its central and dominant component. Such an investigation would miss its object entirely if it were to attempt to inspect Marxism from the vantage of some transcendent position "beyond" Marxism, applying the terms of logical closure, universal noncontradiction, and atemporal validity. The truths of Marxism are not truths of knowing [*Erkennens*],[4] but rather truths of happening [*Geschehen*].[5] The critical question can thus only be posed in the following way: does the framework of theoretical concepts from which Marxism derives truth—that is, the necessity of the historical action it addresses and comprehends—emerge from a full grasp of the phenomena of historicity? Within Marxism, historical materialism refers to the entire domain of knowledge related to historicity[6]—to the being, the structure, and the motility[7] of happening.

A phenomenology of historical materialism sees within this sketch of the givenness of its object a broad outline of the path it will follow. Such a phenomenology begins with the disclosure of the fundamental situation of

Marxism—a disclosure through which a new, revolutionary fundamental attitude [*Grundhaltung*] gains a new view of the whole of social being by coming to know historicity. The discovery of historicity as the fundamental determination of human Dasein opens,[8] through a new understanding of reality, the possibility of radically transformative action. Next Heidegger's foundational analysis in *Being and Time* (1927) is used as a basis for attempting a phenomenological interpretation of historicity. Before the question of whether the statements of historical materialism address the full range of the phenomena of historicity is examined, the methodology of phenomenological interpretation itself will be framed as a problem. The historicity of Dasein demands that phenomenology reorient itself according to the bearings of the dialectical method—a method that shows itself to be the appropriate approach for all historical objects. In this way, the dialectic should also experience a provisional clarification through its methodological application within Marxism. Only then will the phenomenology of historical materialism, which interprets the Marxian theories relevant to the structure of historicity in light of the phenomenon of historicity, be taken up.

2. The Fundamental Situation of Marxism

We will define the fundamental situation of a human being to be that situation in which that person has a clear view of, and can determine, his or her unique relation to the environment and the task that emerges from this relation. If a life obtains its decisive expression through a process of investigation and research, then the determination of the fundamental situation is obtained from its point of departure—from that point out of which originates its method of investigation and its conceptuality, and from which it receives its meaning. (These determinations are intended phenomenologically, not psychologically. It will not be suggested, for example, that Marx saw research as his fundamental task and that his work should be explained wholly in terms of it; rather, the present work sees Marx's investigations and the overall shape they take in his work as the historical material through which the determination of the fundamental situation is to be carried out.) The question whether and to what extent such a determination is possible and of where the measure of its correctness lies can be answered preliminarily by developing the sketch of the modes of givenness of the determination's object already provided in section 1. The Marxian fundamental situation can be "correctly" interpreted once its historical position and the meaning of this historical position are ascertained. This possibility has its foundations in the mode of being of human Dasein as a historical mode of being. Precisely because human Dasein expresses itself in historical situations, situations cannot be repeated; they can, however, be understood by being retraced and reflected on (later, it will be shown under which conditions such reflection is possible). The object of knowledge as it is given does not here "stand over and against" the knower: it is not a different, a "foreign," being (as is the case with objects of the physical world); rather, it "lives with him" and has the same mode of being. Marx frequently refers to this unique quality of historical knowing, which arises out of the fact that human beings are, at once, both subjects and objects of history; to this point as well, it will be necessary to return.

The question of the Marxian fundamental situation must confront still another methodological objection. For even if the investigation restricts its use of sources to the writings of Marx and Engels as the original historical expression of Marxism (as does the present paper), it is clear that even these writings were produced in so many different periods that the idea of a unifying fundamental situation seems to entail, at the very least, a dogmatic prerequisite—namely, the demanded "unity." But it seems to us that one can only address the question of history and its division into periods after one has [phenomenologically] pointed out the fundamental position, because such a historical division of the subject, if it is to be anything other than mechanical and chronological, must relate the different phases of the writings to the fundamental situation. Thus for example, if in considering Marx's lifework, one differentiates among young Hegelian, radical democratic, and scientific communistic periods, then this division must presuppose a value and goal-orientation that emanates from a fundamental position or it will amount to the abstract shattering of the historical totality into fragments connected only by chronology. Given Marxism's dialectical unity, the latter procedure would offer what is probably the most inappropriate method imaginable. The exhibition[9] of the fundamental situation is, by the way, not an attempt to make the goal of this investigation that of establishing, once and for all, the meaning of Marxism; it is, rather, intended simply to demarcate the ground on which such an undertaking must proceed. It is merely a preliminary methodological foray into domains that will only achieve clarity in the course of the investigation.

Let us now sketch out a brief outline of the Marxist fundamental situation: its central concern is with the historical possibility of the radical act—of an act that should clear the way for a new and necessary reality as it brings about the actualization of the whole person. Its standard-bearer is the self-consciously

historical human being; its sole field of action is history, revealed as the fundamental category of human Dasein. Thereby, the radical act proves itself to be
the revolutionary and historical action of "class" as the historical unit.

For the sake of presentation, we must dissect this sketch of the fundamental
situation into a set of decisive partial situations, even while emphasizing that
this is purely a methodological expedient. The interrelation among the partial
situations will prove to be such that the fundamental situation presents a living
unity.

The question of radical action can only meaningfully be posed at the moment when the act is grasped as the decisive realization of the human essence
and yet when, at the same time, precisely this realization appears to be a
factical impossibility—that is, in a revolutionary situation. Even in our initial approach, the fundamental situation reveals itself to be a unity, and this
unity pushes itself immediately into historicity, thus demonstrating that the
fundamental position is eminently historical. Surveying the concrete historical
situation, one sees an endless sum of activities, one next to the other, and each
inextricably bound and determined by the other. All of these activities seem to
be detached from the human actors who, in turn, do not seem to live in them,
but merely to be occupied with them; or—the ultimate absurdity—one sees
actors carrying out actions not to live, but for the sake of mere survival! Here
one sees the "transformation of personal powers into thingly ones,"[10] and what
is left behind is an "abstracted individual [. . .], robbed of all life-content,"[11]
whose "own deed becomes an alien power opposed to him."[12] This Marxian
vision cuts through to the existence of capitalist society: it reaches behind
society's economic and ideological forms to touch the "reality of an inhuman
existence"[13] and to counter this inhumanity by calling for human existence
in its reality, by demanding the radical act. How will one define the qualities
of the radical action that unfolds as a countermovement against capitalistic
activity?

"To be radical is to grasp a matter by its roots. The root of humanity is,
however, humankind itself."[14] Action is comprehended as an "*Existenzial*,"[15]
that is, as an essential mode of conduct of human Dasein and as something
that essentially seeks to fulfill itself in human Dasein. "Social life is essentially
practical. All mysteries which mislead theory into mysticism find their rational
solution in human praxis and in the comprehension of this praxis."[16] Every act
is a human "transformation of circumstances," but not every action also transforms human *existence*. One can change circumstances without transforming,

in its existence, the human Dasein that lives in and is surrounded by these circumstances. Only *the radical act* transforms circumstances as well as the human existence acting within them: "The transformation of circumstances and the transformation of human action coincide only when that transformation is framed as *revolutionary praxis* and is understood as rational." [17]

Radical action is, according to its essence, *necessary*, both for the actor and for the environment in which it is performed. Through its historical occurrence it transforms necessity—transforms something that had become utterly unbearable—and posits in its place precisely the necessity that alone can sublate the unbearable. Any act that does not have this specific character of necessity is not radical and also might just as easily not take place, or might just as easily be performed by someone else. This leads to the last, decisive meaning of necessity: necessity is *immanent* to the radical act. That it must occur right now, that it must be done precisely here and precisely by this person, means that it cannot, under any circumstances, be forced on the doer [*Täter*] from outside; that the doer *must*—in the sense of an immanent *must*—commit it now because the deed [*Tat*] is given along with the doer's very existence. Only under these circumstances does the act become truly necessary, in that its happening does not allow itself to be prescribed from outside, but rather brings itself forth out of itself. But how can one concretely determine this necessity? We have already seen: the act is intended existentially in that it emerges from human Dasein as essential conduct and in that it is directed toward human Dasein. The radical act must (in relation to the doer) happen as a 'concrete' necessity of concrete human Dasein and it must (in relation to the environment) be necessary *for* concrete human Dasein. The sphere of this concrete necessity is history. All determinations of the radical act unite in their foundational determination as *historicity*.

With the discovery of history as the fundamental category of human existence, Marx lays down the concept of *historical existence*, a concept that, in contrast to all factical deviations, he characterizes as the "authentic," "meaningful," and "true" existence: "We know only a single science, the science of history." [18] The "world-historical existence of individuals" is existence "that is immediately bound up with history." [19] Just as human Dasein is essentially practical, so it is also essentially historical; its situation is a historical one, whether it grasps it or not: "As a *determinate* person, as an actual person, you have a *determination*, a task, whether you are conscious of it or not." [20] This determination of existence is a historical one; it is circumscribed by the historical situation of existence, and the prevailing possibilities of concrete human beings are prescribed by it, as are their reality and future. Certainly, there is such a thing as "unhistorical" existence. The isolated individual and the unconscious masses alike can misunderstand their historical situation or rebel against it—but in that case, their existence would lack that necessity that alone can provide the basis for the radical act. Later we shall have to return to examine more fully the fundamental phenomenon of historicity and the Marxist conception of it; at this point we simply wish to emphasize its relations to the question of the radical act.

The radical act only possesses immanent necessity if it is historical—if its necessity is historical—precisely because human Dasein essentially fulfills itself in history and is determined through history. This means that the doer of a radical deed must have historical existence and that the field of action must be history: both the direction and goal of the radical deed must themselves come out of history and must affect historical existence. In order for the concrete possibility of the radical act to be determined, the historical situation within which it should be done must be recognized [*erkannt*]. For this to be possible, it is necessary to clarify both the structure of historicity in general and the fundamental conditions of historical existence.

The exploration of this question in *The German Ideology* begins with the awareness of the fundamental meaning of historicity. Initially, the method is purely phenomenological: the state of affairs of "historical man"[21] is supposed to be exhibited in its full concretion and there are no valid considerations outside of that which can be demonstrated in this historical and human state of affairs: "The presuppositions with which we begin are neither arbitrary nor dogmatic—they are rather the real presuppositions from which one can abstract only by means of imaginative fancy. These presuppositions include the true individuals, their action and their material conditions. . . . These assumptions are therefore ascertainable through purely empirical means."[22] Whether and to what extent this method represents an approach appropriate to its object—this is something that we shall investigate subsequently.

So what is revealed by bringing historical humanity into view? From the very outset, historical humanity does not appear as an isolated individual, but as a human being among other human beings in an environment, as "dependent," "as belonging to a larger whole."[23] In whatever the historical time or space the [phenomenological] gaze is cast, it always discovers *society* as that which is historically concrete, as the historical "unity" (this concept shall initially designate only a unity of individuals that is grounded and concrete in some way or another, thereby leaving open the question of *how* this unity is grounded). Society's limit appears within natural space; its reach extends across a determinate spatial environment (village-city-country). The force and direction of society's effective power is constituted through its *reproduction*, through the constant renewal and constant repetition of its existence.[24] Initially, society concerns itself with the needs related to the preservation of its existence: "the first historical act . . . is the production of material life itself."[25] Production always originally appears as reproduction, as the preservation and propagation of existing society according to the natural conditions prevailing under varying modes of production. With the reproduction of "material life," the "ideal" is also reproduced. "The production of ideas, representations, and consciousness is initially immediately bound up with the material activity and the material intercourse of man."[26] The fundamental historical phenomenon shows the "spiritual" realities of a society to be grounded in "material" realities—to be "dependent": law, ethics, art, science do not, in the historical view, appear as abstract domains lying outside or beyond historical being, but rather as that which has grown out of and is rooted in the concrete being of a concrete society: "Men are the producers of their representations, ideas, etc., by 'men' one means real, acting men, as they are determined through a specific development of their productive forces and of their corresponding forms of intercourse."[27]

Human Dasein, as something that is historical in its being, needs neither otherworldy impetus to set it in motion nor a preset goal toward which to move, because it can be only as happening. "It is not, for example, 'history' which needs people as its means in order to make its way to its goals—as if history were some sort of special and distinct person; rather, history is nothing but the activity of human beings pursuing their own ends."[28] All historical development rests in the immanence of history itself; it is the unfolding of societies as the concrete historical unities propelled by their reproduction and conditioned by the natural environment. At this point we shall forgo a further presentation of the theory of historical development based on Marx's texts, since it is familiar to the readers; only those aspects of this theory necessary for clarifying the fundamental phenomenon of historicity will be mentioned here.

As historical existence, human Dasein is the "succession of . . . genera-tions."[29] In its reproduction, every generation takes the previous generation as its foundation. It receives as its inheritance the "materials" left to it by the previous one—these being the forces of production as well as the relations of production. But the second generation receives these "under completely trans-formed circumstances," since history as the past activity of human beings—as occurred activity [*geschehene Tätigkeit*]—is, in every instance, *transformation*. Therefore, the new generation must either develop or modify the received inheritance [*Erbe*][30]—or, should it no longer correspond to the "transformed circumstances," destroy it. Whichever of these possibilities it embraces, and whatever it elevates to replace that which has been toppled, they can only come to it from history. The new generation can only become the *subject* of history if it recognizes and grasps itself as the *object* of history, if it acts from the knowledge of its singular historical situation.

With the expansion of social reproduction (growth of populations, pressure of spatial expansion, commerce and conflict with other societies) and with the division of labor that results from this expansion, *class* arises as the unify-ing force driving history. In the first approach to the fundamental historical phenomenon, society could still appear as a uniform totality. Considered in a more rigorously concrete manner, however, "*production in general* is an ab-straction."[31] Since there is no uniform reproduction, but rather various forms of it, the totality of concrete historical society disintegrates once more into other unities. Even if a particular society's mode of production should prove relatively uniform, the division of labor nonetheless guarantees that the relative position of an individual vis-à-vis society depends upon his or her place within the process of production, and it is these different positions that constitute *class* as the decisive unity.

Through the development of the forces of production, the national division of labor becomes an international one; the universal character of class becomes visible beyond all national and spatial particularities. This development has reached its zenith in the creation of the modern world market. The "com-prehensive dependency" of the individual in its reproduction transforms the individual's historical existence into a world-historical one: the "transformation of history into world history" is complete.[32]

We have sketched out the Marxian outlines of historical development to the point where the universal class appears as the final bearer of the movement of history. We now believe ourselves to be able to answer the question of who will be the concrete bearer of that radical act that stands at the center of the Marxian fundamental situation. It is the universal class, which is condemned to this action through its historical existence and whose being completes itself in the double necessity of this act: "It is not a matter of what the proletariat might at any given point *imagine* its goal to be. Rather, it is a question of *what the proletariat is* and what, in accordance with this being, it will historically be compelled to do. Its goal and its historical action lie irrevocably prefigured in its own life-situation."[33]

Marx's analysis of historical humanity demonstrated that humanity's consciousness and achievements are parts of the historical-social totality and that they are founded on concrete historical being. Knowledge is also not an act that leads human Dasein out of the immanence of historicity. Even if one may speak of the object of knowledge as being "above" or "beyond" history, the knowing act [*erkennende Akt*] is itself not something that descends from nowhere into concrete being; rather, it is always the product of concrete human beings and the historical situation is the condition of possibility of all knowledge. All true knowledge discloses real objects and states of affairs. As realities, they are valid only if a knowing human Dasein can direct itself toward them in order to make itself "true," to make itself correspond to its historical situation. All genuine knowledge is, in the most profound sense, "practical" knowledge, in that it brings a human Dasein "into the truth." That is the meaning of science—and science's sole task is to fulfill this meaning. Historical existence first becomes complete in the scientific knowledge [*Wissen*] of this existence, in the knowledge of its historical situation, its possibilities, and its task. Only then is it "immediately bound up with history"; only then can it do that which it must do—and do it radically. Only that which must be done can be done radically and it is only through knowledge that human existence can become certain of this necessity. In the historical situation that we have been addressing, class is the decisive historical unity and the knowledge of the unique, historical-social necessity is the achievement of "class consciousness." In class consciousness, the chosen class arises to become the bearer of the historical act. Should the revolutionary situation be at hand, it can only be seized by that class that is conscious of its historical situation.

Thus is fulfilled the immediate unity of theory and praxis to which we have already made reference. Historical necessity realizes itself through human action. Mankind can miss its opportunities for action—recent history has been full of such botched revolutionary situations—and human beings can degrade themselves, can cease to be subjects and become objects of history. Therefore it is the task of theory to free praxis through the knowledge of necessity. At the revolutionary turning points of history, "science" becomes the "conscious product of the movement of history; ceasing to be doctrinaire, it . . . becomes revolutionary."[34] Science becomes reality insofar as it becomes conscious of its historicity. The truth of all genuine reality is fulfilled in its effectiveness and realization. "Philosophers have merely *interpreted* the world; the point is to *change* it."[35]

3. The Historicity of Dasein according to Heidegger's *Being and Time*

We have attempted to show how, in the fundamental Marxian situation, the radical act is set free in its historical necessity. Under the [phenomenological] gaze, historicity reveals itself to be the primary determinacy [*Bestimmtheit*] of human existence; and the concrete ground of historicity is the touchstone to which all intellectual and material objects that have become abstract must return. Human freedom is fulfilled in grasping its own necessity, in the will to that immediate historical existence that realizes itself as the radical act in the revolutionary historical situation. Before we move on to see which method of developing thought (dialectic) and action (revolutionary praxis) is afforded by the position achieved through the Marxian fundamental situation, we must ask the question: how does the "truth" of the Marxian fundamental theses justify itself? How far does its validity extend? From which approach is it possible for a critical analysis to begin to address such questions?

An *immanent* analysis provides the only meaningful approach to a theory that defines human existence as primarily historical and that uses theory only as a way of securing and unleashing the historical act. Such an analysis takes the basic intention of this theory itself as its basis and asks: can human Dasein in general be thought of as primarily historical? If so, has the theory in question brought historicity fully into view?

Since the middle of the last century, the problem of historicity has once again come to be recognized as a central philosophical problem. Droysen, working quite outside the system of Hegel and the Hegelians, threw open the question for debate in his *Outline of the Principles of History*; but it was only with Dilthey that historicity came to be the driving force within philosophical thought. Since then, the problem of historicity has been seized on from all sides, with the increasing awareness that no less than the fundamental question of all of science might be at stake (here we can only list the names: Simmel, Rickert, Troeltsch, Max Weber)—until, finally, Heidegger posed and then answered the question, in all of its radical gravity, from the perspective of a rigorous phenomenology. If, in turning toward Heidegger's *Being and Time*, we linger somewhat longer than might be necessary in this context, it is because this book seems to represent a turning point in the history of philosophy: the point at which bourgeois philosophy unmakes itself from the inside and clears the way for a new and "concrete" science.

The question concerning the meaning of being is Heidegger's starting point and its clarification is his goal.[36] But the entirety of the already published first part of *Being and Time* deals with the interpretation of a privileged be-ing, or "Dasein," which is always understood to mean human Dasein. "This be-ing [*Seiende*][37] which each of us is himself and which includes inquiring as one of the possibilities of its being, we shall denote by the term *Dasein.*"[38] Heidegger's revelation of Dasein's mode of being proceeds according to the stages yielded by the phenomenological course of the investigation. Initially, the constitution of Dasein's being is that of "being-in-the-world." As such, the world is always already "there" along with Dasein's being. The traditional problems of the transcendence, reality, and demonstrability of the world reveal themselves as false problems because Dasein in general is "there" only as being-in-the-world, while the world is originally given only with Dasein's existence— and wholly according to a determinate mode of discovery and disclosure. The first utterance of Dasein is not the *cogito*, with which an *ego* is consequently posited, but rather "*sum*"—and in the sense of "I-am-in-a-world."[39] The riddle of how knowing can be the crossing-over of a (worldless) subject into a world found without is solved once it is demonstrated that knowing is a mode of conduct inherent to the being of primordially world-bound Dasein.

So, which type of being does the world existing with Dasein have? Its fundamental constitution is defined and determined as "meaningfulness," as a "totality of involvements" that is in every case tied to Dasein. Insofar as they are not themselves Dasein, the objects that Dasein encounters in the world partake of the mode of being of "equipment": that of "ready-to-handness."[40] The object-filled environment comes to Dasein as a world of meaning directed toward it; not as rigid *res extensae*, as abstract-physical things independent of Dasein, but rather as related to a Dasein that needs it, that orients itself toward it, that concerns itself with it—and that in every case gives it its meaning, its time and its place. (This statement should not, in the manner of some idealistic philosophical position, be misunderstood to suggest that Dasein creates the world; on the contrary, this argument presupposes the "objective" reality of the world as self-evident and as not worthy of being deemed a philosophical problem. Yet Dasein and world are primordially related to one another in their being, are parts of a concrete totality that cannot be torn asunder. No attempt to posit a temporal or ideal priority should be supposed as a consequence of this argument.) The (theoretical) interpretation of the world as pure present-at-handness does not correspond to the way in which the world is primordially revealed to Dasein. The theoretical mode of conduct that investigates objects as present-at-handness according to their structure and form, relation and movement (examples of which can be found in mathematical physics, in formal logic, and in ontology), is a "derived" and "derivative" mode. It is a modification of the originary[41] understanding of the world as meaningful. The encounter with the world entailed in a practical-needful making-provision[42] is the first and genuine mode and all theoretical, knowing modes of conduct are based on it—even if only in the "manner of turning away from" it.

In the course of a closer interpretation of "being-in-the-world," Dasein is shown to be being-with. "By reason of this *with-bound* [*mithaften*] being-in-the-world, the world is always the one that I share with the conventional self, 'the they.'[43] The world of Dasein is a *with-world* [*Mitwelt*]. Being-in is *being-with* the they."[44] It is from "the they," and from its grounding in this *with-world*, that everyday Dasein receives its determination. The average subject of Dasein is "the they." A thorough analysis shows not only how this "they" assumes for itself, from the very outset, all possibilities and decisions of Dasein, but also how the values and impulses of Dasein are created from its "public interpretation." This "fallenness" of Dasein into its world, this "inauthentic existing" must, importantly, be understood as one of Dasein's essential modes of being (" 'the they' is an existentiale; and as a primordial[45] phenomenon, it belongs to Dasein's positive constitution.")[46] This leads to the central point of the interpretation—to "thrownness." Dasein, according to its being-from-origin, is always already handed-down; its being is laid on it without it having knowledge of its whither and whence. With this thrownness, Dasein is also thrown into its environment and with-world, falling under its sway in a constant turning-away from its own authentic being.

In all of this fallenness, however, there remains, at the ground of Dasein, an understanding—however hidden it might remain—of its own authenticity. For Dasein, the important issue is in fact always its own being, and it is through this existentially grasped "concern" that the authentic being of Dasein is addressed. In this care [*Sorge*] inheres the possibilities of Dasein grasping its own being and of breaking out of inauthentic and into authentic being, despite all thrownness and fallenness. Here we must set aside the interpretation of the being of Dasein as care and of temporality as its ontological meaning, the ground of its possi-

[margin handwriting: Pragmatism]

bility. The exegesis of temporality culminates in the thesis that temporality is neither an a priori form of intuition [*Anschauungsform*] nor an empirical order of objects but rather a fundamental constituent of Dasein through which alone Dasein can be. Having-been, being-present, and the future are Dasein's modes of being, and these together first make possible fundamental phenomena like understanding, care, and resoluteness. Thus, the way is opened up for demonstrating historicity as the fundamental determination of Dasein—the point in Heidegger's phenomenology that is decisive for us.

In the thrownness of being-in-the-world, everyday Dasein derives its possibilities from the handed-down, inherited interpretedness of "the they."[47] In resoluteness, however, Dasein can call itself back to its own authentic being; it can "take over in its thrownness that be-ing [*Seiende*] which it is itself, and take it over wholly."[48] But even in the resoluteness in which the authentic being of Dasein constitutes itself, Dasein remains thrown. Its freedom resides only in an assumption of its inheritance that is steeled in expectation of its own death: in the self-chosen fulfillment of necessity. The "inheritance" remains essentially determining; it makes up the constitutive historicity of Dasein: "The resoluteness in which Dasein comes back to itself discloses current factical possibilities of authentic existing, and discloses them *in terms of the inheritance* which that resoluteness, as thrown, *takes over*. In the resolute return to thrownness, there is hidden a *self-handing-down* of the possibilities that have come down."[49] In resolutely handing itself over to historical inheritance, Dasein grasps its own "fate." It brings itself out of the fallenness of existing inauthentically and into authentic existence insofar as it becomes *historical*: it itself chooses its inherited, historically determined possibility and "recovers" its existence out of this possibility.

But this recovery as resoluteness—a resoluteness that explicitly understands the origins of the possibilities to which it hands itself over—is only possible as "disavowal." It is no mere reliving or recuperation of a decaying, past existence, but is rather something new, a response to and renewing [*Erwiderung*] of past possibilities. As such, moreover, it must necessarily collide with the today [*das Heute*]; it can only be attained as a countermove against that which factically exists in the today.[50]

Even a fate-bound Dasein essentially exists in being-with others and thus its "happening is a co-happening and is determinative of it as *destiny* [*Geschick*]. This is how we designate the happening of the community, of a people."[51] In historicity, Dasein is necessarily rooted in the Dasein of others, and authentic happening of Dasein is Dasein "in and with its 'generation.' "[52]

With its demonstration of authentic existence as authentic historicity and, equally, of the openness to the prevailing historical situation as its most distinguished fundamental attitude, Heidegger's inquiry into the being of Dasein comes to its completion. From this point on, the origins and objects of history as a science are also determined. History is always concerned with a Dasein that has been. All historical facts, everything "material," must be traced back to a Dasein that has expressed itself in these facts according to its own possibilities. Nature, too, is included in history insofar as the structure of the environment as Dasein-related meaningfulness is exhibited in it. Historicity as the basic determination of Dasein demands, moreover, a "destruction" of history as it has existed up to the present point: the preserved facts and their inherited interpretations must be brought back into the living totality of the historical Dasein that belongs to them. Heidegger has already announced that the second half of *Being and Time* will be an attempt of this sort—an attempt at a historical destruction of the history of philosophy.[53]

Numerous objections may certainly be made concerning Heidegger's analyses and his methodological foundations can be rejected outright. Yet every critique of this sort misses the meaning of this work, which remains "true" even if it commits significant errors. Decisive, here, is the new philosophical impetus that these interpretations have brought about. Conscious of its acute necessity, the basic question of all living philosophies is posed: what is authentic existence and how is it possible at all? After choosing many false paths, it is now once again evident that the meaning and essence of man is comprised in his concrete Dasein: "Man's '*substance*' is . . . [his] *existence*."[54] Philosophy has found its way back to its original necessity and it is concerned only with this existence, with its truth and fulfillment. From this foundation, all philosophical problems can now be approached in an effort to rethink them in their genuine relation to Dasein and to explore the degree to which they have expressed existential struggles and needs, the degree to which they point to truths, lies, or masks of being-in-the-world. It is wonderful how, from this point on, problems and solutions that had become rigid are caught up in dialectical motility, taking the form appropriate to the concrete human beings that lived—and live—in them. Concepts such as "knowledge," "truth," "science," "understanding," "reality," the "external world," etc. become clear when their objects are unveiled as the originary modes of conduct of human beings or as

the basic, natural phenomena of Dasein. And if, in the course of such interpretations, the obvious fallenness of everyday existence should once again be
brought back to the possibility of authentic, true existing, then this philosophy
attains its highest meaning as a genuinely practical science: as the science of
the possibilities of authentic being and its fulfillment in the authentic act.

Recognizing the historical thrownness of Dasein and its historical determinateness and rootedness in the "destiny" of the community, Heidegger has
driven his radical investigation to the most advanced point that bourgeois philosophy has yet achieved—and can achieve. He has revealed man's theoretical
modes of behavior to be "derivative," to be founded in practical "making-
provision,"[55] and has thereby shown praxis to be the field of decisions. He has
determined the moment of decision—resoluteness—to be a historical situation
and resoluteness itself to be a taking-up of historical fate. Against the bourgeois
concepts of freedom and determination, he has posed a new definition of being
free as the ability to choose necessity, as the genuine ability to grasp the possibilities that have been prescribed and pregiven; moreover, he has established
history as the sole authority in relation to this "fidelity to one's own existence."
Here, however, the radical impulse reaches its end.

Yet if Heidegger's examination is content to limit its analysis to these exhibitions, does it stay true to its own (historical) meaning? The concrete human
being—in his or her concrete and historical situation—was discovered to be
the basis of all philosophical thought. Historicity proved to be neither a mere
accidental quality of Dasein nor its mere factitious "place" in the world, but
rather the mode of being of Dasein itself, in which its full determination is
grounded. Within these discoveries lies the necessity—for a project with ambi-
tions as radical as Heidegger's—of recourse to the decisive fact of the "today" in
its full historical concretion. It was in and for this "today" that the buried truths
were uncovered: it was not a new attempt to solve the traditional problems of
philosophia perennis, but was rather a fate-bound reflection demanded by the
threatening situation of contemporary human beings. In view of this "today"
and of the recovery of these truths, certain questions thus needed to be asked
and answered: what, concretely, is authentic existence? How is authentic existence concretely possible, if at all? Posed to "Dasein in general," these questions
are empty; that is, they neither require avowal nor entail obligation, which are
two characteristics they must possess as existential questions. Incorporating the
"today" and its situation would have shown both that authentic existence—
which is always possible only as the "*disavowal* of that which in the 'today' . . .

is working itself out as the 'past' in the 'today' " [56]—can only occur "today" as the act that brings about concrete change and that it is the fate of "today" to have to find its way by overthrowing the factically existing situation. Moreover one must undoubtedly oppose Heidegger's attempt, precisely at this juncture, to refer the decisive resoluteness back to the isolated Dasein rather than driving it toward the resoluteness of the act. This resolute act is not just a "modification" of existence as it has been—it is a shaping anew of all spheres of public life.

Furthermore, as thrown being-in-the-world, Dasein is in every case bound to its with-world and environment. In turn, this world is in every case rooted, as a context of meaning, in a Dasein that is concerned with and makes provision in it. But how should this Dasein be more precisely defined for the concrete context? Is it always as individual Dasein, such that there would be as many worlds as individuals? Certainly not; the world that Dasein has is a common world (even though each individual colors and modifies it). But how far does this commonality extend? It has its limits, first of all, in the historical situation. It may be that an all-inclusive "objective" world of nature is there and that it extends through all of history (for example, nature as the object of the mathematical natural sciences exists in this way); yet the historical world manifests itself as relevant only as a context of meanings, as "life-space." [57] Where, then, are the boundaries of the particular historical situation itself? And is the world "the same" even for all forms of Dasein present within a concrete historical situation? Obviously not. It is not only that the world of significance varies among particular contemporary cultural regions and groups but also that, within any one of these, abysses of meaning may open up between different worlds. Precisely in the most existentially essential behavior, no understanding exists between the world of the high-capitalist bourgeois and that of the small farmer or proletarian. Here the examination must confront the question of the material constitution of historicity and in so doing achieves a breakthrough that Heidegger fails to achieve or even gesture toward. It should be remarked that Dilthey has gone further than Heidegger in this direction. Specifically, despite Dilthey's recognition of the particular and unique structure of historicity, the essays published under the title of *The Formation of the Historical World in the Human Sciences* [58] repeatedly find themselves in their analyses running up against the irreducibly material content of history. [59] A short passage may here be quoted: "Each age exhibits a distinctive structure. . . . [Each] involves a system of kindred ideas prevailing in various spheres. . . . But it must be acknowledged that the background of these ideas is a kind of a raw power that cannot be overcome by this higher world. And this is always the case. The facticity of race, of space, and of power-relations provides a matrix that can never be wholly brought under the power of spirit. It is Hegel's dream that each age represents a stage in the development of reason."[60]

4. Draft of a Dialectical Phenomenology

The problematic of historical existence led of its own accord to the material content of historicity. This content is how we have referred, by way of anticipation, to the circle of concrete historical conditions within which a concrete Dasein exists and in which, in every case, Dasein and the totality of involvements [*Bewandtnisganzheit*] of its world are rooted. Marx determined this material content to be the natural and economic basis of society. It is not some kind of unchanging substance that stands outside of the historical movement and operates on it; rather it is itself included in this movement. For Marx, nature has its own history, just as the economy has a history. Both are things that have come to be. Once they are there, however, they constitute a "facticity that cannot be wholly brought under the power of spirit," the basis of concrete Dasein and its totality of involvements. Before we make a transition to the historical materialism that has announced itself in these last sentences, we must first sketch out the method that will direct us in this undertaking. It follows from what has previously been said that Marxism is a historical theory in a double sense: first, because its object is a historical one and is handled in a historical fashion; and second, because it itself intervenes, within a concrete historical situation, in the historical movement. The method with which Marxism approaches its object has been labeled, by Marx, the *dialectical method.*

The relationships between the Marxian and Hegelian dialectic cannot be entered into at the present. Our current task is merely to reveal the dialectic's methodological meaning and, in turn, to ask whether it is adequate to its object.

Marx and Engels repeatedly emphasized that the dialectic is not arbitrarily applied to its object, but rather that it "corresponds to" the movement of history itself. In a celebrated passage at the end of the afterword to the second edition of *Capital*, Marx notes that the dialectic captures "every historically developed form in the process of movement." From the very beginning, thus, the dialectical method sees its object as historical—that is, it regards it in terms of becoming and of transitoriness, as something that has developed in a particular historical situation, that is thus related to the form of Dasein peculiar to this situation, and that is only to be understood by that form of Dasein. The dialectical method thus dissolves abstract historical categories that have become rigidly unequivocal, revealing them to be "forms of existence [*Daseinsformen*], determinations of existence,"[61] leading them back to their unique, living, and concrete ground. This is the methodological meaning of the Marxian dialectic, a meaning that must be insisted on in the face of the foolish uses of the dialectic as a "rattling scaffold" or as a one-size-fits-all schema. Here we will cite two further passages from Engels and Lenin in which this meaning of the dialectical method is clearly laid out: it is "the great, fundamental thought that the world cannot be understood as a complex of ready-made *things*, but rather as a complex of *processes*, in which the things—apparently stable no less than their thought-images in our heads, the concepts—undergo an unceasing process of coming into being and passing away . . ."[62] "Dialectical logic demands that we go further. In order truly to know the object, it is necessary to grasp and to research it from every side, in all of its connections and 'mediations.' . . . Second, dialectical logic demands that the object be taken in its development, in its 'self-movement,' and in its changes. . . . Third, all of human praxis must be included in the 'definition' of the object, not only as a criterion of its validity but also as a practical determination of the connection of the object with that which man requires. Fourth, dialectical logic teaches that 'there are no abstract truths; truth is always concrete.' "[63] Perhaps already in Hegel, but certainly in Marx's work, the specific form of thesis, antithesis, and synthesis indicates in its very method the need to be true to the immanent necessity of historical movement. Rooted in the fundamental character of historicity, this immanent necessity of history finds its clearest expression in the fact that the causes of historical movement from the status quo to that which is to come [*vom Beste-henden zum Kommenden*] are already fully present in the world as it exists in the present and that they develop only out of it. It is only by this principle that transcendent, metahistorical, or ahistorical impulses or interventions are excluded. However, insofar as this development is realized only through the (historical) action of man, that which is to come will always take the form of a "negation of the status quo." We will recall that—as Heidegger made clear—a resoluteness toward authentic existence that is conscious of its fate is only possible as a "disavowal" of the past, a past whose domination always stands in the way in the form of fallenness. This is, when taken in conjunction with the Marxian breakthrough to practical concretion, the theory of revolution. Since it is the case that, up to a certain point of historical development, that which exists in the present necessarily becomes a fallenness that transforms all forms of existence into inauthentic forms, the historical act that makes authentic existence once more possible is, necessarily, a revolutionary act. Therefore, the dialectical method that makes these contexts apparent is "critical and revolutionary in its essence."[64] Marx did not apply the dialectic only to the analysis of social and economic objects in general, but also to the investigation and interpretation of concrete historical situations (particularly in *The Class Struggles in France, The Eighteenth Brumaire of Louis Bonaparte*, the addresses of the General Council of the International). For in looking at the totality of human Dasein, not only the fundamentals of existence are important. One must also look at the concrete situation—the situation in which the dialectic finds its application as revolutionary praxis. Every attempt to rend this totality into two by viewing theory and praxis as if they were modes of conduct that rested upon different ontological foundations contradicts of the essential structure of historicity.

So is the dialectical method an approach that truly corresponds to its objects and, if so, how far does its validity extend? The prerequisite for the genuineness of the method is a historicity appropriate to the being of its objects. We may now recall how phenomenology demonstrated the historicity of Dasein and consider the modification of the phenomenological method required by Dasein's historicity.

Phenomenology means: allowing questions and approaches to be guided by the objects themselves, bringing the objects fully into view. *In being grasped, however, the objects always already stand in historicity*. This sphere of historicity already begins, as a concrete historical situation, in the development of the question as it seeks the object; it includes the unique individuality of the questioner, the direction of his question and the way in which the object first appears. Certainly, there is a scientific method (as for example, that of mathematics and mathematical physics) that begins by viewing its objects in complete abstraction from their historicity and that therefore sees them as principally ahistorical; and this scientific method can and must do this, for the type of being of its object is not historical. Circumventing the sphere of historicity in this way, however, is completely out of place in all sciences that deal with human existence, the modes of this existence, and the domains of meaning that are grasped by them as "objects of significance" [*Bedeutsamkeiten*]. Such a failure to situate a given historicity within a phenomenological analysis signifies that the investigation has failed to bring its object fully into view. But there

is more. Phenomenology should never let its investigation end simply with
the exhibition the historicity of its object, only subsequently to return it to
the sphere of abstraction. Phenomenology must constantly maintain its object
in the most rigorous concretion. This means that as an examination of a historical object—as an examination grounded in historicity—phenomenology
must allow the concrete historical situation, its concrete "material content,"
to work its way into the analysis. Thus a phenomenology of human Dasein
would be lacking in necessary richness and clarity if it were to pass over the
material content of historical Dasein. This, as has already been suggested, is
the case with Heidegger. If Dasein is historical in its very being, then it stands
at every moment in a concrete, historical situation—a situation that must first
be destroyed before its basic structure can be exhibited.

The achievement of the dialectical method is precisely this last concretion.
For this is exactly what is at stake in the dialectical method: doing justice at
every moment to the specific, concrete-historical situation of its object. The
petrified and free-floating *abstracta* become concrete again for the dialectical
method once they are seen reunited with the human existence "that belongs to
them." Moreover, the true dialectic can only then fulfill the demand for ultimate
concretion and (thus) become true to the type of being of human existence
when, on the basis of knowledge of the concrete historical situation, it also
draws correct conclusions for the decisive sphere of human existence: the sphere
of *praxis*. At the same time, the dialectic extends the line of concretion along one
axis to its utmost extreme; it does so by forcing the specific human Dasein that
it addresses in its analyses to take up, with the whole of its existence, a practical
position and to *act* in accordance with its historical situation. The significance
of the dialectical method consists precisely in the fact that it culminates in a
method of action in accordance with knowledge.

If we therefore demand, on the one hand, that the phenomenology of
human Dasein initiated by Heidegger forge onward, coming to completion
in a phenomenology of concrete Dasein and the concrete historical action
demanded by history in each historical situation, we must, on the other hand,
demand that the dialectical method of knowing become phenomenological,
that it push itself it in the opposite direction and thereby learn to incorporate
concretion in the full comprehension of the object. In other words, it must not,
in its analysis of the particular given, remain content simply to determine the
given's historical position or to establish its rootedness in a historical situation of
human existence. Rather, it must push its research further, asking whether the

particular facts exhaust themselves in that which is given or whether that which is given preserves within itself a meaning of its own—if not an extrahistorical one, then at least one that persists throughout all historicity. Though these questions may at first seem unnecessary for the purpose of deciding about a particular historical doing [*Tun*],[65] such work is indispensable if this doing is ever truly to arise out of knowledge.

Only with the unification of both methods—a dialectical phenomenology that represents a method of constant, extreme concretion—is it possible to do justice to the historicity of human Dasein.

With what has been said above, the domain of validity of dialectical phenomenology has already been broadly charted. It extends, first, to a human existence that is historical in its very being—in its essential structure as well as in its concrete forms and configurations. It further encompasses all of the dimensions of meaning shaped by human existence (Dilthey called this phenomenology of culture the "history of spirit" [*Geistesgeschichte*]). The sphere of nature (corporeal world) can also become an object of dialectical phenomenology insofar as those elements of it that are "in historicity" are thematized. There is a dialectical natural science—not, however, in the newer physics, as Engels falsely believed[66]—but rather a dialectical natural science as the history of nature in its active relationship to a particular Dasein. There is also a science, however, that is not dialectical at all: mathematical physics. The question as to which of these sciences is "correct" is a meaningless one, since the objects of each are distinct in accordance with being. It is precisely in abstraction from all historicity that mathematical physics handles its objects—and it can do this meaningfully because the *being* of nature is simply not historical in the way the being of Dasein is. Nature *has* a history, but it *is* not itself history. Dasein *is* history. The fundamental dialectical science is the science of the essence of historicity in general—of its structure and of the rules of movement and the possible forms of existence of historical Dasein. Dilthey tackled this fundamental theme in his *Introduction to the Human Sciences*.[67] Every dialectic presupposes a thematization of historicity of this sort; in fact, the fundamental dialectical insights that determine the further course of the investigation are rooted in it. For Marx, the term "historical materialism" refers to this domain of basic insights into the structure of historicity.

It is in this domain alone, the domain of historicity, that the question of the correctness of Marxism can be meaningfully posed, if by "correctness" is meant a truth valid for every Dasein. All truths pertaining to the structure of historicity in general and of historical Dasein in general are, in this sense, universally valid. But, we should add, only these truths. All other dialectical insights refer to truths that pertain to a particular, concrete historicity and that are only possible to discover and identify through a phenomenology of this historicity.

Within this same context appears the problem of the "pure fact," a problem that has particularly occupied the study of history since Droysen. If by "pure fact" is meant the distillation of univocal facts, such that each fact would be expected to have the same meaning for every historical Dasein that approaches it, then a history of "pure facts" would be equivalent to a complete emptying out of history, for nothing would then remain but a naked, spatial-temporal skeleton (mere data). A fact is first produced in its historical purity when it is situated in the concrete context in which it first became a fact. In the process of being situated, however, the fact takes on a multivalent relation corresponding to the multiplicity of meanings that it possessed for the historical Dasein of the time and this multiplicity of meaning must be preserved.

Herein, however, an inner untruth of the dialectic would seem to be expressed. If all facts are grasped in their historical necessity, are not all facts then affirmed? Does not this dialectical equivalence of values obstruct the truth of decision? Does not such an equivalence of values devastate the inner significance of the action in its radical meaning? From this point onward, the dialectic is ineluctably confronted with the problem of value.

The authentic existential value is the truth of existence—which means existing appropriately within existence's authentic possibility. The authentic possibility, too, is taken over from the historical inheritance. It is an urgent task to differentiate the individual value of a person, his or her existence and contribution, from the historical heritage and the historical-social situation in which the person is found. Even more decisive in our context would be the examination of the relations between value and historicity both in the concrete modes of being-with-one-another and in the authentic historical forms of Dasein and thus also in the sphere of authentic historical action. Here the question should be raised of whether and to what degree concrete historical forms of Dasein (social systems) can be valuable in and of themselves, such that "historical" existing and action might, despite its "necessity," also represent the realization of values. If historicity is really an existential determination of human Dasein, then it is ontologically possible that existential values are bound up with historicity in their very being. Such, for instance, that historical forms of Dasein (social systems) necessarily make the realization of certain existential values impossible—suggesting, in turn, that the realization of these values would only become possible under a new historical form of Dasein.

All these problems are noted here only in order to counter the misinterpretation that the historicity of human Dasein would necessarily require an equivalence of all values that makes no decisions and offers no possibilities. Naturally, the dialectic cannot grasp all realms of value. There are values of the solitary Dasein, values that are won precisely in reaction to historicity and whose grandeur feeds, in large part, on the tragic heroism of the hopeless struggle against historicity. The dialectic can demonstrate the marginality of such figures, forms, and patterns—it says nothing, however, about their immanent value.

These remarks should merely point to that place at which the problem of value presents difficulty—even for the dialectic—and thus refute the objection that the historicity of Dasein would paralyze every decision and thus effectively undermine and discourage the act. It is precisely knowledge of historicity that leads to the most momentous decision: the decision either to struggle for the recognized necessity, even against Dasein's own inherited existence, or to remain in necessarily fallen forms of existence. The alternative ways of defining the act will be taken up and explored further later.

5. Attempt at a Phenomenology of Historical Materialism

The term "historical materialism" designates the entire domain of Marxian insights [*Erkentnisse*] oriented toward the overall structure of historicity and toward the laws of historical movement. We know that these insights are integral to the entire structure of Marxism and play an important role in every concrete analysis; but we can and must mark off this domain as the only one to which the question of the correctness of Marxism can meaningfully be applied. Again, this can only be done in terms of an immanent critique; we must ask whether historical materialism has brought the phenomenon of historicity fully into view and whether it has interpreted it appropriately. Here too we seek to build on Heidegger's analyses, because they have revealed the phenomenon of historicity in its most originary form. The primary historicity of Dasein manifested itself in the fact that the particular, thrown Dasein creates its form of existence out of that which has been, modifies this according to its meaning and thus once again becomes, in the present, a fateful past for the Dasein that is to come. The world, too, is (as natural environment) drawn into this process in that it does not simply stay fixed in pure present-at-handness as a frozen world of things, but rather, as a world of significance, is rooted in the given Dasein. It is self-evident that there exists an objective world of nature that transcends consciousness. As the most originary form of self-evidence, the "objectivity of the external world" poses no problems—the problematic only arises with the question of the relationship "between" human beings and the external world. There are things that are objectively present, toward which Dasein is oriented, that it is concerned with and recognizes; but they always appear to it as significant, as standing in a context of involvement that is a product of tradition and historical becoming. Theoretical modes of conduct can be used to break out of the world of significance, but the knowing [phenomenological] gaze can only ever penetrate the abstract structures and forms of things—only to that about them that can never be "real" and that can never enter into the context of concretion.

Only superficially can these interpretations be confused with some sort of idealistic philosophy of immanence. The weakness of idealistic philosophical interpretations does not lie in their assertion that Dasein and world are interrelated according to being but rather in their failure to move beyond this assertion, their failure to push forward to discover its ontological grounds. It is not *Dasein in general* that is drawn, as thrown being-in-the-world, into its world in every case, and it is not *worldhood in general* that is related, as meaningfulness, in every case to a particular Dasein; rather, there is always a *concrete* Dasein in a *concrete* world, and a concrete world is related to a concrete Dasein. This last abstraction makes it impossible to advance to the material content of historicity. According to its very essence, Dasein is always concrete Dasein in a particular historical situation (spatial-temporal situation) and, as such, it is, according to its very essence, determined by concretely demonstrable material givens. The phenomenological analysis must not come to a standstill once it has discovered Dasein to be the phenomenally ultimate form of thrownness. There is no unitary world of significance that is bound to a unitary Dasein. The bond that exists between Dasein and world is in accordance with being and is not a free-floating *abstractum*; rather, it constitutes itself in concretely historical processes. To be sure, Dasein is thrown being-in-the-world, but as such it is always determined by its world, and not simply in the mode of fallenness in relationship to some "they"—even if this "they" is in accordance with Dasein's being—but rather through the concrete-historical with-world and environment into which it was born. It is this that we call the material content of historicity; it is not only the factical, but also the structurally final determination of Dasein.

Dasein's being-in-the-world means thrownness in a concrete-historical with-world and environment, such that Dasein determines and develops itself in each case out of this world. Let us recall the phenomenological interpretation's exhibition of Dasein's primary mode of conduct as that of a practical, provision-making being: being as setting itself up in its world, directing itself toward its world, utilizing the objects to be found in its world as they prove useful for its provision. This means that concrete-historical Dasein should be understood primarily in terms of how it has provided for itself in its world and according to its world. Dasein's primary care is for itself, for its production and reproduction.

In considering this first principle of historical materialism we must immediately deal with the objections based on mistaken interpretations that seem automatically to come to the fore. At issue is neither the relative priority of value nor the affirmation of one mode of being as the authentic one for Dasein; rather, the question is purely one of phenomenal priority: in view of the simple reality of historical Dasein, the making-provision for the self that expresses itself in production and reproduction proves to be Dasein's "first" mode of behavior. With this, moreover, no ontic-temporal priority is intended or implied, as if (for example) pure production and reproduction somehow existed first and then the "cultural" and "spiritual/intellectual" modes of behavior and objective realms came along afterward. Rather it is the case—and this often forgotten fundamental principle must not be lost—that Dasein, as being-in-the-world, is always already "material" and "spiritual," "economic," and "ideological" at one and the same time (these terms merely serve to indicate the areas among which tradition generally differentiates), such that the ideological realms are already reproduced along with the historical movement of Dasein. (This circumstance is made clear in Karl Liebknecht's *Studies in the Laws of Motion in Social Development*.)[68] Yet there does exist a foundational relationship in accordance with being, such that in every case the ideal objectivities exhibited in the realm of a concrete historical Dasein are grounded in material objectivities. Their foundations are as they are, certainly, *in accordance with being*: that is to say that it is not according to their validity or meaning (so far this argument has yet to make any statement whatsoever concerning meaning and validity) but rather according to their *existence* and (historical) emergence, that they are grounded in concrete historical, "material" objectivities. The concepts of "ideal and material objectivities" are, as already emphasized, makeshift expedients, mere placeholders for something to be developed later, even if they correspond to traditional usage. According to these broad, traditional terms, it would be in the spirit of Marxism to attribute to ideality all objects not provided through the production and reproduction of "material life." To this realm would belong, for example, not only a mathematical but also an aesthetic object! (That is, the aesthetic object precisely insofar as it is aesthetic and not a means of reproduction. For the artisan, it is of course the latter and is therefore not "ideal" in that context.) No one has even begun to clarify these concepts in view of the phenomenon of historicity. This would have to be the object of a separate investigation. By "ideology" we understand the entire domain of ideal objectivities demonstrable in the concrete totality of a concrete, historical Dasein. This demarcation aims in the same direction as the determination given by Liebknecht.[69]

Furthermore, these observations are not directed toward the (abstract) individual Dasein but rather toward the concrete historical unity that is, in every case, a *society*—even if it is still lacking in determinacy. To attempt to explain ideology out of materiality in the case of an *individual* person would be a completely unjustified transgression of the phenomenological self-evidence of historicity. The individual person is not the historical unit of Dasein. It cannot be stressed often enough that these formulations are oriented toward the unit and unity that offers itself in an examination of concrete historicity—that is, of a "society." Moreover, there is no correspondence between what has been said and the claim that the "survival instinct" is Dasein's basic drive or instinct, for no such unitary "drives" can be attributed to society—nor, as will become evident, to a society divided within itself.

In general, the greatest misunderstandings concern the explanation of ideologies. There should, as a matter of principle, be a distinction between the exposition of the immanent meaning of an ideology and its historical meaning (locus). It is one of the fundamental theses of historical materialism that that which an ideology *intends* (its immanent meaning) is by no means the same as its *historical significance*. It is only the latter that interests historical materialism, and it alone is accessible by means of historical materialism's dialectical method. The explanation of the immanent meaning demands an approach directly contrary to that of the dialectic—an approach based on grasping the ideology to be explained as a self-contained, independent unity.

Even though aimed at the kind of misunderstandings that can only be eliminated through detailed analyses, these anticipatory refutations should serve, as much as is possible, to ensure that old confusions are not allowed to encumber an examination just as it is getting underway. We now return to the first theses in which historical materialism expressed itself. The course of the analysis of historicity has made clear that Dasein is always concrete-historical Dasein and that it specifically takes the form of the determinate society (determinate in some form or another, determinate according to Dasein itself) into which the concrete-historical Dasein in its making-provision has been thrown. Dasein's original mode of conduct is practical-active, as production and reproduction, on which the domains of cultural, spiritual, and intellectual objects are founded. It is now our task to add precision to these still largely suggestive remarks.

First of all, what constitutes that "society" which we have already addressed as the authentic historical unity? The answer is that unity that proved itself to be a multiplicity of Dasein, such that individual Dasein only becomes historical as a part of that society. This unity—we now speculate—is at the same time that society in which and for which those worlds of significance are constituted and toward which each of the totalities of involvement of the everyday environment is oriented.

To every concrete-historical Dasein there belongs a concrete-historical "life-space."[70] The thrownness of Dasein is also thrownness into a particular part of the natural world. Out of this part of its natural environment, Dasein first creates the possibilities of its existence as possibilities of production and reproduction. The circle out of which Dasein creates these possibilities is what we call "life-space." This circle is no inviolable barrier: it can be blasted open, expanded, or contracted—but these explosions, expansions, and contractions are, in each case, modifications of this particular life-space and, as such, are determined by the life-space, such that the life-space enters into the historical movement as an inescapable inheritance. It is neither a "form of intuition" nor an empty spatiality of nature but rather is full of the "ready-to-handness" of the Dasein that is concerned with, appropriates, and provisions it. Life-space is filled with everything that Dasein needs and to which it lays claim for its use. Out of this life-space come the objects of Dasein's fears, hopes, and beliefs and from it Dasein receives the impetus for everything Dasein does. From life-space as well come the impulses to movement—to every movement that seizes the whole existence of the society for which Dasein makes provision. This may be the case when the life-space proves no longer sufficiently fertile to bear the production and reproduction of the society concerned with it and is therefore expanded or improved, or when it must be protected from the assault of another society and thereby is circumscribed or destroyed, or when new spaces with new societies appear in its train, which are then drawn into the circle of its provisioning. Life-space appears, in the first instance, as the frontier of concrete-historical Dasein, the historical unity as determinative of society; this becomes most easily and graphically evident in the historical forms of the horde, the tribe, the village community, and the antique city-state. (The question of how much family and clan contributed to the creation of the historic unities will not be explored here. Though their importance cannot be denied, they are not—in a phenomenological sense—primary historical unities, and *factically* they could not have been such unless they possessed, in the sense of complete autarky, their own life-space.) We will later see whether this determination is sufficient for the interpretation of a fully historical Dasein.

Let us now consider how historical society makes provision for itself in its life-space. Heidegger's analysis of Dasein once again exposed the truth that man's substance is his existence. That means that the human being can only fulfill its essence if it fully grasps and shapes its existence. The human being's first concern is for its own existence (and not, moreover, for its existence in the vegetative sense—which would merely be the "instinct of self-preservation"—but rather for the maintenance, formation, and furtherance of being as thrown being-in-the-world, which is to say, with the inclusion of the material and ideal concretions that belong to it existentially). We may designate as "existential needs" the circle of objects comprehended within Dasein's primary concern and we may designate as "economy" the provisioning aimed at fulfilling these needs. The existential needs of society are rooted in the objects whose provision is necessary for the maintenance, formation, expansion, or furtherance of its being.

The meaning of "social production and reproduction" is determined by the totality of existential needs and the modes of provisioning arising from them. Social production and reproduction are truly the most originary and the ultimate constituent of every historical unity because they, without exception, affect its pure existence, and the essential distinction and characterization of human Dasein can only be derived from an existential difference. And one cannot deduce anything more about this totality nor does it allow itself to be further reduced, for it is immediately rooted in the thrownness of Dasein itself in the sense that it is, on the one hand, determined by the natural environment (soil conditions, climate, situation, etc.) into which Dasein is thrown and, on the other hand, determined by the historical inheritance of past generations, to which it is (positively or negatively) committed.

As the expression of the existential needs of a society, the society's mode of production is both the constitutive historical foundation on which it rests and the ground on which the historical movement takes place. Yet it must be remarked ever again that the ideological dimensions of a society are produced ahead of and alongside the economic dimensions—and that is precisely because the former have their foundations in the latter. The old question of what has objective priority, of "which came first"—mind or matter, consciousness or being—not only cannot be answered by a dialectical phenomenology but also becomes meaningless within this framework. What is given is simply always Dasein as historical being-in-the-world, which already includes, at *one and the same time*, spirit and matter, consciousness and being; and it is only on the basis of this evident circumstance that assessments can be made of the foundational relationship that prevails in Dasein. Every attempt to reshape givenness so that it favors the absolutization of one of its parts is dogmatism—a dogmatism that dialectical thought can only hold in contempt, for it constitutes an attempt to begin a dialectical examination with a rigid abstraction, with a *primum absolutum*.

Let us summarize once again. Historical society constitutes itself in the modes of production corresponding to its thrownness, in the modes in which it provisions its life-space in accordance with its existential needs. Only then, when a society truly provisions its life-space in a unified way *as* a society, is it a historical unity, the bearer of historical movement. In the moment when this unity is torn asunder, when the whole society no longer exists in making-provision for its existential needs, and where a *division of labor* is sufficiently advanced that the provision for life-space is no longer regulated through the voluntary act of the whole society, but is rather distributed by means of various coercive measures (such that now the hardest work appears as the activity of the subordinate and the inferior)—in this moment the existential needs, too, grow out of and differentiate themselves from this division of labor within a society that was once unified. As soon as the mode of production of a society is so arranged that it constitutes different strata within the same life-space—strata that exist only in and through their position within the productive process—then these strata become the authentic bearers of historical movement. With the emergence of "classes," new historical unities also arise, which are more originary, more authentically historic than the (seemingly) inclusive communities of the city, the country, the nation, since class exists solely in and through the primary mode of historical Dasein—through the mode of production—and only class is determined through it.

Thus we already stand in the field of inquiry constituted by the problem of *historical movement,* its "ground," its direction, and its goal.

The problem is falsely posed from the very beginning if one seeks to explain the historical movement as something somehow added on to an originally static, historical society (however one characterizes this "original society"). Dasein is, rather, in accordance with its being, historical; and as such, it is always already "motile" [*bewegtes*]: only in historical movement can it exist at all. Provisioning the life-space means, necessarily, altering that which is present-at-hand (pressing natural forces into service, moving between natural positions, seeking out new sources of nutrition, preparing and distributing products, trade, etc.). The whole process by which nature becomes history (cf. *The German Ideology*) belongs to the primary modes of conduct of Dasein and to the fundamental structure of historicity. Furthermore, historical changes are by no means pure changes of location, spatial displacements. Heidegger has forcefully called attention to the "ontological enigma of the motility of happening"[71]: "what 'happens' to equipment and work as such has its own character of movement, and this character has been completely obscure up till now. . . . The motility of happening in which something 'happens to something' is not to be grasped in terms of movement as change of location."[72] In fact, every authentically historical movement proves itself to be "change of *meaning,*" a movement that changes the meaning of the objects it grasps. With the foundation of worlds of meaning (including ideal ones) by the provision-making Dasein, the world of "meaning" is, from the very beginning, drawn into the historical movement.

Every authentic historical movement is always a movement of provisioning Dasein and is, as such, economic movement according to the expression of this historical movement. For only such a movement takes hold of the primary modes of conduct of historical Dasein, reshapes society according to its historical existence and can, therefore, also reshape the worlds of meaning (ideologies) founded on this existence. The direction of the economic movement, however, can only be derived, as historical facticity, from the analysis of the concrete historical circumstances and it is therefore not accessible to a phenomemology of historicity as the fundamental structure of Dasein. Such an economic-historical analysis must always precede every theory of a historical action, for it performs an initial ground-clearing on which the action can subsequently happen as necessary change.

In this context, an attempt can now be made to clarify the concept of historical necessity. If motility (as transformation of the environment) belongs to the fundamental structure of historical Dasein, then talk of the necessity of this change can no longer be misunderstood as suggesting that it is something the world performs on Dasein the way the laws of gravity act on bodies. Historical necessity is not something that happens with or through Dasein; rather, it is characteristic of the being of historical Dasein itself and is always already given with its thrownness. Historical necessity is the necessary act of historical Dasein, the act that becomes mature in recognizing the historical situation and completes itself in seizing the historical situation. This act is neither good nor bad but is merely necessary or unnecessary. It would be a complete misrecognition of the being of historical Dasein if one were to pose the question of whether something can also happen without the act that wills and desires it. Certainly, one would be wholly wrong to suggest that necessity is only necessity when accompanied by this will and desire. "*It*" does not "happen" at all; rather, the acting being of Dasein happens and constitutes the entire realm of happening. (An eclipse of the sun, an earthquake, a storm does not "happen," but rather "enters into happening." The question that is posed by "it happens" comes out of theology and all but cries out for a God who first allows something to happen to Dasein.) The question is simply whether the historical act is done necessarily, that is, whether it is already given in pure historical existence. Here we return to the concept, first developed by Marx and newly interpreted by Heidegger, of "authentic historical existence." Historical Dasein does not by any means always exist as if it were aware of its historical situation, its "fate"—as if it knowingly took that fate upon itself and carried it out. If this were the case, then the historical act would indeed "happen" in the sense of not-being-able-to-exist-otherwise. Factically, however, the possibility of authentic historical existence—of insight into fate and the ability to grasp existence through the act—is only given in specific historical situations. The everyday provisioning of life-space necessarily thrusts Dasein into the provisioned environment and helps render the environment independent, transforming it into a rigid world of mere things, a world that holds Dasein captive within it with the inescapability of a law of nature and dictates Dasein's relation to it. This process of "reification," "depersonalization," "alienation" discovered by Marx, finds its most extreme expression in capitalist society, but is certainly already in force everywhere that the making-provision of the life-space, rather than being unitarily regulated according to the existential needs of the society, is divided within itself and thus robbed of the mastery it once held over its own existence. Once this has come to be the case, then the mode of production of such a society necessarily comes into contradiction with its forms of existence, and the authentically productive class must, on the strength of its sheer existence, break through the reification and sublate the contradiction. Knowledge of one's own historicity and conscious historical existence becomes possible at the moment when existence itself breaks through reification. If, for a particular Dasein, the world is no longer given except as a life-space that must be provisioned; if it no longer exists in anything but this provisioning; if, through its existence, it creates the conditions through which the world is first possible at all as life-space—then it can know that the world is, in accordance with being, related to a provisioning Dasein and that all of the reified objectivities are things that have historically come to be in that they have been objects of provisioning by a Dasein living among them. With the knowledge of the historicity of the world there comes to Dasein as well the knowledge of its own historicity, which, precisely through its thrownness, can create a new world by means of the transforming act. We now understand why it is that bourgeois philosophy must, according to its rootedness in being in bourgeois society, insist on the Dasein-independent objectivity of the environment—or alternatively, in those cases where it did maintain that the world is constituted in Dasein, it needed to contain this constitution within the immanence of consciousness. It is in the moment when revolutionary praxis is known [*erkannt*] as authentic historical existence and when concrete change is recognized as the real movement of the world that bourgeois society can finally be seen in its historical becoming and necessary fallenness. There is a Dasein whose thrownness consists precisely in the overcoming of its thrownness. The historical act is only possible today as the act of the proletariat, because it is the only Dasein within whose existence the act is necessarily given.

Phenomenological analysis demonstrated that human Dasein is essentially historical, and it recognized praxis as Dasein's originary conduct—and therefore opened up to view once again the ways in which "theoretical reason" is grounded in concrete historical existence, not as accidental facticity, but rather as a being-bound to one another in accordance with being. Historical materialism merely provides the concrete interpretation of this state of affairs when it speaks of "social being" (concrete being-in-the-world with each other) as the bearer of historical motility and of its "mode of production" (the praxis of doing things in the environment) as the determining factor of that which happens. However, as soon as this breakthrough from the phenomenological analysis of historicity in general to its concrete-material content was complete, it was only as a theory of revolution that it could gain historical form. In the moment in which praxis is recognized as the decisive attitude [*Haltung*] of human Dasein, as the attitude that authentically creates reality, in the moment when the given historical situation is grasped in its historical fallenness as the "reality of inhuman existence"—in that moment praxis will become the "revolutionary praxis" that leads toward the fulfillment of historical necessity. The motility of history is the happening of human existence. Every new historical reality demands a new human *existence*. Human existence can never become real through a mere change of the present reality, because in that case it would never move beyond the present existence. Indeed, by accepting the present existence as a given, Dasein must necessarily fall into its world of meaning, into its "ideology" (every reform, every revision of the status quo, presupposes acknowledgement of the status quo). "New" existence is only possible as "disavowal." There is so little contradiction between organic, historical development and revolution that revolution appears, rather, as the necessary form of historical motility; for it is revolution alone that can change the *existence* of historical Dasein.

From this point on, the historical meaning of historical materialism in the development of German philosophy can also be explained. But its historical significance was not its philosophical achievement, which was, rather, the proclamation of praxis as the decisive attitude of human Dasein. Marx expressly emphasized that "in contrast to materialism, idealism has always developed . . . the *active* dimension . . . but only abstractly."[73] In order to demonstrate the aptness of Marx's thesis, it suffices merely to mention the fact that both in the Kantian system and in Fichte's philosophy of the act, pure reason is grounded in the practical. The historicity of the world and its dialectical motility already permeate, as living truth, the externally rigid architectonics of Hegel's teachings as well. But idealism cheated human praxis out of its meaning and cheated the act of its decision insofar as it enclosed human knowledge in the world of appearances constituted a priori in consciousness, thereby elevating this a priori constitution above concrete experience. Historical materialism turned this relationship around; not, however, in order to pose the philosophical problem in a new way, but rather because it was forced, out of the necessity of an existence that had become unbearable, to comprehend anew that which happens.

On Concrete Philosophy

We begin our investigation with a consideration of philosophizing as the human activity in which philosophy constitutes itself.[1] Philosophizing, if one takes the meaning of this word seriously, is a mode of human existence. Human existence is in all its modes subject to the question of its *meaning* [*Sinn*]. It is the distinguishing characteristic of human existence that it is not realized through its mere being, that it "confronts" its possibilities in a very specific way, that it must first seize these possibilities and, in this seizing, live in the shadow of the question concerning its "to what end" [*Wozu*]. (All conceptions of this "to what end" as the sphere of the *purpose* that transcends human existence, for the sake of which it would exist, will be avoided here and elsewhere. Even when bracketing any thought of purpose, one can still speak of a "to what end," namely when the "to what end" of existence is grounded in its own being.) This "to what end" in its relationship to human existence is what we mean here by meaning.

Nor can the meaning of philosophizing, with regard to the original understanding of philosophizing, be conceived as the realization of a purpose transcendent to it. All genuine philosophizing has found its meaning in itself and grasped it through itself. Authentic philosophical effort aims at knowledge as the becoming visible of truth. The meaning of philosophizing can be designated provisionally as *the making visible of truth*.

Among the many determinations of truth we first consider that of *validity* [*Geltung*]. Truth *is* not validity, it does not "exhaust" itself in its validity, but validity belongs to the essence of truth. "Invalid" [*Ungültige*] truths, truths that are not valid [*gelten*], do not exist. But what is the meaning of validity? There "is" validity only in relation to human existence. The laws of nature are not valid for a nature that operates in accordance with them, but rather for the humans who understand nature. It is not valid for iron that the magnet attracts it, but rather for the person who observes the iron and the magnet. To say that certain conditions have validity means that I—to the extent that I am concerned with these conditions—must know of them, must be familiar with them, must act accordingly, must adjust myself to them. This "I" is absolutely essential; it points in every case to human existence. Validity does not mean that the valid conditions *are* only for human existence, but it does mean that they can be meaningfully spoken of as *true* only for human existence. The conditions expressed by the laws of nature are not true for nature—for nature they simply *are*—but only for man. A valid set of conditions can be independent of all human existence as far as its *being* is concerned, but validity, as truth, "is" only for man. [2]

If truth is thus related to human existence through validity, this relation receives its existential significance through a phenomenon that is often overlooked: *appropriation [die Aneignung]*. Truth demands by its very nature—however independent from all human existence the being of its conditions may be—an appropriation through human existence. Truths are not sought out and secured, not grasped through the labor of knowing then to be tucked away somewhere and preserved *in abstracto*; rather, in the knowledge of truth lies the demand for its appropriation. [3] Knowledge is an appropriation only for the one who knows primordially, for the one who discovers and achieves mastery over what is known for and in his person, "as if it were the first time." For every individual who fails to repeat this process of original discovery with his entire person, knowledge becomes mere familiarity, truth becomes accepting-as-true. Every genuine truth must be known *[gewußt]* and possessed, and knowing *[Wissen]* and possessing are not temporary acts of human consciousness that appear and then disappear again; rather, they belong to the existing of human Dasein itself, they are a function of existence. Appropriation in no way constitutes the *being* of truth (the true conditions), but it does constitute the *purpose [Sinn]* of truth. The "to what end" of truth is realized only in appropriation.

If its appropriation through human Dasein necessarily belongs to the meaning of truth, and if this appropriation is realized as knowing and possessing in the existing of Dasein itself, then truth must also have an impact in this existing. The existing of human Dasein is, however, at every instant a form of relating to the world: action and reaction. Truth must thus intervene in this actual sphere of existing: Dasein must, in its form of relating, be able to orient itself toward the truth.

Every truth[4] has the existential significance that man can, through its appropriation, exist in a true fashion. That which is being considered here must initially, as long as it is still a question of preliminary, general determinations, be understood very broadly. Even mathematical knowledge can, in all cases in which it has the original character of truth, bring man into a "true" relationship with the world. The mathematical truths of the Greek world, for example, had this existential character: it is palpably evident in the Pythagorean texts and still resonates clearly in some of the Platonic dialogues.

Let us return now to our starting point. If the meaning of philosophizing is the making visible of truth, and if this truth has a fundamentally existential character, then not only is philosophizing a mode of human existing, but philosophy itself is, according to its very meaning, existential. One can delineate the domain of philosophy however one likes, but in its search for truth, philosophy is always concerned with human existence. Authentic philosophizing refuses to remain at the stage of knowledge; rather, in driving this knowledge on to truth it strives for the concrete appropriation of that truth through human Dasein. Care [*Sorge*] for human existence and its truth makes philosophy a "practical science" in the deepest sense, and it also leads philosophy—and this is the crucial point—into the concrete distress [*Bedrängnis*] of human existence. The interconnections sketched out here appear to us to ground the philosophical necessity of asking the following questions: Must not authentic philosophizing prove itself by demonstrating that the appropriation of its truths is of the utmost existential necessity? Is the question of the "fruitfulness" of philosophy perhaps not as "unphilosophical" as it is made out to be? Do philosophical problems and truths also have a "history," not in the merely factual sense that they take shape in "history," but also in the sense that they, historical in their essence, are bound to concrete historical existence and are meaningful and true only from the perspective of and for this existence. By the same token, do philosophical problems and truths also have a specific time, a place and an hour? Is it not possible that concrete human existence in its mode of Dasein and its historical activity has already appropriated for itself truths that have not yet been discovered by philosophical inquiry, such that the task of philosophy would be the emancipation of these truths through the interpretation of concrete existence? On the other hand, does not care for the very concrete possibilities of appropriation of its truths belong to the domain of philosophy? Is it not also the task of philosophy to prepare the ground for its truths and, if necessary, to fight in the sphere of historical existence for this preparation?

Let us summarize the meaning of the questions posed above: does not a necessary philosophical beginning come about when philosophy is once again seen from the standpoint of concrete human existence and is interrogated with concrete human existence as its end?

We believe that an abstract-universal treatment of these questions conceals the crucial, truly urgent significance of the problem, and that only a discussion in the sphere of the most extreme concretion can achieve the necessary clarity. Not the general but rather the concrete necessity of philosophy is at stake. The intrinsic value of authentic philosophizing—this needs to be emphasized once again—is not called into question by this discussion, but is rather presupposed by it. Before the question of the concrete necessity of philosophy can be posed with regard to the current existential situation, however, the general situation in which philosophizing encounters human Dasein must be outlined. We must limit ourselves in this context to only the most necessary preliminary suggestions.

Human existence, the subject of philosophy, always stands in a particular historical situation. The subjects and objects addressed by philosophy are not abstract, "interchangeable" ones; each individual exists in a particular framework of activity (in which he maintains and shapes his existence), in a particular social situation (through which his everyday environment is defined), in a particular state of the community of the people, which has in its turn evolved on the basis of particular natural and historical conditions. From birth onward each individual is delivered up to his historical situation: the possibilities of his existence are prescribed through it. And the objects that "stand over against" Dasein, the things with which it is occupied and with which it fills a life-space, the natural world in which it lives, the structures and forms in which it runs its course—these are not fixed, "unequivocal," independent quantities that manifest themselves in the same way in any given historical situation. Whenever and wherever they appear, they have already been grasped and changed by a concrete existence, have likewise become "history," handed down from one generation to another, shaped according to the necessities of the respective existence.

If one intends to be serious about the philosophical concern for Dasein, then philosophy must not view this conditioning of Dasein through the historical situation as mere facticity, as historical "perspective," as temporal coincidence, or as the realization of an "essential content" [*Wesensgehalt*] (that is itself extra- or supratemporal), but rather as the authentic fate of Dasein, as the concrete fullness of existence itself. Dasein does not "make" history as its product, it does not live in history as if history were its more or less coincidental space or element; rather, the concrete existing of Dasein "*is*" happening [*Geschehen*] that is understood as "history" [*Geschichte*].[5] To regard the ontological historicity[6] of Dasein as mere facticity or something like it would not only mean over-looking the actual life-sphere of Dasein at the very outset of the philosophical undertaking, but would also contravene the findings of phenomenology, which alone may serve to guide it. Let us observe for a moment the situation in the phenomenological reduction. When consciousness is extracted from its natural comportment toward the real world, when every judgment about this world is bracketed out, every transcendent "positing" avoided, then an entirely new area becomes available for study: the flow of consciousness with the fullness of its experiences on the one hand, and the objects, experienced by this conscious-ness as intentionalities, on the other. Here all talk of historicity has suddenly become meaningless, because reality is essentially [*wesentlich*] happening and history (in the sense of transcendent positing). It is entirely possible to restrict philosophy to this area. A wealth of knowledge can be acquired regarding the nature of consciousness, the construction of its acts, the connections among its experiences, the constitution of its objects, and all of this knowledge, if it has been attained with the requisite phenomenological exactitude, must have "supratemporal" validity. But in laying claim to the only field that could provide such knowledge, phenomenology has also made evident the only way in which phenomenological philosophizing is still possible outside of the reduction. The necessary correlate of the phenomenological reduction is the *becoming-historical of philosophy*. At the precise moment when the brackets of the reduction fall away, Dasein and its world in its historical concretion are found standing in front of us.

Let us consider an example. I observe the factory building standing across from me. In the phenomenological reduction I grasp it in its givenness as an object of perception. I exclude all transcendent positing and can now study the constitution of this intentional object in perception, the sequence of the acts through which it is constructed, the laws governing the relations among them, the levels of evidence through which it appears, etc. I can, on the basis of the object of perception "factory building," illustrate the essential laws of the givenness of a thing [*Dinggegebenheit*], as well as the givenness of color, extension, and the like. And now I let the reduction fall away but continue in the execution of the phenomenological method: to allow the "object itself," as it stands before me in total concretion, to be seen and to speak. What I now have is the complex "factory building" in the (more or less abundant) fullness of its concrete meaning: location of economic activity, in which something is "produced," temporary residence of "x" number of workers, property of "y" corporation, modern or obsolete, small or large. The factory appears as integrated into a particular economic system, as one of the elements that results from a long technical development, as the object of bitter conflicts of interest. These are all facts that reveal themselves to me upon closer consideration of the object factory, facts that extend over an ever larger area, but that have their common "location" in the "historicity" of the object factory and the entwinement of its meaning [*Sinnverbundenheit*] with historical human existence.

The historical reality that reveals itself when philosophy addresses Dasein is just as little a facticity, coincidental to a particular Dasein, from which one could abstract, as it is an independent, pure world of things, which could be cognitively detached from contemporaneous existence without damaging its truth. It becomes clear in this context why the ontological historicity of Dasein must also assume decisive significance for the methodology of the "social sciences." Social arrangements, economic orders, and political formations together constitute the happening of Dasein and must be viewed from the perspective of this existence [*Existenz*]. If they are investigated from the outset as "things," with an eye toward their structure, their relationships, and the laws of their development, the observations (most likely undertaken with the model of the natural sciences as their mistaken ideal) that result will be such that the meaning of these constructs cannot even appear. For in and with these constructs a particular Dasein exists in such a way that the very possibility of its "reification" is only given at a specific historical stage of the "fragmentation" of Dasein.[7] It is similarly unacceptable to divide historical reality into a collection of discrete layers or spheres, such that, for example, economic and political and social and artistic and scientific activity are dealt with as self-sufficient, independent "modes of existing." Such a separation may be necessary for the modern scientific establishment, and it may also be objectively necessary for individual empirical investigations—but every investigation that aims at the essence of such constructs must be borne, even at the level of method, by an awareness of the indissoluble unity of historical existence. There are no "economic subjects," "legal subjects," etc., but only individuals or communities, which, as historical unities existing in their respective situations, engage in economic activity, administer and receive justice, pursue the arts and sciences, and so forth. (From this perspective Max Weber's concept of an "ideal type" also requires a correction. If the movements of historical reality are viewed as "deviations" from an ideal type, then one faces the obvious danger that it is precisely these concrete "deviations" that constitute historical occurrence).

We do in fact find striking confirmation of the methodological reorientation suggested here in modern social science as well. Max Weber provides an example, if not in his treatises on the theory of science, then certainly in the execution of his concrete studies, especially on the sociology of religion and in *Economy and Society*. He is deeply committed to a consistently holistic view of all the forces and spaces that historically circumscribe Dasein and to examining these forces and spaces from the standpoint of individual existence. And out of Max Weber's circle came Gottl-Ottilienfeld, with whom the reorientation in social scientific research first achieved full awareness of its methodological implications. His entire struggle is directed against the old approach of national economy, which "thinks in goods" alone, takes facts as data, and, devoid of all historical conscience for the existential character of the economy, lives in pure reification. His draft of a "General Theory of Economics" attempts to return to an understanding of "economics as life," to grasp economic structures as "elements of human communal life." (We cannot pursue here the extent to which even his forward-looking definition of the economy as "a shaping of human communal life in the spirit of a lasting harmonization of needs and their fulfillment" recreates the risk of the elements of the economy being viewed from the position of an abstract "economic subject.")

Having sketched out a general approach, we will now attempt to concretize the question of the existential significance of philosophy in terms of the present situation of Dasein: in the current historical situation, can one demonstrate that a particular mode of philosophizing is "necessitated" by the present form of existence, and which mode of philosophizing is it that proves to be necessary?

With this formulation of the question a problem immediately arises. Is it even permissible to speak of a particular historical situation as a "unity"? And, by the same token, of *a single* present existence and *a single* necessity? Or does the inquiry, precisely in its concrete form, rather run up against a multiplicity of present existences with a multiplicity of necessities in a multiplicity of historical situations? So that the formulation given above ends up leading to an abstraction that either ignores or does violence to concrete existence? When a particular historical situation is addressed, it is already viewed as something differentiable and differentiated and its specific difference in the flow of historical occurrence is accentuated. Decisive here is the visible line of demarcation from what has been: a concretely demonstrable state of economic and social development, which can be differentiated from the previous state in its *structure*. This difference is to be demonstrated first on the basis of the "material content" of the situation under consideration:[8] the mode in which the Dasein in question produces and reproduces, the structure of social stratification that corresponds to this mode, and the forms of social being. Numerous variations among individual classes, peoples, countries, etc. may become apparent in the process—but they are all merely variations within a unity that provides their foundation, different positions and developments within the same economic and social being. And only as far as the unified structure of this being extends can one speak of a unified situation.

To such a unified situation, however, there must also correspond a "unified" human existence. All individuals, all "communities" of a certain epoch, however different they may be, are united by the essential fact that they occupy the same historical situation. To be sure, there are as many modes of existing as there are individuals, and thus also just as many existential possibilities and necessities. But the individuals are by no means the ultimate unities on which the analysis of historical existence must rely. To begin this investigation with them would be to veer off arbitrarily when one is only halfway to the intended object (concrete historical existence). What appears under phenomenological scrutiny as a historical unity are "higher unities": "communities" or "societies" in their respective life-spaces (an attempt to clarify these concepts will be undertaken later). Thus, if the question concerning the type of philosophizing necessary for a concrete historical existence is posed here, it must aim at an existence that can be addressed as a unity for the reason that and insofar as the historical situation "in which it is based" demonstrates a unified structure in the sense suggested above. A specific type of philosophizing would then be necessary for concrete existence when this existence finds itself in a state of existential distress [*Not*] (that is to say, distress that concerns and takes hold of it as existence), a type of philosophizing that could help ameliorate this distress. It will be necessary to return later to the reasons why philosophizing is restricted here to the role of contributing, of helping.

The historical situation in which "contemporary" existence finds itself, and in view of which this investigation was begun, is determined in its structure through the structure of capitalist society at the stage of high capitalism (organized capitalism, imperialism). These concepts, which are intended to outline the situation, are by no means meant to refer to merely political or scientific circumstances; rather they seek to address the existential determinations of the present Dasein. In capitalist society, a particular mode of human existing, one that belongs only to that society, has become reality. The economic system has drawn all areas of life into the process of reification, which has detached forms of life and unities of meaning [*Sinneseinheiten*], previously bound up with the concrete individual, from any form of individual personality, and has created a force [*Gewalt*] that operates between and above individuals. Having been established, this force now subsumes all forms and values of the individual and the community under itself. The modes of being-with-one-another [*Miteinandersein*] are emptied of any essential content and are regulated from without according to "foreign" laws: fellow humans are primarily economic subjects and/or objects, professional colleagues, citizens, members of the same "society"; the essential relationships of friendship and love, any authentic form of human community is restricted to the small sphere of life that remains separate from general occupation [*Geschäftigkeit*]. At the same time as this situation drives individualism to the fore (which in no way contradicts a pronounced collectivism of the economy!), the individual is also separated from his "activity," which is "assigned" to him and is carried out without any possibility that it could actually lead to personal fulfillment.

The world in which this Dasein lives is also evolving to an ever greater degree into a "business" [*Betrieb*]. The things encountered in it are viewed from the outset as "goods," as things that one must use, but not in the sense of using them to meet the needs of Dasein. Instead, they are used to occupy or to fill an otherwise aimless existence, until they actually do become "necessities." In this way more and more existences are consumed simply in order to keep the "business" operational. The form of existence of all classes has hollowed itself out in such a way that it becomes necessary to place existence itself on a new foundation.

These remarks were not intended to depict the worldview and the "position" of capitalist society at the stage of high capitalism. The aim was merely to indicate that the crisis of capitalism is a crisis of existence, which has truly been shaken to its foundation. And even this is not yet the crucial aspect of the present situation for our purposes. It is rather this: science [*Wissenschaft*][9] in this situation is in a position to understand this crisis, its causes, and its resolution—or perpetuation. The foundations of contemporary existence, its historical contours, the general conditions that have led to this existence, and the historical consequences that accompany it have all become accessible to science. In these circumstances philosophy is burdened by existence with the enormous task of making this knowledge [*Wissen*] concrete, of presenting the necessity of its truths to this threatened existence. Whenever Dasein has found itself in an existential crisis, all genuine philosophy has understood its truths as existential and has seen its task as demonstrating, through the communication of those truths, its necessity for contemporaneous Dasein. We will attempt to clarify what this means.

Present existence is not only universally connected to all Dasein contemporaneous with it, but is also determined at its very roots by a universal historical inheritance. As this universal web of connections that originated in the economic structure of society has become more dense, two developments have occurred. On the one hand, the existentially binding truths of each society and its specific elements (status groups, classes, peoples) have become more differentiated, in their historical particularity. On the other hand, the "universally valid" truths have dissipated into abstractions [*abstrakte Sachverhalten*]. If we add to this the existential distress of contemporary Dasein mentioned above, which is determined by the structure of capitalist society, then it becomes clear that for this Dasein not a single truth can be established in existential concretion as absolutely binding and necessary. The responsibility of philosophy and its duty to dedicate itself to this existence only grows in these circumstances. To be sure, philosophy can continue to occupy itself with establishing essential laws for ethical behavior or being, for the world of values and its construction, and so forth. But if the problems thus "solved" are then lived through in their existential concretion, it will become clear that contemporary Dasein lacks entirely the possibility of maintaining and realizing these laws in its existence. It is easy to dismiss this problematic by saying that this Dasein is simply "not genuine" and not in truth, and thus it is not the task of philosophy to be concerned with it. Precisely this, however, is the goal: that philosophical investigation once again directs its attention toward the *possibilities of appropriation* of truth that are available to a given Dasein. If this Dasein is in a situation whose historical structure (the concrete way in which Dasein maintains and shapes itself socially) makes the appropriation of such truths impossible, then it is the task of philosophy to seek out Dasein and to attempt take it *out of this situation* and "bring it into truth." An example: in the intoxication of power that has accompanied advancements in technology and rationalization in contemporary society, it has been overlooked that the *personal* power of humans over nature and "things" has not increased, but decreased! Just as humans as "economic subjects and objects" find themselves in thrall to a commodity economy that has become a self-sufficient "entity," rather than in a situation where their industry is an appropriate mode of their existing, so it is that their tools—machines, means of transportation, electricity, light, power—have become for them so large and burdensome that, seen from the perspective of the individual, those people who use these tools must increasingly adapt their existences to suit them, must enter into their service. Indeed, it becomes clear that ever more lives are being consumed in order to keep them "functioning"!

This is just one aspect of the fact that in capitalist society all personal values have been lost or have been put into the service of technological and rational "objectivity." If philosophizing is to have any possibility of being existentially necessary for such a Dasein, it must attempt to bring this Dasein into a situation in which it can grasp and maintain the truths of its essential laws. Knowledge of the historical possibilities of contemporary Dasein must be achieved: this must include both a comprehension of its origins and a demarcation of the range of its transformations. After supplying a precise analysis of present existence, philosophy has the task of investigating which of these possibilities ensures a "true mode of existence." It must carefully observe every movement of existence: it must drive forward those that represent a movement toward truth and hinder those that lead to fallen modes of existence.

In this way the noblest desideratum of all philosophizing—the unity of theory and praxis—can become reality. With this we believe to have pointed to the location in which philosophy can become necessary for present Dasein. We will now attempt to characterize the direction and the task of such philosophizing. It is the process of *philosophy becoming concrete*, whose most important stages shall be sketched out in the following discussion.

This philosophizing is directed toward the specific Dasein contemporaneous with it. Its task is to bring this Dasein into the truth of existing. Now in order to even be able to approach Dasein, in order to be able to take hold of it in its existence, concrete philosophy must *become historical*, it must insert itself into the concrete historical situation. The becoming historical of philosophy means, firstly, that concrete philosophy has to investigate contemporaneous Dasein in its historical situation, with an eye toward which possibilities for the appropriation of truths are available to this Dasein, which truths it can realize, and which are necessary to it. Investigate should not be understood here in the sense of an opportunistic philosophy of utility that places itself, as a scientific discipline, in the service of contingent [*faktischen*] Dasein, allows itself to be used by it—the truths of philosophy are not grounded in facticity, even though they must in each case also be realized by contingent Dasein. Concrete philosophy knows that truths can never be taken in abstract form and arbitrarily grafted on to any Dasein; rather, they must be grasped out of the midst of the existing Dasein and maintained in existence. For this reason, concrete philosophy incorporates into its "teaching" the entire concrete situation of contemporaneous Dasein in the complete determinateness of the social structure. Only when it knows how Dasein thus determined suffers and acts, what its real difficulties are, which modes of existing and which paths for change are prescribed to it by the situation, only then can it bring Dasein into truth, become for it an existential necessity. But is not such an analysis of contemporaneous Dasein in terms of its historical situation the task of the actual historical sciences: history, sociology, economics? Certainly, concrete philosophy will make extensive use of the material provided by these sciences, will find it necessary to effect a radical break with the long practice of isolating itself from these sciences. Yet despite all of this, one must not forget that the method of philosophical analysis is the phenomenological method, and that a particular method also corresponds to a particular object domain. The object of concrete philosophy is contemporaneous Dasein qua existing, human Dasein in the mode of its existing. In the case of history, the focus is the contingent political situation of this Dasein, in the case of economics, the contingent mode of its economic activity, in the case of sociology, the contingent mode of its social being, or, in each case, the focus is the respective *theory* of these contingent modes as historical formations (political, economic, social structures), but not *existence itself.* In concrete philosophy, the focus is *Dasein* in the concrete fullness of its *existence*, which includes all of these contingent modes—precisely as modes in which Dasein exists. The authentic philosophical character of this analysis further reveals itself in the fact that the deconstruction [*Destruktion*] of contemporaneous Dasein into its historicity must be completed under constant consideration of the ontological structure of Dasein and the world. A concrete historical phenomenon such as a scientific system, a hierarchy of values, a social order can be recognized in its existential significance only when it is compared in its facticity to the ontological structures of a "scientific system," a "hierarchy of values," etc., which can only be ascertained by way of the phenomenological method.

In addition, the analysis of contemporaneous Dasein outlined here must be assigned to philosophy and not to the historical sciences for the reason that such an investigation cannot remain at the level of mere analysis, but must rather be carried through to the point of establishing normative guidelines for action. If concrete philosophy truly wants to bring Dasein into truth, then it must take hold of it in the only sphere in which existential decisions can occur: in the sphere of action. The existing of Dasein in its concrete form as "happening" is always a changing, a transforming of conditions, an affecting, in other words, an acting. Even a "bios theoreticos," as long as it gives expression to an "authentic" existing, as long as it is concerned with existential necessities, will entail a changing and thus an affecting [*Wirken*] and acting, even where such an "effect" [*Wirkung*] is in no way its intent. The guidelines for action in which concrete philosophy culminates will never contain—this will have already become clear from the preceding discussion— abstract norms, empty imperatives. They will necessarily have been drawn from the necessities of concrete existing in its historical situation and will in every case be addressed, not to an abstract universal, but to a concrete, existing subject. The question that now arises is this: how does philosophy arrive at such guidelines for action and what type of subject will follow them? How can philosophy approach concrete existence at all? Certainly not by confronting existence with truths, taken from who knows where, that are presented as unconditionally binding and stopping short at the proof or the demonstration of these truths. If philosophy in the appropriation of truths is committed to a real movement of existence, then it cannot be satisfied with the knowledge of truth as an impetus for this movement. Human Dasein does not exist on the basis of knowing, but rather on the basis of fateful happening in a particular situation in the shared and surrounding world [*Mit-und Umwelt*]. Knowledge can only give rise to an existential movement (which is always a transformation in happening) when it intervenes in the concrete fate of the Dasein it addresses: when it takes upon itself the historical situation of this Dasein, together with its possibilities and its reality, and initiates the movement within and out of this situation. Only by this path can knowledge find and make manifest the concrete necessities of Dasein. And such knowledge will complete and realize itself in a real transformation of the structure of historical existence and its world: not in the vague sense of some or other influence of the "idea" on historical reality, but rather in the sense of a conscious transformation of this reality with the real means made available by the situation.

Concrete philosophy can thus only approach existence if it seeks out Dasein in the sphere in which its existence is based: as it *acts* in its world in accordance with its historical situation. In becoming historical, concrete philosophy, by taking the real fate of Dasein upon itself, also *becomes public*. It must take upon itself the existence of the Dasein contemporaneous with it, and this is at bottom only a grasping of its own fate. For "contemporaneity" [*Gleichzeitigkeit*] does not mean a mere temporal juxtaposition, but rather is always an existing-with-one-another [*Miteinander-Existieren*], a sharing of fate. To say that philosophy is in a relationship of contemporaneity with a concrete Dasein is to say that philosophy must concern itself with the thoroughly concrete struggles and difficulties of this Dasein, that it is burdened by the same cares regarding a life that must exist in this and no other way.

Kierkegaard saw most clearly this existential character of contemporaneity and the profound obligation it entailed for philosophy: "For contemporaneity is the tension that prevents one from allowing the matter to remain undecided; rather, it forces one either to be offended or to believe."

It provides "the proper qualitative pressure; distance, in contrast, helps both to make something into nothing and to make something, more or less from nothing, into the extraordinary."[10] Concrete philosophy grasps the situation of contemporaneity as a demand for relevance. If contemporaneous Dasein is to be brought into truth, then this must occur as the movement of a present existence: Dasein's present existence in the fullness of its historical uniqueness, under the full strain of its historical position. With this, philosophy's occupation with [*Sich-Kümmern*] existence becomes a concern for [*Bekümmerung*] the thoroughly concrete difficulties of this existence. Philosophy, once it has found itself in a situation of contemporaneity with its Dasein, can no longer philosophize as in a vacuum, in generalities "without qualitative pressure"; existing in reality, it will be forced to take an unequivocal position, to make decisions, to choose its point of view, visibly and tangibly, ready to submit itself to any test. Concrete philosophy will exist in the public realm, because only by so doing can it truly approach existence. Only when, in full public view, it grabs hold of existence in its daily being, in the sphere in which it actually exists, can it effect a movement of this existence toward its truth. Otherwise, only an absolute authority, which is believed unconditionally to be in possession of revealed truth, can call forth such a movement.

The phenomenon indicated above can be illuminated by considering the final development of Kierkegaard's philosophy as a becoming-public of concrete philosophy. Seldom has a philosophizing torn open so deep a chasm of meaning between the eternal, absolute, divine and the historical Dasein of man as did Kierkegaard's; seldom has it aligned itself more deliberately with the idea of the eternal and judged from this perspective, or denounced more vociferously, as cowardly escapism and irresponsibility all grasping of historicity, all attempts to address historical-social being as the true world of humans. Yet at the same time, seldom has a philosopher been as concerned, from the very outset of his philosophizing, with the truth of concrete existence; seldom has a philosopher been so convinced that the foundation of all philosophizing is found in the tribulations of simple existing. And so it necessarily came to pass that Kierkegaard, at the end of his career, came to recognize and understand the public sphere, where contemporaneous Dasein existed in an active state, as the authentic sphere of activity even for a philosophizing entirely aligned with the eternal. He takes leave of his solitude: he, who had always addressed himself only to the "individual," for whom the public impact of his books was completely unimportant, takes to the streets, in a truly Socratic act. He writes article after article for a daily newspaper, publishes pamphlets, and focuses his entire struggle on the central decision of the historical moment. And this struggle in the public realm does not take the form of Kierkegaard abstractly opposing the truth of the eternal to concrete existence and addressing existence from the realm of the eternal. On the contrary, he directs his efforts with absolute precision toward the achievement of a concrete movement of contemporaneous Dasein, a "real" transformation of its existence, and his attacks and demands are thus always directed at the concrete forms and tasks of this existence, keeping in sight the full range of possibilities for such achievement available at that moment. Only when one grasps how very important the immediacy of a real decision was for Kierkegaard in realizing the meaning of his concrete philosophy, to what degree he strove for a real movement and transformation of contemporaneous existence, only then can one understand the ferocity of his attack, the agitational force of his public appearance, the deliberate collision with representative public figures, the revolutionary concreteness of his demands (such as that its members should secede from the state church). In addition, only then can one understand how deeply Kierkegaard necessarily suffered from the absence of an impact, how agonizing he found the silence of the attacked, and how he tried again and again to break this silence.

The question concerning the reason for Kierkegaard's public collapse leads us to a problem that lies once again within the scope of our general investigation. How can the becoming public of philosophy become actual *in concreto*? To which concrete Dasein can philosophy address itself and where can it grab hold of concrete existence? Is there a guarantee of the possibility of an existential impact? Concrete philosophy is concerned with the truth of contemporaneous human existence. The bringing-into-truth of Dasein means, concretely, a "real" change in existence: not just a (peripheral) change of its contingent forms and formations (forms of life and culture in the sense of the customary terminology), but rather a change in the mode of existing itself, which constitutes the foundation of all these forms in the first place. The concrete mode of existing is the true sphere of happening: "history." It is the mode in which a given Dasein grasps and lives its fate in its world, a fate, moreover, that unfolds in a particular historical situation, one that can be identified and distinguished through its particular economic and social structure.

If concrete philosophy intends to elicit a real change in existence, it must seek out existence in this sphere of historical occurrence. Only the true subject of historical occurrence can be the subject of such change. Concrete philosophy must first inquire as to the subject of historical occurrence. And here it becomes clear that the subject of historical occurrence is not "the individual." Human Dasein, as something historical, is in its essence a being-with [*Mit-sein*] with others, and the historical unity is always a unity of being-with-one-another, of "social" being—it is always a "society." The limits of being-with-one-another, the constituents of society, are different in the different historical situations and must in each case be demonstrated for a specific situation.

In accordance with these circumstances, concrete philosophy must address itself to the society contemporaneous with it, seek it out in its historical situation, analyze its forms of existence and the realms of meaning and value seized by it, and in this way work through to the truth of this society. But is this not precisely the attempt to flee that Kierkegaard opposed so adamantly, a flight into world history from the very personal difficulties of existing, an avoidance of the final, absolutely unequivocal decision, which in every case the individual can make only for himself? For if philosophy truly and in absolute concretion has existing as its object—existing is something that is always done only by the individual, and no society can take his authentic existence away from him —the legitimacy of this objection is incontrovertible. It is true that the meaning of philosophizing is not limited to the "individual," but it can only be realized by each individual and is grounded in the existence of each individual. The concretion of philosophy in the existence of each individual must never be pushed off on to an abstract "they" subject [*Mansubjekt*][11], the decisive responsibility deferred to some universal category.

But precisely because concrete philosophy is concerned with concrete existence, it must ask itself this question: how is it possible, in concrete terms, to approach this individual? Does the individual even exist in the historical situation of contemporaneity? If so, then it is not enough to write books whose addressee is always merely an abstract universal, books that do not concern themselves with the question of who appropriates their truths and for whom this appropriation is possible. Socrates could still address the individual in the marketplace and philosophize with him, because the individual still existed in the society of the Athenian city-state. His questions are binding for every individual with whom he speaks and they force this individual to bear the full weight of decision. Whom do the philosophical books oblige to make a decision? Concrete philosophy must not suppose the existence of the individual to be such that its appeal can reach and impact him and his interiority "just like that." To be sure, philosophy must take hold of the "interiority" of the individual existence, and it must struggle to establish itself in this arena, but interiority is not some abstraction that stands beyond historical space and historical time. Both the world of the individual, precisely as a specific, historically determined surrounding and shared world, and the world of nature and society in the fullness of its unique situation, belong ontologically to the Dasein of the individual, even if it is grasped as contrary to them. And this world of the individual is by no means a function of him, such that it could be changed through a simple change in the individual himself. On the contrary, in the "thrownness" of his Dasein, the individual is given over to this world in such a way that his decisions are prescribed to him by it (without thereby relieving the individual of the seriousness of decision and transferring it to "fate" or society.) Society is neither a determinately existing [*daseiendes*] subject alongside the individual nor the sum of individuals; rather, society is in a very concrete sense each and every individual, it is the concrete-historical mode of individual Dasein. Thus it is precisely when philosophy intends to become serious about its concern for the individual that it must not lose sight of the world in which the individual's Dasein realizes itself. The individual exists as an individual only in a particular situation of the surrounding and shared world, in a particular situation of social being. This situation is never merely coincidental, such that it could or must first be "stripped away" in order to gain access to the "authentic" existence of the individual. It is the reality of his existence itself and only through it can the individual truly be addressed, be affected. Admittedly, the question can now be posed whether the path of philosophy must not nevertheless lead from the individual to his surrounding and shared world rather than vice versa: whether or not meticulous care on the part of the individual for the truth of his existence must serve as the starting point from which the truth of his surrounding and shared world can then be grasped. Aside from the fact that both points of departure, when separated in this way, are abstractions, aside from the fact that the main idea of concrete philosophy, in contrast, is a consistently synthetic consideration of the individual together with his surrounding and shared world, this question can only be answered from within the context of the historical situation in which it becomes urgent for philosophy. There are historical situations in which the individual can serve as the foundation for a construction of existence, in which revolutionizing the individual can lead to a social revolution. And there are historical situations when this is no longer possible in any fashion because the contemporaneous mode of social being precludes the authentic existence of the individual. In such cases revolutionizing the individual can only be achieved by transforming society. In such cases the individual is no longer the point of departure, but rather the goal of philosophy, because individuality itself must first be made possible again. In such a society the Dasein of the individual is necessarily false, because no essentially true individuals can exist in an essentially false society. In both situations philosophy can only impact the individual in his existence when it grasps him not as an abstract subject, but rather in the fullness of his unique historical determinacy: when it impacts and grasps together with him a contemporaneous shared and surrounding world, a social being. Philosophy must intervene, on the basis of the knowledge of truth accessible to it, in the distress of contemporaneous existence; it must propel existence forward in accordance with its historical possibilities. The becoming-concrete- of philosophy is impossible without philosophy's commitment to contemporaneity (in the Kierkegaardian sense). And this is the crucial point: this commitment can never remain on a merely theoretical level. If philosophy is truly concerned with existence, then it must take this existence upon itself and, existing together with it in a state of contemporaneity, fight for truth. The philosopher must know that he has not only the right, but also the duty, to intervene in the entirely concrete difficulties of existence, because the existential meaning of truth can only be realized in this manner. Thus, at the endpoint of every genuine concrete philosophy, one finds the public act: the accusation and defense of Socrates and his death in prison; Plato's political interventions in Syracuse; and Kierkegaard's struggle with the state church.

The task that remains is to explain the philosophical possibility of linking knowledge and truth with historical contemporaneity. The necessary presupposition is that philosophy can only intervene in contemporaneity by means of *knowledge*, that every attempt to "animate" the concepts of philosophical knowledge by subordinating them to "life," by trying to make them duplicate the movements of life, means abandoning philosophy. Furthermore, the relation of concrete philosophy to contemporaneity is not to be understood in the sense that contemporaneity is in each case the "truth" to which philosophy must accommodate itself. On the contrary, as corresponds to the existential character of truth, a given human existence has a very particular relation to its possible truths, whether of falling short of or achieving realization, proximity or distance, striving toward or concealing. To the extent that philosophy constantly opposes the truths that have become known to the state of contemporaneous existence, it lives in the crucial tension out of which alone it can become necessary and productive. Rather than being comingled in an artificial manner, the true interconnectedness of knowledge and "life," truth and contemporaneity, will be established when completed knowledge is propelled forward toward the realization of its truth in contemporaneity, after knowledge itself has been achieved on the basis of genuine care for existence. The concrete tension of philosophy will not lead in every historical situation to public acts, to an intervention in the sphere of happening. But in situations where contemporaneous existence has actually been shaken to its foundations, that is to say, where a struggle is actually taking place over new possibilities of being, it would be a betrayal by philosophy of its *own meaning* (not, as some would claim, of "history") to stand on the sidelines and continue to occupy itself with "timeless" discussions. Philosophy lives up to its traditional title as the "first science" only when it takes the lead at precisely this moment.

On the Problem of the Dialectic

Part 1

In the framework of this journal, the full-length acknowledgment and review of a book with purely philosophical intentions is justified by the central position that the dialectic occupies within Marxism, and through the insights that could be obtained if one considers contemporary philosophy from a dialectical perspective relating philosophy to contemporary society and to the entire socio-historical situation.[1] This approach underlies the following critical remarks. It is not a question of analyzing Marck's particular examinations of systems of modern philosophy and his reactions to them. Instead, it ought to be asked whether and to what extent the basic problem of the dialectic is developed in these works, and whether a "cross-section of current philosophy, from the viewpoint of the problem of the dialectic" is at all possible. To anticipate, Marck's particular examinations are of a level of accuracy and penetration that is seldom found in modern histories of philosophy. Even though the basic intentions and meaning of the systems Marck presents vary widely, his book is distinguished by his constant effort to find the correct approach and to achieve a genuine understanding of each one. In contrast to all putatively value-free "objective" descriptions, which view all types of philosophizing as equally disinterested, Marck succeeds in illuminating the internal vitality and limitations of many types of philosophizing, because he examines them from the standpoint and in view of a real problem. This is the case even when Marck's critical presuppositions lead the analysis astray, as in the last chapters of the section on Heidegger. The meaning and intention of Heidegger's philosophizing is not captured by the "opposition of existentialism and Platonism," which is as little correct as substituting for validity or the metaphysical concept of being a "concept of being derived from Dasein." The a priori dualism of "ego and is" [*Ich und Ist*], of validity and existence, is disastrous for Marck here. We shall return to this dualism, whose "unresolved tension" Marck sees as the root of the dialectic.

In the first half-volume Marck treats the following philosophers under the heading of "perspectives on the problem of the dialectic": Rickert, Lask, Kroner, Kierkegaard, Borth, Gogarten, Brunner, Tillich, Lenin, Lukács, Grisebach, and Heidegger. J. Cohn, Hönigswald, Bauch, Natorp, N. Hartmann, Cassirer, and M. Adler are announced for the second volume, and Scheler, Driesch, Litt, Spranger, W. Stern, and O. Spann are also to be examined. When one considers that Marck proposes no ordinary sketch of contemporary philosophy, but an analysis aiming at *one* particular problem, the combination of these philosophers is cause for astonishment. Even when one bears in mind that the first volume treats the opponents and the second volume the advocates of the "critical dialectic"—which is the position and the standard of the author—it is still surprising. What on earth has the inner meaning of the philosophizing of Rickert to do with the religious socialists? What have Heidegger, J. Cohn, Lukács, Natorp, Bauch, and Adler to do with each other?! What is it about the dialectic that it is able to bridge such chasms? Our initial assumption was the central position of the dialectic within Marxism—so, has all of current philosophy suddenly become Marxist? Or, since we do not believe that it has, what does Marck actually mean here by his use of the term "dialectic"?

Marck's investigation is directed not at the dialectic per se, but at the "critical dialectic." He characterizes its meaning as "insight into the irreconciliability of the contradictions in the foundation of philosophy, and as preservation, not 'sublation,' of the contradictions resulting from this." An essential aspect of this meaning is "the unresolvable tension between the existing subject and the realm of validity, the rejection of the construction of an ideal subject."[2] It follows that the dialectic belongs, in a not yet elucidated manner, to the foundation of philosophy and more specifically, to the foundation of a particular philosophy, namely critical philosophy. Its meaning is an "insight" and its dimension the knowing that resides in the tension between ego and the realm of validity. This tension is preserved in its progression and its result and therefore functions, as it were, as a guide and as a medium of knowing. So far as it is evident from this first half-volume, this philosophical foundation to which the dialectic belongs retains from critical philosophy the a priori constitution of the world and the self-enclosed "realm of validity" that "stands opposed" to the ego, but forgoes the "construction of an ideal subject," that is, pure consciousness or consciousness in general. A sufficient portrayal and critical analysis of this foundation is made even more difficult by the fact that its systematic underpinnings will be presented only in the second volume. For our purposes these remarks can and must suffice. They make clear the direction from which this dialectic comes and the region in which it is at home. The direction is critical philosophy, the region epistemology, and only on this basis is something like a dialectic of be-ing [*Seinde*]³ itself, of reality, formulated.

The word "dialectic" and the concept of it have been so abused in recent philosophy and in Marxist theory and praxis that it has become necessary to reconsider its origins. Philosophy appears to view the dialectic as a panacea that will allow it to escape from the helpless confusion and lifelessness that it has brought on itself. Philosophy grasps the dialectic in a confused manner as the necessity of contradiction, tension, and movement partly in knowing, partly between knowing and reality, ego and world, ego and validity, partly within reality itself. It appears that unequivocal decisions can thereby be avoided; everything can be incorporated into such a "dialectical system," and everything remains in an unresolved state. Dialectics is used within Marxism in a similar manner. To some, this development is "only a historical contingency," a moribund residue of Hegelianism in Marx and, for that reason, something that can without detriment, indeed with profit, be removed from Marxist theory and practice. To others, it is an essential part of Marxism, but—and this point is decisive—what for Marx was the meaning and essence of historical movement has become a fetter in the present. Through a faulty dialectic each mistake, each step backward, can be justified and can be claimed as a necessary link in the dialectical movement, so that in the end the same thing results as with bourgeois philosophy—decisions are avoided. In view of this, one should either abandon all talk about the dialectic or make an effort to reappropriate its originary meaning. This exercise tries to make a small contribution in this direction.

If we now begin with an examination of Plato, we do this not merely out of a desire to see the manner in which the dialectic has been treated historically, but because we believe that Plato has understood the meaning of the dialectic in its most fundamental sense, and that Hegel, at least in the *Phenomenology of Spirit* and in the *Science of Logic*, started from the Platonic tradition when laying the foundation for his dialectic. It should be clear that only preliminary suggestions can be made here.

When we examine the passages in which Plato discusses the meaning of the dialectic (in regard to the proper ordering of Plato's writings, we will use

Stenzel's interpretation in his *Studies on the Development of the Platonic Dialectic*,[4] even though we are not in agreement with it in all respects), we see right away that the dialectic always addresses "true being," be-ing as it "really," authentically is, in contrast to all that is "apparently real" or "not authentic be-ing." The dialectic belongs to the highest level of human knowledge, "reason" [*Erkenntnis*] (although one must dismiss all the more recent rationalistic interpretations of reason as mere conceptual knowledge), in other words to Logos itself, precisely in double meaning of the original Greek: as the Logos of be-ing and as the Logos of human speech that makes be-ing visible. Reason makes apparent what each be-ing is as such (*Republic* 511b, 531–532). It is a "capacity" [*Vermögen*] of human reason to see be-ing as it is in "truth" (*Republic* 511b; *Philebus* 15d); it is, therefore, by no means an "instrument of knowledge" or a method of knowledge that everyone can use at all times. In the *Philebus* (15–16), Plato sharply opposed such abuses of the dialectic. Since for Plato, true be-ing does not consist in the multiplicity of objects of sensual experience and everyday opinions, but rather in a "commonality and unity" that is not immediately apparent yet is the foundation of this multiplicity, the dialectic is necessary to comprehend it (*Republic* 531–532c, *Phaedrus* 265–66). *Comprehension of true be-ing* requires the *dialectic*, because this be-ing itself is given to men as *dialectical being*: it is concealed in a state of inauthentic dispersal and togetherness that can be clarified only through a difficult process of genuine unifying and separating. Stenzel has conclusively demonstrated that in the great dialogues after the *Republic*, particularly in the *Theaetetus*, *Sophist*, and *Philebus*, the dialectic acquires a deeper meaning and with it a more central position in Plato's philosophizing. Beginning with the *Theaetetus*, the dialectic stands in an essential union with *becoming*, which attains a new significance in the Platonic system. "The things of which we naturally say that they 'are,' are in the process of coming to be, as the result of movement and motility[5] and blending with one another. We are wrong when we say they 'are,' since nothing ever is, but everything is coming to be." (*Theaetetus* 152d).[6] And what is still more important is that this motility and unification is no longer attributed merely to sensual reality as its mode of being [*Seinsart*], to "things that come to be or perish" (*Philebus* 15a) as their mode of being, but also to the Ideas as authentic be-ing itself.[7] The uniqueness, isolation, and unambiguous determination[8] of be-ing (the Idea) is replaced by its ontological multiplication, relatedness, and complexity, in which, however, unity and determinacy are still constituted (*Sophist* 153d). This is the central problem: how can the one be many and yet be one (*Philebus* 16)? The realization that all be-ing consists in the one and the many is considered so profoundly important that it is seen as a gift to mankind from the gods comparable to the fire of Prometheus (*Philebus* 16). Everything depends on not misunderstanding the decisive investigations in the *Sophist*, as though they were concerned with a logical question, a theory of concepts or judgment, the meaning of "definition," or the like. In the *Sophist* it is sufficiently clear (234d-e) that the issue is capturing the being of be-ing itself, the mode of being of the universality of objects as reality and the related problems of true and false being, of appearance and truth, and of be-ing and nonbe-ing. This inquiry culminates in the assertion that be-ing is neither movement nor permanence, neither sameness nor difference, but something distinct and different from all that. And since everything is only by being different from everything else, everything must also be different from *be-ing*, and thus in a certain way *not be* (although nonbe-ing is not the opposite, but rather that which is other than, different from, be-ing). Thus to every be-ing "belongs" ontologically nonbe-ing, otherness, difference (256d-e).

In this way the meaning and purpose of the dialectic acquires a deeper justification. The purpose of the dialectic no longer consists merely in discovering true be-ing by removing it from the obscurity and dispersal of the inauthentic be-ing of sensual reality and revealing its unity, determinacy, and permanence. Rather the being of this be-ing has itself become problematic and with it its relation to sensual reality, to which it is no longer opposed as unified and permanent be-ing to a diverse and flowing (inauthentic) nonbe-ing. Be-ing has divided mysteriously into types, which reunite or separate according to their respective natures, and in this motility, through this process, form new unities of be-ing. This be-ing is neither motility nor permanence, and yet it *is* only in motility and permanence (*Sophist* 250c). The major objective of the dialectic, as described in the *Sophist* (253), is capturing this be-ing in its multiplicity, which is recognized as its type of being. This is accomplished through a very complex procedure of "classification" in terms of the "types" of be-ing. In due course, through increasingly narrow classificatory divisions, the desired unities of be-ing become visible together with the nonbe-ing (differences) that "belongs" to them.

The fundamental analyses of be-ing and the dialectic in the *Sophist* have so far hardly been recognized as foundational, much less clarified, because their misinterpretation as logical and epistemological inquiries have always stood in the way. That they have, nonetheless, been drawn on here in such a superficial manner can be justified because without pointing to the location of the problem it would be completely impossible to demarcate the original basis of the dialectic, even if this means merely showing where the dialectic is not located. With this in mind, we will now attempt to summarize our findings.

For Plato, the dialectic is a capacity (cognition [*Erkennen*], knowledge [*Wissen*])[9] of human reason to comprehend be-ing as it is, in its true being. It is not based on human reason or on the relation of reason as knowledge to the "world," but rather in the being of be-ing itself. Every be-ing *is* in a state of diversity, indeterminacy, and motility only when it is ontologically related to other be-ings, or when it separates itself from be-ing in order to build a new unity of being with some other be-ing. It *is* simultaneously with its other, with nonbe-ing, with difference only through limitation and determination. Be-ing is only in this motility, change, and multiplicity and is only in them as unity, permanence, and sameness. Be-ing is inherently dialectical and for that reason can only be comprehended dialectically.

For an understanding of the further development of the problem of the dialectic, one needs to be aware that in Plato the exploration of the dialetic's decisive significance occurs together with a turning to the problematic of becoming as a mode of being of reality. The plurality and motility of be-ing is no longer dismissed as mere appearance and opposed to the permanent unity of true being (of the Ideas); instead it is recognized as a mode of being of be-ing itself. This finds its clearest expression in the statement that to all be-ing necessarily belongs the existence of its other, what is different from it and nonbe-ing, through which alone it can be determined and limited. In *Philebus* the essential relation of the dialectic to the knowledge of having-become [*Gewordensein*] is demonstrated even more clearly than in the *Sophist*. In *Philebus* the problem of how be-ing can be both unity and plurality also stands in the foreground. It is explicitly emphasized that this problematic is truly grasped only when be-ing as unity becomes a problem not only in "coming to be and perishing" but also in the idea of be-ing in itself (*Philebus* 15a). We learn from the resolution of this problem that all being is unity and plurality and has united determinacy and indeterminacy in itself (limit and unlimitedness) throughout be-ing as such, not just in the world of sensible reality. The task of the dialectic is to identify the unities of be-ing as determinacies, first by perceiving in each be-ing the one comprehensive Idea. But it does not stop there; it continues to investigate how many new determinacies as unities this primordial Idea has divided itself into, a process that is relatively infinite because every be-ing contains unlimitedness in its being (*Philebus* 15–16). Next, there is a general classification of be-ing into three types: determinate and limited be-ing, indeterminate and unlimitable, and that which arises when both are "mixed together": indeterminate be-ing that has become determinate.[10] The following point is decisive: only the latter is designated as authentic, true, and essential being (*Ousia*), and only is this true being designated as *having become* [*gewordenes*]. "What makes is always leading in the order of nature, while the thing made follows since it comes into being through it" (26e); "in third place comes the being which is mixed and generated out of those two [the unlimited and the limited]" (27b).[11] Not until this point, when having-become and motility are incorporated in the being of the essence [*Wesenheit*], is the real purpose of the dialectic fulfilled: to reveal this having-become and motility as the highest stage of knowledge.[12] From the dialectic of be-ing understood in this way, the next step is an understanding of the historicity[13] of be-ing, on which this plurality and motility is based. Hegel was the first to complete this step, to attain a knowledge of historicity that cannot be found anywhere in Plato's philosophy. Plato's incorporation of the dialectic into his theory of Ideas barred the way to any development beyond the horizon of the Greek world. Whenever the discussion has not been advanced to the level of historicity, this has also led to a condemnation of the dialectic as a pseudoscience. We must skip these developments here and take up the problem of the dialectic where it enters into the consciousness of philosophy in a new and original way—in Hegel's philosophy.

We now want to show where Hegel took up the problem of the dialectic again (and in so doing, we must omit the important point that Kant made in his *Critique of Pure Reason*, namely, that the dialectic, which was considered for so long as mere appearance without essence, is still appearance, but is also necessarily rooted in human reason. First one should note that for Hegel—as already for Plato—the dialectic is a capacity of knowledge and a method of knowledge only because and insofar as be-ing itself, the true reality, is inherently dialectical. "The abstract and unreal are not its [philosophy's][14] element, on the contrary, it is the real, i.e., that which posits itself, that which lives in itself: *Dasein in its concept*. It is the process that creates its own moments and passes through them. The entirety of this movement constitutes its positive element and its truth."[15] The dialectical method as a philosophical method is nothing other than the expression and representation of this necessary motility, the necessary becoming of reality itself. Its highest principle is "surrender to the life of the object."[16] The dialectical method should free all be-ing from its apparent ossification and isolation and comprehend it as a necessary moment in its totality, as a result of becoming and in this way comprehend be-ing in its genuine essence. With this knowledge of the essential having-become of all be-ing one also understands its essential "limits," its "negativity," and its transition into a new and "higher" be-ing. The comprehension of reality as a necessary becoming—not only reality as a whole, but each real particular— views each be-ing, which has developed out of something different and will become something different later, as it really exists, as a "unity of opposites." Thus for Hegel the origin and basis of the dialectic lies in be-ing itself. It is— as Hegel continually stresses—not a method, which is applied to be-ing by the ego, the knowing subject, not simply an instrument of knowledge, but is "nothing different from its object and content; for it is the content in itself, the dialectic that the content *has in itself,* that moves it forward. . . . It is the motion of thing itself."[17]

When each real particular is comprehended as it has become and is be- coming, as a process and a moment of the totality, as an outcome "which contains essentially that out of which it results,"[18] the essential historicity of reality is disclosed at the same time. While the mode of being is recognized as historicity with the comprehension of that which has become and is becoming as the authentic being of be-ing, one can hardly find a truer understanding of historical being than one that states that it contains essentially that out of which it resulted. Hegel's determination of the "substance of reality" as "subject" shows how seriously he took the historicity of reality. Perhaps it is possible to clarify the difficult and oft misinterpreted understanding of authentic being, of the (absolute) substance as *subject,* only when one keeps this insight in mind, namely that only being with the mode of being of a subject (for which be-ing is being for it and which has a self and knowledge [*Wissen*] of itself and of be- ing) can be essentially historical. But Hegel explicitly emphasizes this essential historicity of the "absolute and concrete individual" in this context: "Since the substance of the individual, the world-spirit itself, has had the patience to pass through these forms [i.e., forms of reality] over the long passage of time, and to take upon itself the enormous labor of world-history, in which it embodied in each shape as much of its entire content as that shape was capable of holding, and since it could not have attained consciousness of itself by a lesser effort, the individual certainly cannot by the nature of the case comprehend his own substance more easily."[19] These comments must suffice for what we want to now add: as the origin of the dialectic lies in being, in reality itself, the foundation of the dialectic lies in the ontological historicity of being, of reality. Only because and insofar as the real is historical is it dialectical, and it can and must be comprehended through the dialectical method.

We now ask what is meant by "dialectical" as a determination of the essence of historical be-ing and to what extent the designation of such be-ing as dialectical is an accurate characterization of its real being. And secondly, can and should all be-ing, be understood as historical and thus also as dialectical or, if not, which be-ing can and should be? Both questions lead beyond what has been said in the context of Hegel's philosophy to Marx's treatment of the problem of the dialectic, on the one hand, and to the general formulation of the problem, on the other.

With respect to the first question, what is meant when we designate historical be-ing as dialectical? As an answer we always hear, among other things, something about opposition and unity, recognition and preservation of contradiction, of movement and thesis, antithesis and synthesis, but it is not at all apparent what this has to do with the historicity of the real and why it has anything to do with it. The revolutionary significance of such a determination remains completely opaque, and it does not help to appeal to Marx, as long as the original meaning of the dialectic in Marx's theory has not been reappropriated. Let us now examine the presence of a concrete historical be-ing, for perhaps this a good approach to understanding its "dialectic."

Let us take as our example a large-scale modern factory. At first glance, there does not seem to be anything ambiguous about this factory's presence. It is "the same" for everyone who sees it and sets foot in it, not only as a totality but also in its machinery, its workers, the parts of its building, and so forth. But when I really see the factory and the parts and people in it, I have to know what they "mean," what factory, machine, worker is and ought to be, what their significance and purpose is. If I do not know these things (this knowledge is, of course, usually completely "unconscious," an unnoticed, "habitual knowledge"), I do not see a factory, machinery, workers, and so forth but only a pile of stones, iron, people, etc. I do not know what it really is or what it is supposed to mean. When we consider that in all of our everyday perceptions, these habitual and familiar meanings shape our perception and experience, and that without them we could see nothing at all, the unambiguous presence of such an object suddenly becomes doubtful. Is the factory really the same for the workers employed in it, for its owners, for the idle traveler who happens upon it, and for the architect who built it? Or is it not each time the same and yet something quite different: for one, a place of compulsory labor imposed by social relations, a place one enters reluctantly and leaves exhausted; for the other, a source of great profit, stressful and demanding, but nonetheless a place one visits gladly and misses when one has left; for another perhaps the disfigurement of a beautiful area, something foreign and at best uncanny; for yet another a work of art that, executed with the most modern architectural means and designs, may make its builder famous? When we extend the scope of our considerations we see how different a factory is for the economy of a people, for the competitive struggle of the large trusts, for the small merchants and dealers dependent on it for their livelihood, and for the industry of the neighboring state! No objections should be made to the effect that all these are all "subjective" moments that have nothing to do with the factory as such. Such objections emerge from preconceived theories that do not begin to see the concrete object in its real entirety. When one eliminates all these moments from the object, what remains? Certainly not a factory in the dimension of meanings that are always present in a concrete approach not falsified by theory. Indeed, such objects *are* only in an abundance of different meanings. A continuous tradition belongs to their respective being, a long period of becoming, which has placed them within an extended life-space and world-space. They continue to develop in this space, determining and being determined by it, steadily altering. In addition to this multiple motility and determinacy, such objects are characterized by a strange duality, even multiplicity. Their reality, their effect on human Dasein within their space and time, is such that it splits this Dasein into contradictions that are grounded in these objects themselves. Consider the following preliminary outline of these contradictions: human Dasein evaluates its reality as positive or negative, as declining or promising; it takes hold of these contradictions in order to shape its existence, or it struggles with them or it remains indifferent to them, and this multifaceted movement toward the objects drives them to change constantly. The factory expands or closes down or is paralyzed by a strike; it is bought out and remodeled, a technical or chemical discovery revolutionizes its operation, interest groups struggle over and within it, etc. And all this is not simply an event that "happens in the factory" or takes place around it as if the "factory itself" was not affected by all this. On the contrary, all this happens in and to the factory itself and is actually what constitutes its total being, its entire reality. To comprehend a historical object completely in its concrete reality, one has to grasp the motility of its happening[20] in its totality. Such a comprehension is made impossible from the beginning when an object is removed from its historical context and treated as a fixed and isolated entity with an identity free of contradictions "through the passage of time" instead of being seen as a multifaceted becoming, acting, and passing away in time. Comprehension is also impossible when only the positive moments of the object are brought into view and the negative moments, which equally belong to it, are overlooked. What the object has been, what it will be, and what it is not all help constitute its reality, since they determine and move it.

These remarks are intended only to indicate the location where the historical dialectic can become visible. By no means do they exhaust the possibilities for analysis in any area. They are intended simply to indicate the areas that must be researched in more detail. This much perhaps has already become clear: a procedure that designates the historical object from the outset as a "unity of opposition" or, even worse, places it within the schema of thesis, antithesis, and synthesis always does violence to its historical complexity. In any case, this procedure does not belong to the original meaning of the historical dialectic; it does not appear until much later. Each historical object by no means stands in such a twofold or threefold relationship from the very beginning. Its relations can be grasped only from within a comprehensive, larger historical totality (periods, evolutionary stages), and this presupposes the dialectic and dialectical knowledge.

We now come to the second question: which objects are historical in their mode of being and hence dialectical or are all objects, indeed, is all of reality, dialectical? Hegel chose the latter answer, and in view of his system it is evident that absolutizing historicity or historicizing the absolute in this way forces both the essence of historicity and the essence of reality into a tidy construct. When we now attempt to answer the question about the positive domain of historicity, it must be said that such an answer necessarily presupposes further inquiries into ontology. We can mention here only the results of these inquiries, although this shortcoming can be remedied by pointing to the fundamental examination of this problematic by Dilthey (especially also in his correspondence with the Graf Yorck v. Wartenburg) and more recently by Heidegger (*Being and Time*).

Only human Dasein and all the objects seized, formed, created, and animated by this Dasein in its existence are ontologically historical, such that their entire being, their entire reality exists only in history and as historicity.

This would be true of human life in all its ways and forms, of all of its works and creations, but also of nature as an occupied life-space and a power to be used. The ontologically nonhistorical would include the objects of mathematical and physical science (whose being is constituted in abstraction from their relatedness to human Dasein), and not just nature as an object of physics, but also as far as its mode of being is different from that of human Dasein and insofar as it is objectified in this mode (as is it can be, for example, in our "experience of nature"). Thus the dividing line between historicity and nonhistoricity is ontological, not merely arbitrary. All objects can become historical or nonhistorical objects, even human existence (although since human being is thoroughly historical, this is possible only on the basis of a very particular negation of reality that results in an unreality, as when a person becomes an object of art, for example). In the true sense of the word only human Dasein can be called historical because knowledge [*Wissen*] of one's own existence and a knowing [*wissendes*] (not merely cognizing [*erkennendes*]) relation to reality belong to authentic being-historical.

It now becomes clear how things took a new turn on the path from Hegel to Marx. When Marx "set the Hegelian dialectic rightside up," this was no mere correction of a part of Hegel's philosophy, no mere selective appropriation of method, no materialist reinterpretation, but the return of the dialectic to its proper domain and, hence, the scientific discovery of the authentic dimension of history, which now, since the dialectic had also been rediscovered, could be grasped in its basic structure. Marx was the first to grasp the authentic historicity of human Dasein using the only approach appropriate for this purpose. In a much deeper sense, Marx is the heir of German idealism because this philosophy was only able to become authentic again by way of and through the historicity of human Dasein.

Our results so far are summarized in the following theses. The theses are by no means proved in the text above, but are rather only meant as a guide for further discussion of the problem.

1. The dialectic is not a method or form of knowledge based on some philosophical or sociological theory nor is it a means of knowledge, but rather the designation for a mode of being of be-ing itself. Only because and insofar as a mode of being of be-ing is dialectical can research on this mode of being be dialectical. Only such research can be understood as dialectical.

2. Not all be-ings are dialectical in their mode of being; rather only those whose being is historicity are.

3. Only authentic historical be-ing is in the true sense dialectical: human existence in its reality, in its happening, and in the world it takes hold of and shapes.

4. The idea of a tension or opposition between the human ego, on the one side, and a "posited" world of being, "superbeing" [*Überseins*] (God . . .), or validity, on the other, is never dialectical because such an interpretation abandons the fundamental basis of the dialectic at the very outset in its approach. It counterposes concrete (historical) human existence, which is viewed from the beginning as an isolated entity, to an ontologically ahistorical world (and in this way the wholeness of the world is torn to pieces, so that it can be bound together again afterward in unity or tension).

If these theses apply to the original location and meaning of the dialectic, the following theses concern its concretization in the happening of human Dasein, in history, and hence its "application." The primordial unity of theory and practice becomes visible, which Marx, once again, was the first to grasp in the dialectic.

5. If the dialectic is based on historicity and only human Dasein is authentically historical, such that it exists only in a concrete-historical way, that is, determined by the respective concrete historical situation, then the full meaning of the dialectic can be found only in the concrete history of human Dasein (history in the true sense of the term).

6. The concrete dialectic is concerned with happening as the mode of being of human Dasein. It can by no means be assumed that all events occurring in history can be grasped dialectically and termed dialectical (the worst abuses occur here), for the term applies only to those actions and events that are concerned with historical Dasein in its *being*.

7. Insofar as the concrete dialectic displays the multiplicity, development, and limitations of the historical modes and forms of Dasein, it implies the taking of a certain stance toward these modes and forms of Dasein and their reality. Insofar as each historical reality as reality carries within itself and makes a claim to constancy, de-

terminacy, and validity, the dialectical stance must be critical and must undermine such claims. Concrete dialectics as an objective, value-free science is an absurdity.

Let us return now to Siegfried Marck's book. An examination of a problem like the dialectic, which is so unclear, and in which so much is concealed, must give at least a provisional determination of what it means by the dialectic. It will not do to console the reader with a reference to the second volume, because a historical review, "from the standpoint of the problem of the dialectic," is meaningful only on the basis of such a determination. But if we take the brief allusions as well as the other relevant points that were developed in the course of the first volume as a preliminary determination of what is meant here by "dialectic," one can, based on preceding considerations, say the following.

Marck tries to locate the dialectic in philosophy or more exactly in the "philosophical foundation," and then in a tension between ego and is [*Ich und Ist*], knowing and reality. The presuppositions of such a determination have already been briefly touched on. It is, of course, possible to arrive at a meaning of the dialectic from a philosophical foundation and then to examine various forms of philosophizing accordingly, but only those forms whose intent is the demonstration of historicity in the sense suggested above ought to be considered. Given this, a number of forms of contemporary philosophizing that Marck treated in the first volume can be discarded right away, such as "antidialectical criticism" (Rickert and Lasch), theology, and E. Grisebach. What is decisive is not the extent to which history and historicity "are present" in these systems (this is the case in Rickert, to be sure, to a considerable extent), but whether or not the inner meaning of the philosophizing in question is oriented toward history and historicity. But this question must be answered in the negative. Perhaps one must answer negatively also in the case of Heidegger, if, as Marck argues, the entire existential analytic in the first part of *Being and Time* is only a starting point for the elaboration of fundamental ontology and metaphysics (an interpretation that Heidegger himself appears to have adopted since his recent publication of *The Essence of Reasons* and *Kant and the Problem of Metaphysics*).[21]

All these question go unanswered here, since they can only be clarified within the framework of philosophical discussion. It is our intention now only to consider Marck's critique of Lukács, which brings the problem back onto Marxist ground. Here, finally, a long-standing and gross injustice is redressed:

Lukács's book, *History and Class Consciousness*, is recognized and appreciated as a contribution to the development of Marxism that is essential and whose importance cannot be overestimated.[22] Marck finally puts an end to the primitive "critique" according to which Lukács's analysis can be refuted by calling it "metaphysics," which has been recited in its worst form precisely by the communist side. His critique also pinpoints the weakness of Lukács's dialectic: the concept of "correct class consciousness." This concept is (as is the very idea of class consciousness) a violation of the dimension of historicity in its the fixation of a point "outside" of what happens from which an artificial and abstract connection with history is subsequently made. But it seems to us that Marck's objection to Lukács's treatment of the "problem of nature and the problem of value" is not correct.[23] Lukács's polemic against Engels (whose false interpretation of the mathematical-physical sciences as "dialectical" was shown to be indefensible by the partial publication of the *Dialectics of Nature*) in particular shows that Lukács did indeed clearly recognize the duality of the being of nature—completely ahistorical as an object of physics, historical as the life-space of human Dasein—and by no means interpreted nature "as purely a product of society." Finally, Marck's objection that Lukács posits "value-transcendence" completely misses the point of Lukács's book, whose aim is concrete dialectics not philosophical foundations.

After these critical observations, the great value of Marck's book must once again be emphasized. We see its value not only in the aforementioned accuracy and depth of his individual analyses, but also in his disentanglement of contemporary philosophy and his exposition of its true problematic, which, despite the problems with this exposition, clearly demonstrates the contemporary relevance of this problematic. Hence, Marck's book can become the source of fruitful discussion especially for Marxism, because it shows that contemporary philosophy cannot be found where both old and new Marxist theory has normally looked for it, and that a critical confrontation with contemporary philosophy is no mere "shadow boxing," but a necessity for Marxism in particular.

On the Problem of the Dialectic

Part 2

Also a Contribution to the
Question of the Sources of the Marxian Dialectic in Hegel

I

The critique of the second half-volume of Marck's work[24] must pass over the very lively and penetrating depiction of the various "dialectical" movements in contemporary philosophy even more than it did with regard to the first volume, and must instead limit itself to Marck's "systematic explanations of the concept of the critical dialectic." The *controversy over the Hegelian dialectic* is the central issue at stake. The concept of the "critical" dialectic—which Marck sees as the single "genuine" dialectic—is derived positively by differentiation from the "speculative" dialectic of Hegel.

"The relation to Hegel is immanent in any work on dialectics." This is true in a most decisive sense insofar as the Hegelian dialectic is not a free-floating and arbitrarily variable methodology but is inseparably rooted in Hegel's whole metaphysics. Marck clearly articulates the consequences of this position: "it is only possible to accept or reject this speculative dialectic in its entirety."[25] The question still remains, however, whether and how a *non*-Hegelian dialectic is possible. Marck affirms such a possibility. Indeed, he is convinced of the "superiority" of the critical dialectic "to every form of metaphysics." But we shall attempt to demonstrate that in the course of his investigation Marck ends up basing this critical dialectic, precisely in its positive determinations, on the Hegelian dialectic (which he rejects) by grounding his position in a limiting transformation of the speculative dialectic. In this way Marck undermines his own thesis that there are a "plurality of dialectical methodologies" and a variety of "dialectical positions."[26] Our criticism is intended to show how far such a limiting transformation of the Hegelian dialectic discloses new and fruitful philosophical problems or reveals old problems in a new light.

To arrive at a determination of the concept of the critical dialectic Marck wishes to posit "the unacceptable aspects of the Hegelian dialectic and oppose the positive aspects to them."[27] These unacceptable aspects are for him: 1) the "complete fusion of consciousness and object" and thus also the interpretation of "substance as subject," as well as the transformation of the object into a "process" through which its structure becomes identical with the structure of the ego (consciousness); 2) the "progress from finite to infinite consciousness," the "sublation of the finite spirit in the infinite spirit" (Hegel's central concept of the "absolute"); 3) the "sublating" (neutralizing) power of negation, particularly the sublating power of the human ego, of self-consciousness.[28] All these moments are internally related. Rejecting them does indeed undermine the entire foundation of the Hegelian dialectic. Marck would then have to prepare a new foundation for the critical dialectic. First, let us see how he establishes the unacceptability of these moments of Hegel's philosophy.

Marck maintains that the two major theses of Hegelian metaphysics, the "fusion" of consciousness and object and "the transition from finite to infinite reason," are based solely on the "mystical-pantheistic belief" in the unity of spirit and world, God and man—a conviction that can only be "directly" believed or "intuitively grasped."[29] But if these theses are only the "expression of a mystical conviction," then it is strictly speaking impossible to criticize them *philosophically*, since such a conviction *precedes* any "speculative proof" and any "mediation"; "it is given before the first step of thinking begins."[30] It is given not in the sense of an objective basic assumption (hypothesis), whose correctness is then demonstrated by the philosophical investigation, and not in the sense of "self-sustaining evidence requiring no further proof"[31] either. Instead, it is given in the sense of an "incomprehensibility without the aid of the mystery."[32]

As essential as it is to move beyond the idle talk of the rationalism and panlogicism of the Hegelian system and to expose the true sources of his philosophy, which lie elsewhere, tracing them back to a "mystery" threatens to destroy the foundations of any discussion of Hegel. But even apart from this, such an approach cannot be justified. It is true that Hegel's philosophy was fed by religious sources that remained strong through his final systematic investigations, but they flow into a purely *philosophical* foundation, are treated on this *philosophical* basis, and do not eliminate the necessity of purely philosophical arguments. Many of Hegel's later philosophical concepts are already present in his early theological writings. Not a mystical conviction, but a critical confrontation with ancient (especially Aristotelian) metaphysics, carried out in a rigorously conceptual manner, gives Hegel's system its inner form. I have attempted to work out these connections in an interpretation of the *Phenomenology of Spirit* and the *Science of Logic* that will be published soon. Here I can only convey some of my findings.

Neither the unity of consciousness and object nor the interpretation of substance as subject nor the positing of an absolute reason, of which human consciousness and its object are only modes of existence, grows out of a mystical-pantheistic conviction. They were discovered via the difficult path of pure philosophical investigation, guided by the specifically Hegelian questioning about the meaning of being in general. These concepts are not preconceived axioms. Instead, they are presupposed only after they have been established through philosophical investigation. In his analysis of metaphysical questions (about the meaning of being) Hegel takes as his first point of reference the Kantian problem of the I-think that first makes possible all objective [*gegenständliche*] [33] be-ing; the transcendental synthesis is one source of the Hegelian dialectic. His second point of reference is the fundamental discoveries of antique metaphysics, particularly the determination of being as *motility*; grasping motility conceptually as the fundamental character of being is the second source of the Hegelian dialectic. Both of these sources merge in the conceptualization of being as "*life*" on which the *Phenomenology of Spirit* is based and toward which Hegel had already begun working in his early theological writings. The original proof of the unity of consciousness and object, of the subject-character of substance, and of "reason" as the authentic being of be-ing is completed in an exposition of the being of life and its historical occurrence in the world. The primordial basis of the Hegelian dialectic is the being of *life* and its specific motility.

The "highest point" of Kantian philosophy—the "original synthetic unity" of the I-think (which in the process of its thinking being first makes objectivity possible)—and the knowledge of the central determination of being as motility, both become concrete in the concept of life. From this position Hegel also formulates the concept by which he intends to comprehend the essence of being: that concept is "*equality-with-self-in-otherness*" [*Sichselbstgleichheit im Anderssein*]. All be-ing exists as motility but cannot be reduced to it; it preserves itself in the various conditions of its motility as one and the same thing. This oneness and sameness, which determine what the being really is, develop only in this self-preservation in motility. Be-ing becomes different in its existence and is always different in its existence from what it is "in itself." These differences, into which it "falls" along with other be-ings it affects and is affected by, belong to its own being. Only in these differences does it maintain and conduct itself as a self, and only in this conducting-oneself [*sich-verhalten*][34] in otherness does it fulfill its essence.

These very rough suggestions are intended to begin to clarify how Hegel came to the conceptualization of being as "equality-with-self-in-otherness." This formulation is one that already contains in germinal form the basic meaning of the dialectic, which presumes in an absolute sense that concept of being and reveals the most formal and general basis of the "identity" of consciousness and object. This is true insofar as the structure of "equality-with-self-in-otherness" determines both the essence of consciousness and of the object-being [*Gegenstand-Seins*] and addresses both modes of being as the same mode of motility.

But this equality-with-self-in-otherness is only the most general and most formal determination of being. This determination receives its authentic meaning only when Hegel proves that all modes of being are concrete modes of this equality-with-self, that is, that they are concrete modes of conducting-oneself in motility. For the sake of this proof, life is presumed to be that being which most authentically fulfills the posited meaning of being as such and can therefore have validity as absolute being. In the early theological writings Hegel already wrote "pure life is *being*."[35] That which lives [*Das Lebendige*] is in a notable sense equal-with-itself in the various conditions of its living [*Lebendigkeit*] insofar as it produces, preserves, and continues *itself* as this unity. It represents therefore the most interior and at the same time realest identity [*Selbigkeit*] in motility. And life achieves this kind of unity and identity essentially as knowing [*wissendes*] being, as "consciousness." It achieves it by bringing before itself ("imagining" [*vorstellt*]) the various states of its living and of the world that affects it as *ego*. It is not simply absorbed in these conditions but is able to transcend them by recurring to ("reflecting") its ego-like self [*ichhaftes Selbst*] and in this way behave as a real self. (Hegel's concept of "consciousness" should always be understood so broadly that it can embrace the entire basic conduct [*Grundverhalten*] of life. It means above all not mere thinking, knowing, etc., but a concrete manner of existence that includes both practical and theoretical behavior, that is, thinking and acting.)

The unity of the Kantian I-think experiences in this way a decisive new meaning. The "highest point" of philosophy is now no longer that transcendental "pure consciousness," whose cognizing [*Erkennen*] first makes the world recognizable [*erkennbar*], but rather the being of life, through whose happening the world first becomes alive. The "other" of all objectivity, against which and for which be-ing becomes objective in the first place, is for Kant the transcendental self-consciousness of "pure apperception." For Hegel it is the living self-consciousness of concrete life. This general formulation alludes to the way in which the transcendental synthesis of pure thought becomes the living synthesis of the being that is in itself "dialectical." The dialectical unity of being is the "positive" unity ("posited" in and by itself) of the living (ego-like) substance, and this of course is the "result" of the concrete happening of living [*Lebendigkeit*]. It is always merely a result of a constant "sublation" ("negation") of the otherness in which life finds itself at the time.

Hegel develops this dialectical motility of life in the *Phenomenology of Spirit* but not for the purpose of formulating a "philosophy of life [*Lebensphiloso-phie*]," a philosophy of history, or the like but rather with the intention of laying the foundations for metaphysics in general. If Hegel posits the being of life as unity of life and world, consciousness and object (in Marck's terms: "ego and is"), this is due to his objective [*sachlich*] orientation toward an apparent "primordial phenomenon": Hegel bases the *epistemological* unity of conscious-ness and objectivity on the *living* unity of ego and the world. It is not a "total melting together," a unification that excludes the "correlation" (i.e., difference) of the unified[36] but rather a unification that always allows difference to endure. This is evident from the fact that Hegel believes that "consciousness" inherently demands an *opposing* being-for-consciousness! Consciousness is only possible vis-à-vis an "other" being standing-opposed [*gegen-ständlichen*] to it. A total merger of consciousness and object would eliminate both the concept of ob-jectivity [*Gegen-ständlichkeit*] and the concept of consciousness as well! Hegel himself has thus already corrected this moment that was unacceptable to Marck and moved him to attempt a correction of the Hegelian dialectic.

It is possible to understand how life can enter into the "middle" of being and can be valued as the fulfillment of the meaning of being only if one is clear about the fact that Hegel understood the being of life as *knowing* [*wissendes*] being, that is, as "self-consciousness." By this means Hegel integrates the Kantian discovery of the a priori constitution of the world into self-consciousness and follows this Kantian discovery to its final consequences. The necessity of an orientation of the concept of life to *human* life (in which consciousness first be-comes self-consciousness) and to the "rationality" of the ego ("reason", "spirit") is entailed by this position. We cannot address these issues in more detail here. But the sources of these determinations drawn from the concept of life cannot be overemphasized for understanding the positing of substance as reason. In sections 170–77 the *Phenomenology*, Hegel provides the general determinations of life as the "universal medium" and "universal substance" of be-ing.[37] The following sections of the work are basically only an exposition and concretization of these definitions. The exposition begins with the unmediated existence of life in the world immediately present to it. The happening of life has the inner meaning of discovering and taking hold of this world as "its own," as well as comprehending and taking possession of it as its own "arbitrary" existence—which can be more or less conducive to its potentialities—and therefore also as its own "otherness." The necessity of life lies in "mediating" the world of its immediate existence with its essence, sublating its otherness and uniting with its own authentic being. The unification of ego and world, consciousness and object takes place first through the relations of "mastery and servitude" and "desire and labor." The world is infused with life for the first time in the process of this unification; this is the first realization of life as "universality." The master and slave relationship is the first (incomplete and untrue) form in which the individuals opposing each other in a life and death struggle meet in a first "universality." Living self-consciousness seizes and subjugates objective be-ing (thingness) for the first time through desire and labor and in this way takes it into the universality of life.

From the discussion of this immediate mode of life's historical occurrence it will become clear what is meant by the determination of life as a "universal medium" and "universal substance." Life is a universal medium of be-ing insofar as all be-ing becomes apparent and real only through the mediation of living self-consciousness. And life is a universal substance insofar as being really "exists" [*besteht*] only through the mediation of life. Living self-consciousness is that through which and in which all be-ing first becomes full "reality;" its omnipresence first makes present be-ing as something real.

In the further development of the *Phenomenology* Hegel shows how life realizes itself in the movement from the immediate and incomplete to the true and complete forms of universality and substantiality. In the process he provides the crucial determination of knowledge [*Wissen*] that is certain of itself in its truth: "reason." Life can represent true universality and substantiality only as rational subjectivity. Only if it constantly knows itself and its other, and only if it lives continually according to this knowledge [*Wissen*], can it really maintain its identity in its motility (in its "falling" into otherness) and in this equality-with-self-in-otherness knowingly [*wissend*] mediate all be-ing with itself.

When life has realized itself as rational subjectivity and has effected [*er-wirken*] the world as its reality, "spirit" is realized as the substance of be-ing. In the *Phenomenology* the concept of spirit *grows out of the concept of life*. Spirit is articulated as the authentic being of substance only on this foundation. This remains true despite Hegel's assessment, in anticipation of the fulfillment of all be-ing in the spirit, of the various modes of being (inorganic nature, organic, and historical life) as (more true or less true) modes of spirit, which makes spirit into the true being at the basis of all be-ing, hence an "absolute." This is not mutually contradictory, for this spirit, which is always already at the basis of all be-ing as truth, realizes and reveals itself only in the historical occurrence of life, in living self-consciousness. Despite the fact that Hegel posits all modes of being from the outset of his philosophy as modes of absolute spirit, this is not an unsubstantiated basic assumption but a result that follows necessarily from the entire conception of the problem of being and is verified in the course of his investigation.

But this does not change the fact that with the interpretation of authentic being as "spirit" the "transition from infinite to absolute reason" has, as Marck notes, become "unavoidable," and finite human consciousness is unified with the infinite consciousness (of God).[38] Hegel's dialectic is indeed an "absolute" dialectic insofar as it attempts to represent the essence and motility of be-ing in and for itself and not for "our thinking:" "the bare truth, as it is in and for itself."[39] In this absolutizing of finite thought lies the second moment of Hegel's dialectic that is unacceptable to Marck. "The inner experience of the finite ego, the certainty of our thought," on which the critical dialectic, as opposed to the speculative, must rely, "stands opposed to the speculative desire to advance from finite to infinite consciousness."[40]

But by invoking the experience of the finite ego, Marck faces the task of establishing a *new* foundation for the dialectic, which can no longer be accomplished by merely correcting Hegel; in fact, in cannot orient itself at all—not even in a negative way—toward Hegel's absolute dialectic. Let us now examine the positive determinations Marck makes regarding the critical dialectic to see if they provide a new foundation for the dialectic, or at least point in that direction.

The positive determination of the critical dialectic in its possible "systematic unity" brings together once again "Hegelian motifs" that Marck himself refers to only as "modifications of the dialectical method." "The dialectic of self-consciousness is preserved" in the critical dialectic "together with the dialectic of the process of knowledge, the dialectical motif in all totality thinking [*Ganzheitsdenken*], and the dialectical function of the passage through contradiction for the thought result achieved."[41] Both of the latter moments refer back to the first: "the dialectic of self-consciousness is central to the critical dialectic."[42] In what sense is the being of self-consciousness for Marck the basis and center of the dialectic?

Marck answers this question by referring to the major thesis of Hönigswald's "psychology of thinking."[43] For Marck this is "in a real sense critical dialectic."[44] We are treating here only the results of thought psychology that Marck has incorporated into his work and which are supposed to provide a foundation for the critical dialectic.

Consciousness and being, "experience and object" exist in essentially "correlative relationships" to each other. The "law" of these relationships is determined by their character as "meaning." "In meaning the abstract concepts of object and ego are both overcome. Meaning is supposed to make apparent the ego in existence [*das Ich im ist*] and the existence in ego."[45] The object in itself has the possibility of being experienced: as the content of an experience [*Erlebnis*] to mean something and to be known in this meaning by the experiencing ego. On the other hand, the experiencing ego is in itself also a possible object of knowledge [*Wissens*] and comprehensible as meaning. "The entire argument can be summarized in the formula that says that existence can be represented in the ego as the known [*Gewußte*] and that the ego can be represented in existence as the possibility of knowing [*wissen*] the object."[46]

The ego and the object are thus for Marck tied together as a unity, which is not, as in Hegel, "total merging" but "at the same time separation." The object always remains an object and the ego always remains the "other" of the object. "The basic difference between a metaphysical and critical dialectic remains that between actual-absolute and potential-relative unity. The object is not experience, but experienceable, the experience is not object, but it can be objectified [*vergegenständlicht*]."[47] These relationships thus remain full of tension." Their parts are "connected in a heterogeneous medium." And all essential relationships, like that between "temporal and atemporal" (temporally determined ego and in itself atemporal truth) are based on this fundamental and inherently dialectical relationship between ego and object. "The basic relationships of philosophy are thus always those in a heterogeneous medium."[48] They must appear, therefore, as inherently dialectical and be so understood.

This "dialectic of self-consciousness" preserves the finiteness of "our think-ing" insofar as it is based on the presence and otherness of the object vis-à-vis the ego, which cannot be sublated or negated by the power of the concept. Referring to this, Marck correctly emphasizes that the critical dialectic must drop from the Hegelian concept of "sublation" at the moment of the "negation of the negation."[49] "Our ego cannot sublate, it remains tied to that which is present, that which is given."[50] But it must be emphasized that this theory of finite self-consciousness does not go beyond a theory of *cognizing* [*erken-nend*] self-consciousness; it grasps the relationships between ego and object primarily as relationships of *cognition* [*Erkennen*]—which makes perfect sense within the framework of thought psychology. So even though the concepts of meaning and experience [*Erlebnis*] have been substantially deepened vis-à-vis traditional psychology, they are nonetheless still left in the realm of the knowing ego. The full being of the ego (as Hegel had incorporated it into the concept of the being of life) is not incorporated into this theory. This di-alectic of self-consciousness remains, therefore, a dialectic of cognition [*Erken-nen*] even when it aims at a "reconstruction of psychological principles,"[51] or when it attempts to establish a general philosophical "doctrine of principles."[52] And both other moments—"the dialectical motif in all totality thinking" and the "passage through contradiction"—by which Marck intends to delimit the critical dialectic formulate only the most general determinations of cognitive [*erkennenden*] thought.

But the question must be asked, whether referring to such determinations of cognition [*Erkennen*] with the term "dialectic" is justifiable based on the history of the problem, if—as Marck emphasized in the preface—"dialectic" is to retain its primary meaning as a philosophical "basic method" [*Grundmethode*]. The dialectic as "basic method" cannot be separated from the deep-seated premises of its historical problematic; those premises must be incorporated into the new foundation of the dialectic. Perhaps the decisive historical premises of the dialectic lie precisely in that which *leads beyond* the realm of knowing thought—in "metaphysics"!

We already alluded to these kinds of unavoidable premises in the critique of the first half-volume during our discussion of Plato, Kant, and Hegel. A new founding of the dialectic can be developed from each of the stages of its historical development signified by these names. At first it seems as if Marck were selecting the Kantian dialectic as the starting point for the critical dialectic. But Marck's dialectic of self-consciousness does not take that set of problems, in which Kant situated the transcendental dialectic of "pure reason," as its own point of departure. It is not, for him, a question of the dialectic as "transcendental appearance," as a "natural and unavoidable *illusion* of human reason"(§B 354).[53] It is not the transcendental dialectic that Marck appropriates from the Kantian critique but the transcendental analytic, conceived as a foundation of cognitive thought (of the finite ego).

But in our opinion the intellectual-historical [*problemgeschichtlichen*] premises of the dialectic do not justify treating this as "dialectic," especially if one rejects—as Marck correctly does—a "separation of the systematic and the historical" and proposes a study of the history of the problem.[54] Seen from the perspective of the history of the problem, neither the "potential-relative unity" of knowing ego and knowable object nor the passage of knowing through contradiction nor the knowable synthesis of unity and diversity is sufficient to establish the dialectic. But the synthetic unity of *self-consciousness* can indeed provide such a proof. Marck formulates the following historically correct guiding principle: "the dialectic arises in the ego and returns to the ego."[55] But this is true only when self-consciousness (ego) is made the origin of the dialectic not only in its conduct [*Verhalten*] as knowing thought, but also—as in Hegel—in its *full being* unified with the full being of the "world" that is its object. This is intended to help clarify the following remarks on the historical problematic of the dialectic. The following remarks on the history of the problem of the dialectic are an attempt to elaborate this point. They are at the same time intended to clarify and complement the theses presented in the first part of this essay.

2

The origin of the problem of the dialectic within the metaphysics of antiquity[56] can be summarized briefly in the following way. With regard to the question of what comprises the essence of be-ing (what it is itself, what remains constant as opposed to its multiple variations and its changing diversity in the process of becoming and passing away), the investigation comes up against the circumstance that this "true" being of be-ing itself contains a plurality in its unity. It has varied relationships with other beings, and these relationships are not accidental and superficial but are the very foundation of its essence. The being of each be-ing is only together with that which it is not and which is an other. It is only together with its nonbe-ing and otherness and can only be grasped in the passage through that which it is not and what is other. But this set of relations only becomes "dialectical" and demands a "dialectic" as access to it ("method") under the following conditions, which were already present in the premises of ancient philosophy.

1. The truth of be-ing is revealed and preserved by human speech (Logos, *legein*).
2. Human speech is essentially talking with another about something; only in this talking through [*Durchsprechen*] with another can it fulfill its revealing and preserving function.
3. The essence of be-ing revealed and preserved in human speech is supposed in its truth to be available and convenient for human life and its happening. Humans have to have and to understand the essence and the truth of being for the production of things, as well as for coming to terms with and confronting nature (in the broadest sense) and the state.

It follows from these points that the philosophical inquiry has by no means come to an end by recognizing the circumstance outlined above, but has instead only arrived at its authentic beginning. It becomes dialectical and thus a genuine means of accessing the essence of be-ing only when it has made this circumstance in all its "parts" and in its various concrete manifestations recountable in human discourse and therefore secure in its availability. This results in the demand to return the inherently plural unity of essence to its last, no longer variable basis and secondly to allow this last basis to unfold itself into the multiplicity of be-ing established by it, in other words, to retrace the genesis of this multiplicity in its particular "countable" stages. Only then when the last basis of be-ing is recognized, on the one hand, and the multiplicity emerging from this basis has become "countable" in all its parts, on the other, do the preconditions exist for making available and preserving the discovered truth in human life.

We can derive from this the following premises for the history of the origin of the dialectic:

1. The dialectic arises *only in a mediated way* from the ego, insofar as its immediate first origin lies in a particular state of the essence of be-ing itself and in the resulting necessity for human life to come to terms with and to confront this given state of affairs.
2. This "ego" of human life, to which the dialectic thus "returns," is not primarily knowing thought but the full being of life happening

in the world. The necessity of the dialectic lies in the necessity of this life to be able to control reliably the essence of be-ing in all life situations. The "dialectic of self-consciousness" is not a free-floating dialectic of knowing; it is tied to the concrete being and action of human life.

3. The synthesis of unity and plurality, being and otherness [*Anderssein*] that is carried out in the dialectic is not just any synthesis of knowing. Above all it does not lie in the dimension of diverse appearances, of becoming and passing away, but concerns the essence of be-ing (the "idea") even in its possible relation to human life which through speaking-with-each-other [*Miteinander-reden*] discovers and makes available this essence.

It lies beyond the scope of this essay to demonstrate how in Hegel's philosophy the decisive elements of the dialectic of antiquity return on a new foundation determined by Kantian philosophy. We single out instead only one aspect of the dialectic in which all the others are based and from which the radical transformation of the Hegelian dialectic by Marx can best be understood. Only through an interpretation of the first Hegelian writings and the *Phenomenology of Spirit* can one prove that the full being and happening of human life constitutes for Hegel the authentic basis of the dialectic. Here are a few indications that must suffice for now.

It has already been indicated above the extent to which the concept of the being of life forms the fundamental basis of the metaphysics Hegel established in the *Phenomenology of Spirit*. Even in the *Science of Logic* life is still the first "unmediated" form of the "idea," that is, of that "which is in and for itself true." The "idea" is "to be apprehended and known in this determinacy in which it is *life*, so that its treatment will not be something empty and devoid of determinate content."[57] Life in its "simple relation to itself" is true equality-with-self-in-otherness. It maintains and comports itself as selfness and oneness in the various states of its living. And in this happening it makes itself into the "universal substance" and "universal medium" of be-ing, because it "mediates . . . the preexistent external world with itself."[58] It "seizes control" of being outside of it and "appropriates" it in such a way that it makes this be-ing "into its means and gives subjectivity to its substance."[59]

The concepts explaining this "life process," such as "seizing control," "appropriation," "need," "production and reproduction," already indicate that we are dealing here not only with a process of knowledge, but also with a really changing and realizable process of all life. This becomes fully clear in the presentation of this same happening in the *Phenomenology*. The happening of life is here primarily the dialectic of *knowing* [*wissenden*] *action*, of changing "doing" [*Tun*].

Although Hegel determines the being of life from the outset as "self-consciousness," thus as a mode of "spirit" with reference to the "rationality" of life, nevertheless the full concretization of happening life is contained in the concept of self-consciousness. Self-consciousness is at once *knowledge* [*Wissen*] *and action, theoretical and practical* reason (just as in the *Science of Logic* the "idea of knowing" is at once theoretical and practical "idea," indeed the theoretical idea is only completed in the practical idea). The concepts used in the *Phenomenology* to describe the unfolding of life express the concrete unity of the entire structure of life: "desire and labor," "observing, legislating and law-testing reason," "action of all and each one," "work," and the "thing itself," etc. This basis of the Hegelian dialectic will now be clarified by examining more closely one of its central concepts, namely the *concept of "sublation."*

Marck distinguishes the critical dialectic from the Hegelian precisely with this concept of sublation.[60] The "negation of the negation" appears to him as the clearest expression of a metaphysics of absolute spirit that oversteps all boundaries of the finite ego and identifies God and man. "Our thinking" can only preserve the contradiction, *not sublate it*: "it cannot remove that which has been posited."[61]

This is undoubtedly correct as long as the ego of *knowing thought* is meant; this ego cannot, of course, sublate. It remains tied to preexisting conditions. Hegel himself emphasized this strongly. He says of "knowing as such": "this knowing is *finite*, because it has as its precondition a *pre-existing* world; thus its identity with this world is not for itself. The truth to which it can come is therefore also only finite."[62] For Hegel it is precisely in this point that the motive to go beyond simple "knowing as such" lies. Mere knowing is not yet the true form of the "idea" because of this preexisting presence [*Gegebenheit*] of the object that can never be sublated by it. It leads of its own to a demand for the "practical idea" of action as its fulfillment and completion.

For the acting (and, indeed, the knowing [*wissend*]-acting) ego *really can sublate*, can remove that which is "posited." The will of the acting ego can truly create and change. It can remove that which is present in order to put its own "work" [*Werk*] in its place. The way in which this fact is related to the foundations of the dialectic becomes the actual basis of the disagreement between Marx and Hegel.

The concept of sublation made concrete in this way aims at the unique mode of motility of human life in the preexisting world in which it finds itself. This life can only happen by *going beyond* the particular "determinacy" of its existence in which it finds itself (and that always necessarily stands in a negative and "accidental" relationship to its further possibilities); it must overcome its own immediately present situation and draw on its own possibilities to drive itself to a higher situation. It can only fulfill its essence if it mediates its entire immediate existence (which, measured against its actual possibilities is essentially an "otherness," a "loss of its self") with its self-being; it makes this existence its own by changing it, "appropriating it" ("assimilating it"). Only in this change through the process of sublation does the living ego remain equal to itself in otherness.

This motility (grounded in the elaboration of the concept of life in the *Phenomenology* and *Science of Logic*) of life is at play not only in single individuals, but is at the same time and necessarily always a confrontation of the individuals among themselves and with the objective world. The sublation of otherness that happens in the life process always means a happening that truly changes the respective human and objective environment. The "dialectic" of the process of life has essentially such a "real" character. It is not a dialectic of pure cognition [*Erkennens*], but a dialectic of (knowing [*wissend*]) *doing*.[63] Hegel's concept of doing has the decisive meaning of expressing precisely the *essence* of living self-consciousness and its reality: "Things are undertaken because doing is in and for itself the essence of reality,"[64] and the "absolute matter [*Sache*]" is a reality "whose existence is the *reality* and the *doing* of self-consciousness."[65]

Let us give just one example here of the essential character of "sublation"[66] as an *act* [*Tat*].[67] In the *Phenomenology* the first (still incomplete) "sublation" of objectivity, and hence the first union of consciousness and object, takes place through the "labor of the slave."[68] By "working" on things the slave *sublates* the form of their mere objectivity (their pure negativity and otherness vis-à-vis living consciousness). The thing already worked on no longer stands opposed to living self-consciousness as pure otherness and negativity, but rather stands as something belonging to it, available to it for "pleasure" and possession.

Furthermore, the things continue to exist in the form that the self-conscious labor of the slave has given them (and only in this form). The laboring self-consciousness is their "substance," through which they first become concrete reality. Thus the "thingness which the form gets in labor . . . is no other substance than consciousness."[69] The original "negation" of consciousness is now negated and taken into the unity of living self-consciousness.

At the same time as this "sublation," there occurs in the process of work yet another sublation. When the slave recognizes that the things have permanence and reality only in the form that *his labor* has given them, he—who previously only stood in the "service of the master"—becomes conscious of his own independence. Through this "rediscovery of himself by himself" the slave's self-consciousness, which until then had been in the service of *another,* "realizes that it is precisely in . . . [the slave's] work wherein he seemed to have only an *alienated existence* that he acquires his *own existence.*"[70] "In this way laboring consciousness comes to the perception of independent being as its own self."[71]

It is already evident from this example that Hegel is concerned here with the process of reification and its transcendence as the basic happening of human life, which Marx then represented as the basic law of historical happening. This process stands in an essential relation to the dialectical concept of "sublation." It is revealed in a different form at each stage of the *Phenomenology.* The contradiction of knowing consciousness and object of knowledge is only one of the many forms of this process which is grounded in the essence of human life.

From this standpoint the theses advanced in the first essay about the connection between dialectic and historicity also lose their apparent arbitrariness and violence. The being of self-consciousness, as developed by Hegel in the *Phenomenology,* is essentially *historical* being and was originally seen as such by Hegel. The dialectic is inherently related to historicity precisely insofar as it "arises from the ego" and is the dialectic of self-consciousness. For the full essence of self-consciousness is determined by historicity. This does not mean, as Marck thinks, that "the expansion of human existence is carried through to an absolute Logos"[72]; on the contrary, such an expansion is totally out of the question. For constituting the *totality* of be-ing in the historical being of human life forbids precisely any statement about "absolute being" and any determination of be-ing from the standpoint of "absolute Logos." Hegel's dialectic, which was originally based on the concept of life, could only become an absolute dialectic when this original historicity of life came to a standstill within his system.

A historical examination of the relationship between the dialectic and historicity would above all have to investigate this peculiar duality in the foundations of the Hegelian dialectic. Life in its full historicity originally provides the guiding concept of being, but then this being moves beyond its own historicity and brings it to a standstill—it becomes "absolute spirit." This duality appears already in the *Phenomenology* given that *absolute* spirit has a *history*. It realizes and fulfills itself at a particular stage in the history of life so that it can, once thus realized and fulfilled, preserve and determine all past and future history.

The first side of this dual foundation—the being of life in its historicity— is developed in the first sections of the *Phenomenology*. These sections portray the being of life (for Hegel, self-consciousness) in its relationship to preexisting be-ing (the "world"), which always already accompanies being. These sections also show how in the history of life the totality of be-ing is realized in that form that, as "spirit," constitutes the truth of all be-ing and completes its history. The history of life that realizes itself and the world as spirit ends with the existence of the "free people": "in the life of a people the concept of self-conscious reason's realization . . . has its complete reality."[73]

The fact that the history of spirit begins with the history of the people, and that the "life of the free people" is the first form of the realization of the spirit, already points to the *historical happening* of life as the basis of the *Phenomenology of Spirit*. Of course, "history" cannot be understood here in a factual sense, as if Hegel were applying his metaphysics to factual human history and philosophizing about it (as he did in a certain sense in his later lectures on the philosophy of history). The *Phenomenology of Spirit* is not a history of philosophy, which always comes *post festum*. Hegel outlines in this work the history of life in its basic structure, which *precedes* all factual history—precedes in the sense that all factual history is a (respectively different) realization of this basic structure. In our example the process of reification and its transcendence ("sublation") is not a unique historical fact but a happening rooted in the essence of human life that repeats itself at each stage of factual history in another form. The same is true of the relationship between "mastery and servitude," individual and general "work," "state power and wealth."[74]

It is a serious mistake to interpret Hegel's understanding of history based primarily on the *Lectures on the Philosophy of History* or the *Philosophy of Right*— this is a mistake that has concealed the internal relationship between Hegel and Marx to the present day. Both works presuppose the *Phenomenology*, on the one hand, and the *Science of Logic*, on the other, in the sense that they already represent an attenuation of the original discoveries of the *Phenomenology* and the *Logic*. The historical concept that operates in them is a curtailment and transformation of the original concept of history. In the *Philosophy of Right* and the *Philosophy of History*, history is still only a partial unfolding [*Teilgeschehen*] of the absolute spirit, and indeed a partial unfolding only of a particular form of this spirit.

A sufficiently in-depth interpretation of Marx would have to show that his critique of Hegel starts at exactly the point where Hegel began falling away from the original and full concept of history. Marx recovered the original concept of history and the essential character of historical life, but not—and this *separates his work decisively not only from Hegel but from all philosophy*—to establish a philosophical determination of life within all be-ing. Instead Marx undertakes an analysis of the contemporary historical situation of this life with the aim of a revolutionary upheaval. This is why Marx explicitly limits his description of the process of reification and its transcendence to the historical stage decisive for this revolutionary situation: the reification of life in capitalist commodity production.

Thus with his radical transformation of the Hegelian dialectic Marx did not simply extract the philosophical method from a particular philosophical system but rather rediscovered the dialectical motility of historical life that Hegel had discovered but then covered up once again. The dialectical relationship of thesis, antithesis, and synthesis is only the general expression of a basic law of the historical motility of life. It is an expression of the necessary "sublation"—that is, a sublation grounded in the being of life—of the particular historical reality in which life finds itself (thesis) and that necessarily represents a deterioration [*Verfall*] of its possibilities (negation), and, finally, the progress to a higher and truer reality that eliminates the first (antithesis). This happening does not just sublate, it "preserves" at the same time. It integrates the positive possibilities that have been realized at the present [*gegeben*] historical stage (synthesis). In a crucial sense it is bound to this present [*Gegebenheit*] insofar as the preserving sublation can only happen based on the particular possibilities present and on the *knowledge* [*Wissen*] of their having-become, their deterioration, and their future.

Even the concept of "knowledge" [*Wissen*], as it appears in Hegel's philosophy in the determination of life as "self-consciousness" has an originally *historical* content, which is expressly developed in the *Phenomenology of Spirit*. The "mediating" movement of consciousness in which consciousness "merges" its present individual existence (the form of its respective particular existence) with the "universal spirit" (the totality of being in its true form) takes place only by way of the "system of the forms of consciousness" present at that time, "which has its objective existence as *world history.*"[75] Life as self-consciousness is "a development which systematizes itself." Knowing [*wissendes*] life does not, like organic nature, "fall straight from pure universality into the brute singularity of existence;" instead it *gives itself* its reality from the knowledge [*Wissen*] of the preexisting, already realized "forms" of the world and in the confrontation with the particular "objective existence" that has preceded it. And insofar as it does this, insofar as this preserving sublation constitutes its essence, it is *history*. And precisely on the basis of this, its historicity, it distinguishes itself from organic nature that has "no history" because precisely this movement directed by *knowledge* [Wissen] is lacking in it.[76]

From this point of view the criticism often directed against both Hegel and Marx can be refuted—namely, that they do not apply their dialectic to themselves, that their method "comes to a halt" (as Max Weber puts it) before their own position. So little as the dialectic allows an arbitrary coming to a halt, just as little does it permit an arbitrary continuation. The Hegelian dialectic is rooted in Hegel's own system in such a way that it cannot transcend that system. It has no basis outside of his self-enclosed philosophical system. The Marxian dialectic cannot be applied to the situation in which Marx rooted it as long as this situation itself is not sublated and a new dialectical movement established in a new situation. Only on the basis of the realized proletarian revolution could the question regarding the possibility of a new dialectic of happening be raised.

These suggestions are meant to show that Marck really raises the genuine problems of the dialectic and uncovers the precise preconditions necessary for raising the question of the Marxian dialectic.

New Sources on the
Foundation of Historical Materialism

The publication of the *Economic and Philosophical Manuscripts* written by Marx in 1844 must become a crucial event in the history of Marxist studies.[1] These manuscripts could put the discussion about the origins and original meaning of historical materialism, and the entire theory of "scientific socialism," on a new footing. They also make it possible to pose the question of the actual connections between Marx and Hegel in a more fruitful and promising way.

Not only does the fragmentary nature of the manuscripts (substantial sections seem to have been lost and the analysis often breaks off at crucial points; there are no final drafts ready for publication) necessitate a detailed interpretation that constantly relates individual passages to the overall context, but the text also demands an exceptionally high level of technical knowledge on the part of the reader. For, if I may anticipate, we are dealing with a philosophical critique and foundation of political economy as a theory of revolution.

It is necessary to place such strong emphasis on the difficulties involved right at the outset in order to avert the danger that these manuscripts will once again be *taken too lightly* and hastily put into the usual compartments and schemata of Marx scholarship. This danger is all the greater because all the familiar categories of the subsequent critique of political economy are already found together in this work. But in the *Economic and Philosophical Manuscripts*, the original meaning of the basic categories is clearer than ever before and it could become necessary to revise the current interpretation of the later and more elaborate critique in the light of its origins. Perhaps this provisional review of the *Manuscripts* will suffice to show the inadequacy of the familiar thesis that Marx developed by moving from providing a philosophical to providing an economic basis for his theory.

We are dealing with a *philosophical* critique of political economy, for the basic categories of Marx's theory here arise out of his emphatic confrontation with the philosophy of Hegel (e.g., labor, objectification, alienation, sublation, property).[2] This does not mean that Hegel's "method" is transformed and taken over, put into a new context, and brought to life. Rather, Marx goes back to the problems at the root of Hegel's philosophy (which originally determined his method), independently appropriates their real content, and thinks the philosophy through to a further stage. The great importance of the new manuscripts further lies in the fact that they contain the first explicit documentary evidence of Marx's critical reception of Hegel's *Phenomenology of Spirit,* "the true point of origin and the secret of the Hegelian philosophy."[3]

If Marx's discussion of the basic problems of Hegel's philosophy informed the foundation of his theory, it can no longer be said that this foundation simply underwent a transformation from a philosophical to an economic basis and that in its subsequent (economic) form philosophy had been overcome and "finished" once and for all. It is rather the case that the foundation includes the philosophical basis in *all* its stages. This is not invalidated by the fact that its sense and purpose are not at all philosophical but practical and revolutionary: the overthrow of the capitalist system through the economic and political struggle of the proletariat. What must be seen and understood is that economics and politics have become the economic-political *basis* of the theory of revolution through a quite particular, philosophical interpretation of human essence [*Wesen*][4] and its historical realization. The very complicated relationship between philosophical and economic theory and between this theory and revolutionary praxis, which can only be clarified by an analysis of the entire situation in which historical materialism developed, may become clear after a full interpretation (which I only want to introduce in this essay) of the *Economic and Philosophical Manuscripts.* A rough formula that could be used as a starting point would be that the revolutionary critique of political economy itself has a philosophical foundation, just as, conversely, the philosophy underlying it already contains revolutionary praxis. The theory is in itself a practical one; praxis does not only come at the end but is already present at the beginning of the theory. To engage in praxis is not to tread on alien ground, ground external to the theory.

With these introductory remarks we can proceed to describe the overall content of the *Manuscripts.* Marx himself describes their purpose as the *critique of political economy*—a "positive" critique,[5] and thus one that, by revealing the

mistakes of political economy and its inadequacy for the subject, also provides
it with a basis to make it adequate to its task. The positive critique of political
economy is thus a critical *foundation* of political economy. Within this critique
the idea of political economy is completely transformed: it becomes the science[6]
of the necessary conditions for the communist revolution. This revolution itself
signifies—quite apart from economic upheavals—a revolution in the whole
history of man and the determination of his essence [*Wesensbestimmung*]:[7] "This
communism . . . is the *genuine* resolution of the conflict between man and
nature and between man and man—the true resolution of the strife between
existence and essence, between objectification and self-confirmation, between
freedom and necessity, between the individual and the species. Communism
is the riddle of history solved, and it knows itself to be this solution."[8]

If political economy can gain such central importance, it is clear that it must
be treated from the outset as more than just another science or specialized scientific field. Instead it must be seen as the scientific expression of a problematic
that affects the entire essence of man. Thus we must begin by considering more
closely *in which way* political economy is subjected to criticism here.

Political economy is criticized as the scientific justification or obfuscation
of the total "estrangement" and "devaluation" of human reality as it appears
in capitalist society—as a science that treats man as "something unessential"[9]
[*ein Unwesen*] whose whole existence is determined by the "separation of labor,
capital and land" and by an inhuman division of labor, by competition, by
private property, etc.[10] This kind of political economy scientifically sanctions
the transformation of the historical-social world of man into an alien world of
money and commodities; a world that confronts him as a hostile power and in
which the greater part of humanity ceases to be anything more than "abstract"
workers (torn away from the reality of human existence), separated from the
object of their work, and forced to sell themselves as a commodity.

As a result of this "alienation" of the worker and of labor, the realization of all
man's "essential powers" becomes the loss of their reality; the objective world is
no longer "truly human property" appropriated in "free activity"[11] as the sphere
of the free operation and self-confirmation of the whole of human nature. It
is instead a world of objects in private possession that can be owned, used,
or exchanged and whose seemingly unalterable laws even man must obey—in
short, a world of the universal "domination of dead matter over mankind."[12]

This whole situation has often been described under the heading of "alienation," "estrangement," and "reification" and is a widely known element of

Marxist theory. The important point is, however, to see how and from what angle Marx interprets it here at the starting point of his theory.

At the beginning of his positive critique of political economy, at the point where he takes up the matter of alienation and estrangement, Marx states: "We proceed from an economic fact of the present."[13] But are alienation and estrangement "economic facts" like, for example, ground rent or the price of commodities in its dependence on supply and demand or any other "law" of the process of production, consumption, and circulation?

Bourgeois political economy, as criticized here, does *not* regard alienation and estrangement as such as a fact (the circumstances to which these words refer are covered in the bourgeois theory under quite different headings); for socialist political economy this fact will only "exist" if and insofar as the theory is placed on the foundation that Marx worked out in the context of the studies we are discussing. We must therefore ask what sort of fact this is (since it is essentially different from all other facts in political economy), and on what basis it becomes visible and can described as such.

The description of the circumstances of alienation and estrangement seems initially to proceed completely on the ground of traditional political economy and its theorems. Marx significantly starts by dividing his investigation into the three traditional concepts of political economy: "the wages of labor," "the profit of capital," and "the rent of land."[14] But more important, and a sign pointing in a completely new direction, is the fact that this division into three is soon exploded and abandoned: "From page xxii to the end of the manuscript Marx wrote across the three columns, disregarding the headings. The text of these six pages (xxii–xxvii) is given in the present book under the title, 'Estranged Labor.' "[15]

The development of the concept of labor thus breaks through the traditional framework for dealing with problems; the discussion continues with this concept and discovers the new "fact," which then becomes the basis for the science of the communist revolution. Our interpretation must therefore take Marx's concept of labor as its point of departure.

When Marx depicts the manner of labor and the form of existence of the worker in capitalist society as complete separation from the means of production and from the product of his labor, which has become a commodity, the balancing of wages around the minimum for mere physical survival, the severance of the worker's labor (performed as "forced labor" in the capitalist's service) from his "human reality"—all these features can in themselves still denote simple economic facts. This impression seems to be confirmed by the fact that Marx, "by analysis from the concept of alienated labor," reaches the concept of "private property" and thus the basic concept of traditional political economy.[16]

But if we look more closely at the description of alienated labor we make a remarkable discovery: what is here described is not merely an economic matter. It is the alienation of man, the devaluation of life, the inversion and loss of human reality. In the relevant passage Marx identifies it as follows: "the concept of alienated labor, i.e. of alienated man, of estranged labor, of estranged life, of estranged man."[17]

It is thus a matter of man as man (and not just as worker, economic subject, and the like), and of a process not only in economic history but also in the history of man and his reality. In the same sense he writes about private property: "Just as private property is only the sensuous expression of the fact that man becomes objective for himself and at the same time becomes to himself a strange and inhuman object, . . . so the positive sublation of private property [is] the sensuous appropriation for and by man of the human essence and of human life."[18]

It is not because Marx is limited by a particular kind of philosophical terminology that he so often speaks here of "human essential powers" and "the essence of man" or, for example, that he calls "the established objective existence of industry . . . the open book of man's essential powers" or wants to grasp industry's "connection to the essence of man"[19] and, in the places quoted above, uses *philosophical* concepts to describe labor and private property. His interpretation rather attempts to make it clear that the whole critique and foundation of political economy was developed on a philosophical basis and grew explicitly out of a philosophical dispute, and that the philosophical concepts used cannot be regarded as remnants that were later discarded or as a disguise that we can strip off. As the result of an idea about the essence of man and its realization that evolved out of Marx's dispute with Hegel, a simple economic fact appears as the inversion [*Verkehrung*] of the human essence and the loss of human reality. *It is only on this foundation* that an economic fact is capable of becoming the real basis of a revolution that will genuinely transform the essence of man and his world.

What we are trying to show is this: from the outset the basic concepts of the critique—alienated labor and private property—are not simply taken up and criticized as economic concepts, but as concepts related to a decisive happening in human history; consequently the "positive abolition" of private property by the true appropriation of human reality will revolutionize the entire history of mankind. Bourgeois political economy has to be basically transformed in the critique for this very reason: it fails to recognize man who is its real subject. It disregards the essence of man and his history and is thus in the profoundest sense not a "science of man" [*Wissenschaft vom Menschen*] but of inhuman beings [*Unmenschen*] and of an inhuman world of objects and commodities. "Crude and thoughtless communism"[20] is just as sharply criticized for the same reason: it is not grounded in the reality of human essence either but operates instead in the world of things and objects and thus remains in a state of "estrangement." This type of communism only replaces individual private property with "universal private property";[21] "it wants to destroy everything which is not capable of being possessed by all as private property. It wants to do away by force with talent, etc. For it, the sole purpose of life and existence is direct, physical possession. The task of the laborer is not done away with, but extended to all men."[22]

The objections to the absolute economism of Marxist theory, which have been thoughtlessly raised time and again right up to the present day, were already raised here by Marx himself against the crude communism that he opposed: for him the latter is merely the simple "negation" of capitalism and as such exists on the same level as capitalism—but it is precisely that level which Marx wants to abolish.

Before beginning with our interpretation we need to avert another possible misunderstanding. If Marx's critique of political economy and his foundation of revolutionary theory are here dealt with as *philosophy* this does not mean that thereby "only theoretical" philosophical matters, which minimize the concrete historical situation (of the proletariat in capitalism) and its praxis, will be considered. The starting point, the basis and the goal of this investigation is precisely the particular historical situation and the praxis that is revolutionizing it. Regarding the situation and praxis from the standpoint of the history of man's essence makes the acutely practical nature of the critique even more trenchant and sharp: the fact that capitalist society calls into question not only economic facts and objects but the entire "existence" of man and "human reality" is for Marx the decisive justification for the proletarian revolution as a *total and radical* revolution, unconditionally excluding any partial upheaval or "evolution." The justification does not lie outside or behind the concepts of alienation and estrangement—the justification is rather precisely this alienation and estrangement itself. All attempts to dismiss the philosophical content of Marx's theory or to gloss over it in embarrassment reveal a complete failure to recognize the historical origin of the theory: they set out from a point of an essential separation of philosophy, economics, and revolutionary praxis, which is a product of the reification against which Marx fought and that he had already overcome at the beginning of his critique. We begin now with the interpretation of the concept of labor.

I

In capitalist society labor not only produces commodities (i.e., goods that can be freely sold on the market), but also produces "itself and the worker as a commodity," the worker becoming "an ever cheaper commodity the more commodities he creates."[23] The worker not only loses the product of his own labor and creates alien objects for unknown people; he is not only "reduced spiritually and physically to the condition of a machine" through the increasing division and mechanization of labor, so that "from being a man [he] becomes an abstract activity and a stomach,"[24] but he also even has to "sell himself and his humanity,"[25] that is, he must himself become a commodity in order to exist as a physical subject. So instead of being an expression of the whole man, labor is his "alienation;" instead of being the full and free realization of man it has become a "loss of realization." "So much does labor's realization appear as loss of realization that the worker loses realization to the point of starving to death."[26]

It should be noted that even in this depiction of the "economic fact" of alienated labor the simple economic description constantly breaks through to man's reality: the economic "condition" of labor is cast back onto the "existence" of working man[27]; beyond the sphere of economic relations, the alienation and estrangement of labor concern the essence and reality of man as "man" and only for this reason can the loss of the object of labor acquire such central significance. Marx makes this quite clear when he states that the fact he has just described is the "expression" of a more general state of affairs: "This fact expresses merely that the object which labor produces—labor's product—confronts it as something alien, as a power independent of the producer. The product of labor is labor which has been embodied in an object, which has become material: it is the objectification of labor."[28] He also makes this clear when he says: "All these consequences" (of the capitalist economic system) "result from the fact that the worker is related to the product of his labor as to an alien object."[29] The economic fact of estrangement and reification[30] is thus grounded in a particular attitude by man (as a worker) toward the object (of his labor). "Alienated labor" must now be understood in the sense of this kind of relation of man to the object and no longer as a purely economic condition: "The alienation of the worker in his product means not only that his labor becomes an object, an external existence, but that it exists outside him, independently, as something alien to him, and that it becomes a power on its own confronting him. It means that the life which he has conferred on the object confronts him as something hostile and alien."[31] In what follows it will also become apparent that the economic fact of "private property" too is *grounded* in the situation of alienated labor, understood as the activity of man: "Private property is thus the product, the result, the necessary consequence, of alienated labor, of the external relation of the worker to nature and to himself."[32]

An astonishing, idealistic inversion of the actual facts seems to have taken place here: an economic fact is supposed to have its roots in a general concept and in the relation of man to the object: "Private property thus results by analysis from the concept of alienated labor."[33] This is Marx, not Hegel writing! The apparent distortion expresses one of the crucial aspects of Marx's theory: the breakthrough from economic fact to human factors, from fact [*Tat-"sache"*] to act [*Tat-"handlung"*], and the comprehension of fixed "situations" and their laws (which in their reified form are out of man's power) in motion, *in the course of their historical development*, out of which they have fallen and become fixed (see the programmatic introduction of the new approach to the problem on p. 92 [pp. 118–19]). We cannot go into the revolutionary significance of this method here; we shall continue to pursue the line of approach outlined at the beginning.

If the concept of alienated labor includes the relation of man to the object (and, as we shall see, himself) then the concept of labor as such must also cover a human activity (and not an economic condition). If the alienation of labor signifies the total loss of realization and the estrangement of the human essence, then labor itself must be grasped as the real expression and realization of the human essence. But that means once again that it is used as a *philosophical* category.

Despite the above development of the subject we would be loath to use the often misused term "ontology" in connection with Marx's theory, if Marx himself had not expressly used it here.[34] He says that only "through the medium of private property does the *ontological* essence of human passion come into being, in its totality as in its humanity," and he suggests that "man's feelings, passions, etc., are not merely anthropological characteristics . . . but truly ontological affirmations of his essence (nature)."[35]

Marx's positive determinations of labor are almost all given as counter-concepts to the determination of *alienated* labor, and yet the ontological nature of this concept is clearly expressed in them. We shall extract three of the most important formulations: "Labor is man's coming-to-be for himself within alienation, or as alienated man," it is "man's act of self-creation or self-objectification," "[and it is man's] life-activity, productive life itself."[36] All three of these formulations, even if they did not occur within the context of Marx's explicit examination of Hegel, would still point to Hegel's ontological concept of labor.[37] The basic concept of Marx's critique, the concept of alienated labor, does in fact arise from his examination of Hegel's category of objectification, a category developed for the first time in the *Phenomenology of Mind* around the concept of labor.[38] The *Economic and Philosophical Manuscripts* are direct evidence of the fact that Marx's theory has its roots in the center of Hegel's philosophical problematic.

We can deduce the following from these determinations of labor: labor is "man's act of self-creation," that is, the activity through and in which man really first becomes what he is, according to his essence, as man. He does this in such a way that this becoming and being are there *for himself*, so that he can *know* and "regard" himself as what he is (man's "becoming-for-himself"). Labor is a knowing [*wissende*] and conscious activity. In his labor man relates to himself and to the object of his labor; he is not directly one with his labor but can, as it were, confront it and oppose it (through which, as we shall see, human labor is fundamentally distinguished as "universal" and "free" production from the "unmediated" production of, for example, the nest-building animal). The fact that man in his labor is there "for himself" in objective form is closely related to the second point: man is an "objective" or, more exactly, an "objectifying" being. Man can only realize his essence if he realizes it as something *objective*, by using his "essential powers" to produce an "external," "material," objective world. It is in his work in this world (in the broadest sense) that he is real and effective. "In creating a world of objects by his practical activity, in his work upon inorganic nature, man proves himself a conscious species being."[39] In his activity man shows himself as the human being he is according to his "species" as distinct from animal, vegetable, and inorganic being (we will examine the central concept of objectification at a later stage below). Labor, understood in this way, is the specifically human "affirmation of essence" in which human existence is realized and confirmed.

Thus even the most provisional and general characterization of Marx's concept of labor leads far beyond the economic sphere into a dimension in which the subject of the investigation is human essence in its totality. The interpretation cannot progress any further before this dimension has been described. We must first answer the question of how and from what starting point Marx defines man's existence and essence. The answer to this question is a prerequisite for understanding what is really meant by the concept of estranged labor and for understanding the whole foundation of revolutionary theory.

2

There are two passages in the *Economic and Philosophical Manuscripts* in which Marx gives an explicit determination of man, encompassing the totality of human being.[40] Even if they are only a rough outline, these passages give a clear enough indication of the real basis of Marx's critique. On several occasions Marx describes "positive communism,"[41] which will achieve the abolition of estrangement and reification, as "humanism"—a terminological hint that for him the basis is a particular kind of realization of the human essence. The development of this humanism, as far as it is a positive determination of the human essence, is here primarily influenced by Feuerbach: as early as in the preface we read "positive criticism as a whole—and therefore also German positive criticism of political economy—owes it true foundation to the discoveries of Feuerbach"[42] and "it is only with Feuerbach that positive, humanistic and naturalistic criticism begins."[43] Later the "establishment of true materialism and of real science" is described as Feuerbach's "great achievement."[44] In our interpretation, however, we shall not follow the road of philosophical history and trace the development of "humanism" from Hegel through Feuerbach to Marx, but attempt to unfold the problem from Marx's text itself.

"Man is a species being, not only because in practice and in theory he adopts the species as his object (his own as well as those of other things), but—and this is only another way of expressing it—also because he treats himself as the actual, living, species; because he treats himself as a universal and therefore a free being."[45] The determination of man as a "species being" has done a lot of damage to Marx scholarship; this passage is so valuable because it exposes the real origins of Marx's concept of "species." Man is a "species being," that is, a being [*Wesen*] that has the "species" (his own and that of the rest of be-ing)[46] as its object. The species of a be-ing is that which this be-ing is according to its "stock" and "origin"; it is the "principle" of its being that is common to all the particular features of what it is: the general essence of this be-ing. If man can make the species of every be-ing into his object, the general essence of every be-ing can become objective for him; he can have every be-ing as that which it is in its essence. It is for this reason (and this is expressed in the second half of the sentence quoted) that he can *relate* freely to every be-ing. He is not limited to the particular, actual state of the be-ing and his immediate relationship to it, but he can take the be-ing as it is in its essence beyond its immediate, particular, actual state. He can recognize and grasp the *possibilities* contained in every be-ing. He can exploit, alter, mold, treat, and take further ("produce") any be-ing according to it "inherent standard."[47] *Labor*, as the specifically human "life activity," has its roots in this "species being" of man; it presupposes man's ability to relate to the "general" aspect of objects and to the possibilities contained therein. Specifically human *freedom* has its roots in man's ability to relate to his *own* species: the self-realization and "self-creation" of man. The relationship of man as a species being to his objects is then more closely defined by means of the concept of free labor (producing freely).

Man as a species being is a "universal" being [*Wesen*]; *every* be-ing can become for him objective in its "species character." His being consists in a universal relationship to objectivity. He has to include these "theoretically objective things in his praxis; he must make them the object of his "life activity" and work on them. The whole of "nature" is the medium of his human life; it is man's means of life, it is his *prerequisite*, which he must take up and reintroduce into his praxis. Man cannot simply accept the objective world or merely come to terms with it; he must appropriate it. He has to transform the objects of this world into organs of his life, which is manifested in and through them: "The universality of man appears in practice precisely in the universality which makes all nature his inorganic body—both inasmuch as nature is (1) his direct means of life and (2) the material, the object, and the instrument of his life activity. Nature is man's inorganic body—nature, that is, in so far as it is not itself the human body."[48]

The thesis of nature as a means for man implies more than merely that man is dependent simply for his physical survival on objective, organic, and inorganic nature as a means of life or that under the direct pressure of his "needs" he "produces" (appropriates, treats, prepares, etc.) the objective world as objects for food, clothing, accommodation, etc. Marx here explicitly speaks of "spiritual, inorganic nature," "spiritual nourishment," and "man's physical and spiritual life."[49] This is why the universality of man—as distinct from the essentially limited nature of animals—consists in *freedom*, for an animal "produces only under the dominion of immediate physical need" while man "only truly produces in freedom therefrom."[50] An animal thus only produces itself and "what it immediately needs for itself or its young. It produces one-sidedly, whilst man produces universally."[51] Man does not have objects merely as the environment of his immediate life activity and does not treat them merely as objects of his immediate needs. He can "confront" any object and exhaust and realize its inner possibilities in his labor. He can produce "in accordance with the laws of beauty" and not merely in accordance with the standard of his own needs.[52] In this freedom man reproduces "the whole of nature," and through transformation and appropriation furthers it, along with his own life, even when this production does not satisfy an immediate need. Thus the history of human life is at the same time essentially the history of man's objective world and of "the whole of nature" ("nature" in the wider sense given to this concept by Marx, as also by Hegel).[53] Man is not *in* nature; nature is not the *external world* into which he first has to come out of his own inwardness. Man *is* nature. Nature is his "expression," "his work and his reality."[54] Wherever we come across nature in human history it is "*human* nature" while man for his part is always "human *nature*" too. We can thus see provisionally to what extent consistent "humanism" is immediately "naturalism."[55]

On the basis of the unity thus achieved between man and nature Marx moves toward the crucial determination of *objectification*, through which the specifically human relationship to objectivity, the human way of producing, is more concretely determined as universality and freedom. Objectification—the determination of man as an "objective being"—is not simply a further point appended to the determination of the unity of man and nature, but is the closer and deeper foundation of this unity. (Objectification as such belongs—like his participation in nature—to the essence of man and can thus not be "sublated;" according to revolutionary theory, only a particular form of objectification—reification, "estrangement"—can and must be sublated.)

As a natural being man is an "objective being [*Wesen*]," which for Marx is a "being equipped and endowed with objective (i.e. material) essential powers,"[56] a being who relates to real objects, "acts objectively," and "can only *express* his life in real, sensuous objects."[57] Because the power of his being thus consists in living out (i.e., through and in external objects) everything he is, his "self-realization" at the same time means "the establishment of a real, objective world, which is overpowering because it has a form external to him and is thus not part of his being."[58] The objective world, as the necessary objectivity of man, through the appropriation and sublation of which his human essence is first "produced" and "confirmed," is part of man himself. It *is* real objectivity only for self-realizing man, it is the "self-objectification" of man or human objectification. But this same objective world, since it is real objectivity, can appear as a precondition of his being that does *not* belong to his being, that is beyond his control, and that is "overpowering." This conflict in the human essence—that it is in itself objective—is the root of the fact that objectification can become reification and that externalization [*Äußerung*] *can become alienation* [*Entäußerung*]. It makes it possible for man to "lose" completely the object as part of his being and to let it become independent and overpowering. This possibility becomes a reality in alienated labor and private property.

Marx then attempts to implant objectification and the conflict appearing within it even more deeply into the determination of man. "An objective being . . . would not act objectively if the quality of objectivity did not reside in the very essence of his being [*Wesensbestimmung*]. He creates, posits objects alone because he is posited by objects—because at bottom he is nature."[59] The quality of being posited by objects is, however, the fundamental determinant of "sensuousness" [*Sinnlichkeit*] (to have senses, which are affected by objects) and thus Marx can identify objective being with sensuous being, and the quality of having objects outside oneself with the quality of being sensuous: "To be sensuous, i.e. real, is to be an object of the senses, a sensuous object, and therefore to have objects outside oneself which are subject to the operations of one's senses"; furthermore, "To *be* objective, natural and sensuous, and at the same time to have object, nature and sense outside oneself, or oneself to be object, nature and sense for a third party, is one and the same thing."[60] (The second identification also included here will be discussed below.) Thereby "sensuousness" for Marx moves to the center of his philosophical foundation: "Sensuousness (see Feuerbach) must be the basis of all science."[61]

It will already be clear from the above deduction that "sensuousness" is here an ontological concept within the determination of man's essence and that it comes before any materialism or sensualism. The concept of sensuousness here taken up by Marx (via Feuerbach and Hegel) goes back to Kant's *Critique of Pure Reason*. There it is said that sensuousness is the human perception through which alone objects are *given* to us. Objects can only be given to man insofar as they "affect" him. Human sensuousness is affectibility (§B 33).[62] Human cognition [*Erkenntnis*] as sensuousness is receptive and passive. It receives what is given, and it is dependent on and needs this quality of being given. To the extent that man is characterized by sensuousness he is "posited" by objects, and he accepts these prerequisites through cognition. As a sensuous being he is a receptive, passive, and suffering being.

In Feuerbach, to whom Marx explicitly refers in the passage quoted, the concept of sensuousness originally tends in the same direction as in Kant. In fact, when Feuerbach, in opposition to Hegel, wants to restore the receptivity of the senses as the starting point of philosophy, he initially almost appears as the preserver and defender of Kantian criticism against "absolute idealism." "Being is something in which not only I but also others, above all the *object*, participate."[63] "Only through the senses, and not through thought itself, is an object given in a true sense become"; "an object . . . is given . . . not to the 'I,' but to my 'not-I' in me; for only when I am . . . passive, does the conception of an activity existing apart from me . . . arise."[64] This being that is accepting, suffering, needy, and dependent on given things finds expression in man's sensuousness, and is developed by Feuerbach into the "passive principle"[65] and placed at the apex of his philosophy—although he goes in a direction quite different from that of Kant. The definition of man as purely "suffering" and "needy" being is the original basis for Feuerbach's attack on Hegel and his idea of man as a purely free, creative consciousness: "Only a *needy* being is a necessary being. Existence *without needs* is superfluous existence. . . . A being without distress is a being without ground. . . . A being without *suffering* is a being without being [*Wesen ohne Wesen*]. A being without suffering is nothing other than a being without sensuousness and matter."[66]

The same tendency to go back to sensuousness is now also discernible in Marx—a tendency to comprehend the way man's being is defined by needs and his dependence on preestablished objectivity by means of the sensuousness in his own being. This tendency in turn is subject to the aim of achieving a real, concrete picture of man as an objective and natural being, united with the world, as opposed to Hegel's abstract "being," freed from preestablished "naturalness," which posits both itself and all objectivity. In line with Feuerbach, Marx says: "as a natural, corporeal, sensuous, objective being [man] is a *suffering*, conditioned and limited creature,"[67] and "to be sensuousness is *to suffer*. Man as an objective, sensuous being is therefore a *suffering* [*leidendes*] being—and because he feels what he suffers, a *passionate* [*leidenschaftliches*] being."[68] Man's passion, his real activity and spontaneity, is ascribed to his suffering and neediness, insofar as it is an aspiration to achieve a preestablished object existing outside him: "Passion is the essential force of man energetically striving for its object"[69]; furthermore, "The rich man is simultaneously the man *in need of* a totality of human manifestations of life—the man in whom his own realization exists as an inner necessity, as *need.*"[70]

We can now understand why Marx emphasizes that "man's feelings, passions, etc. . . . are truly ontological affirmations of his essence (nature)."[71] The distress and neediness that appear in man's sensuousness are no more purely matters of cognition than his distress and neediness, as expressed in estranged labor, are purely economic. Distress and neediness here do not describe the individual modes of man's behavior at all; they are features of his whole *being*. They are ontological categories (we shall therefore return to them in the connection with a large number of different themes in these *Manuscripts*).

It was necessary to give such an extensive interpretation of the concept of sensuousness in order to point once again to its real meaning in opposition to its many misinterpretations as the basis of materialism. In developing this concept Marx and Feuerbach were in fact addressing one of the crucial problems of "classical German philosophy." But in Marx it is this concept of sensuousness (as objectification) that leads to the decisive turn from classical German philosophy to the theory of revolution, for he inserts the basic traits of *practical* and *social* being into his determination of man's essential being. As objectivity, man's sensuousness is essentially practical objectification, and because it is practical it is essentially a social objectification.

3

We know from Marx's *Theses on Feuerbach* that it is precisely the concept of human *praxis* that draws the line of demarcation between himself and Feuerbach. On the other hand, it is through this (or more exactly, through the concept of labor) that he reaches back beyond Feuerbach to Hegel: "The outstanding achievement of Hegel's *Phenomenology* and of its final outcome . . . is thus . . . that Hegel . . . grasps the essence of labor and comprehends objective man— true, because real man—as the outcome of man's own labor."[72] Things are thus not as simple as we would expect; the road from Feuerbach to Marx is not characterized by a straight rejection of Hegel. Instead of this, Marx, at the origins of revolutionary theory, once again appropriates the decisive achievements of Hegel, transforming them.

We saw that man's sensuousness signified that he is posited by preestablished objects and therefore also that he *has* a given, objective world to which he *relates* "universally" and "freely." We must now describe more closely these ways of having and relating to the world.

For Feuerbach man's having and relating to the world remain essentially theoretical, and this is expressed in the fact that the way of relating, in which man really has reality, is "perception" [*Anschauung*].[73] For Marx, to put it briefly, labor replaces this perception, although the central importance of the theoretical relation does not disappear; it is combined with labor in a relationship of dialectical interpenetration. We have already suggested above that Marx grasps labor, beyond all its economic significance, as the human "life-activity" and the genuine realization of man. We must now present the concept of labor in its inner connection to the determination of man as a "natural" and "sensuous" (objective) being [*Wesen*]. We shall see how it is in labor that the distress and neediness, but also the universality and freedom of man, become real.

"Man is directly a natural being. As a natural being and as a living natural being he is, on the one hand, endowed with natural powers of life—he is an *active* natural being. These forces exist in him as tendencies and abilities— as instincts. On the other hand, as a natural, corporeal, sensuous, objective being he is a suffering, conditioned and limited creature. . . . That is to say, the objects of his instincts exist outside him, as *objects* independent of him; yet these objects are objects that he *needs*—essential objects, indispensable to the manifestation and confirmation of his essential powers."[74] Objects are thus not primarily objects of perception, but of needs, and as such objects of the powers, abilities, and instincts of man. It has already been pointed out that "need" is not to be understood only in the sense of physical neediness: man needs a "totality of human manifestations of life."[75] To be able to realize himself he needs to express himself through the preestablished objects with which he is confronted. His activity and his self-affirmation consist in the appropriation of the "externality" that confronts him, and in the transference of himself into that externality. In his labor man sublates the mere objectivity of objects and makes them into "the means of life." He impresses on them the form of his being [*Wesen*] and makes them into "his work and his reality." The objective piece of finished work is the reality of man; man is as he has realized himself in the object of his labor. For this reason Marx can say that in the object of his labor man sees himself in objective form, becomes "for himself," perceives himself as an object: "The object of labor is, therefore, the objectification of man's species life [*Gattungsleben*]: for he duplicates himself not only, as in consciousness, intellectually, but also actively, in reality, and therefore he contemplates himself in a world that he has created."[76]

Marx speaks here of the objectification of the "species life," for it is not the isolated individual who is active in labor, and the objectivity of labor is not objectivity for the isolated individual or a mere plurality of individuals—rather it is precisely in labor that the specifically human *universality* is realized.

Thus we can already discern the second basic characteristic of objectification: it is essentially a "social" activity, and objectifying man is basically "social" man. The sphere of objects in which labor is performed is precisely the sphere of common life-activity; in and through the objects of labor, men reveal themselves to *one another* in their reality. The original forms of communication, the essential relationship of men to one another, were expressed in the common use, possession, desire, need and enjoyment, etc. of the objective world. All labor is with and for and against others, so that in it men first mutually reveal themselves for what they really are.[77] Thus every object on which a man works in his individuality is "simultaneously his own existence for the other man, the existence of the other, and that existence for him."[78]

If the objective world is thus understood in its totality as a "social" world, as the objective reality of human society and thus as human objectification, then through this it is also already defined as a *historical* reality. The objective world that is in any given situation preestablished for man is the reality of past human life, which, although it belongs to the past, is still present in the form it has given to the objective world. A new form of the objective world can thus only come into being on the basis and through the sublation of an earlier form already in existence. The real human and his world arise first in this movement, which sublates the past into the present: "History is the true natural history of man," his "act of origin," "the creation of man through human labor."[79] Not only man but also nature "comes to be" in history, insofar as it is not something external to and separated from the human essence but belongs to the transcended and appropriated objectivity of man: "world history" is "the transformation of nature for man."[80]

It is only now, after the totality of the human essence as the unity of man and nature has been made concrete by the practical-social-historical process of objectification, that we can understand the determination of man as a "universal" and "free" species being. The history of man is at the same time the happening[81] of "the whole of nature;" his history is the "production and reproduction" of the whole of nature, the furtherance of objective be-ing through the renewed sublation of its current form. In his "universal" relationship[82] to the whole of nature, therefore, nature is ultimately not a limitation on or something alien to and outside of him to which he, as something other, is subjected. It is his expression, confirmation, activity: "externality is . . . sensuousness *externalizing itself* and opening itself to the light and to the sensuous human."[83]

We now want to summarize briefly the determinations brought together in the concept of man as a universal and free being. Man "relates" [*verhält sich*][84] to himself and what exists, he can sublate what is given and preestablished, appropriate it and thus give it his own reality and realize himself in everything. This freedom does not contradict the distress and neediness of man, of which we spoke at the beginning, but is based on it insofar as it is freedom only as the sublation of what is given and pre-established. Man's "life-activity" is "not a determinacy with which he directly merges"[85] like an animal; it is "free activity," since man can "distinguish" himself from the immediate determinacy of his existence, "make it into an object," and sublate it. He can turn his existence into a "means," can himself give himself reality and himself "produce" himself and his "objectivity." It is in this deeper sense (and not only biologically) that we must understand the sentences that "man produces man" and that human life is genuinely "productive" and "life-engendering life."[86]

Thereby Marx's determination [*Bestimmung*][87] returns to its starting point: the basic concept of "labor." It is now clear to what extent it was right to deal with labor as an ontological category. As far as man, through the creation, treatment, and appropriation of the objective world, gives himself his own reality, and as far as his "relationship to the object" is the "manifestation of human reality,"[88] labor is the real expression of human freedom. Man becomes free in his labor. He freely realizes himself in the object of his labor: "When, for man in society, the objective world everywhere becomes the world of man's essential powers—human reality, and for that reason the reality of his *own* essential powers— . . . all objects become for him the objectification of himself, become objects which confirm and realize his individuality, become *his* objects; that is, *man himself* becomes the object.[89]

4

In the preceding sections we have attempted to present in its context the determination of man underlying the *Economic and Philosophical Manuscripts* and to reveal it as the basis of the critique of political economy. It almost appears, despite all protestations to the contrary, as if we are moving in the field of philosophical investigations, forgetting that these *Manuscripts* are concerned with the foundation of a theory of revolution and ultimately with revolutionary *praxis*. But we only need to put the result of our interpretation next to its starting point to find that we have reached the point where the philosophical critique in itself directly becomes a practical revolutionary critique.

The fact from which the critique and the interpretation set out was the alienation and estrangement of the human essence as expressed in the alienation and estrangement of labor, and hence the situation of man in the historical facticity of capitalism. This fact appears as the total inversion and concealment of what the critique had defined as the essence of man and human labor. Labor is not "free activity" or the universal and free self-realization of man, but his enslavement and loss of reality. The worker is not man in the totality of his life-expression, but something unessential [*ein Unwesen*], the purely physical subject of "abstract" activity. The objects of labor are not expressions and confirmations of the human reality of the worker, but alien things, belonging to someone other than the worker—"commodities." As a result of all this the existence of man does not become, in estranged labor, the "means" for his self-realization. The reverse happens: man's self becomes a means for his mere existence. The pure physical existence of the worker is the goal that his entire life-activity serves. "As a result, therefore, man (the worker) only feels himself freely active in his animal functions—eating, drinking, procreating, or at most in his dwelling and in dressing-up, etc., and in his human functions he no longer feels himself to be anything but an animal. What is animal becomes human and what is human becomes animal."[90]

We have seen that Marx describes this estrangement and loss of reality as the "expression" [*Ausdruck*] of a total inversion, in his relationship to the product of his labor as an "alien object exercising power over him" and simultaneously in the relationship of the worker to his own activity as "an alien activity not belonging to him,"[91] of the conduct of man as man. This reification is by no means limited to the worker (even though it affects him in a unique way); it also affects the nonworker—the capitalist. The "dominion of dead matter over man" reveals itself for the capitalist in the state of private property and the manner in which he has and possesses it. It is really a state of being possessed, of being had, slavery in the service of possessions [*Besitz*]. He possesses his property [*Eigentum*] not as a field of free self-realization and activity but purely as capital: "Private property has made us so stupid and one-sided that an object is only *ours* when we have it—when it exists for us as capital, or when it is directly possessed, eaten, drunk, worn, inhabited, etc.,—in short, when it is *used* by us. . . . The life which they (this type of possessions) serve as means is the life of private property, labor, and conversion into capital."[92] (We shall return presently to the determination of "true property" that underlies this description of "false having.")

If historical facticity thus reveals the total inversion of all the conditions given in the determination of the human essence, does it not prove that this determination lacks content and sense, and that it is only an idealistic abstraction, which does violence to historical reality? We know the cruel derision with which, in his *German Ideology*, which appeared only a year after these *Manuscripts*, Marx destroyed the idle talk of the Hegelians, such people as Stirner and the "true socialist," about *the* essence, *man*, etc. Did Marx himself, in his determination of human essence, give in to this idle chatter? Or does a radical change take place in Marx's fundamental views between the *Manuscripts* and the *German Ideology*?

There is indeed a change, even if it is not in his fundamental views. It must be emphasized again and again that in laying the foundations of revolutionary theory Marx is fighting *on various fronts*: on the one hand, against the pseudoidealism of the Hegelian school, on the other against reification in bourgeois political economy, and then again against Feuerbach and pseudomaterialism. The meaning and the purpose of his fight thus varies according to the direction of his attack and defense. Here, where he is principally fighting reification in political economy, which turns a particular kind of historical facticity into rigid "eternal" laws and so-called essential relationships, Marx presents this facticity in contrast to the real essence of man. But in doing this he brings out the truth of this facticity, grasps it within the context of the real history of man and reveals the necessity of its being overcome.

These changes, then, result from shifts in the terrain of the conflict. But the following point is still more decisive. To play essence (as the determinants of "man") and facticity (his given concrete historical situation) off against each other is to miss completely the new standpoint that Marx had already assumed at the outset of his investigations. For Marx essence and facticity, the situation of essential history and the situation of factual history, are no longer separate regions or levels independent of each other; the historicity[93] of man is *taken up into the determination of his essence*. We are no longer dealing with an abstract human essence, which remains equally valid at every stage of concrete history, but with an essence that can be defined in *history* and *only* in history. (It is therefore quite a different matter when Marx speaks of the "essence of man," as opposed to Bruno Bauer, Stirner, and Feuerbach!).[94] The fact that despite or precisely because of this it is always man himself that matters in all man's historical praxis is so self-evident that it is not worth discussing for Marx, who grew up in a direct relationship with the most lively period of German philosophy (just the opposite seems to have become self-evident for the epigones of Marxism). Even in Marx's extremely bitter struggle with German philosophy in the period of its decline, a philosophical impetus lives on that only complete naiveté could misconstrue as a desire to destroy philosophy altogether.

The discovery of the historicity of the human essence does not mean that the history of man's essence can be identified with his factual history. We have already heard that man is never directly "one with his life-activity;" he is, rather, "distinct" from it and "relates" to it. Essence and existence *separate* in him; his existence is a "means" to the realization of his essence, or—in estrangement— his essence is a means to his mere physical existence.[95] If essence and existence have thus become separated and if the real and free *task* of human praxis is the unification of both as factual realization, then the authentic task, when facticity has progressed so far as totally to *invert* the human essence, is the *radical sublation* of this facticity. It is precisely the persistent focus on the essence of man that becomes the inexorable impulse for the initiation of radical revolution. The factual situation of capitalism is characterized not merely by economic or political crisis but by a catastrophe of the human essence; this insight condemns any mere economic or political *reform* to failure from the outset and unconditionally requires the cataclysmic sublation of the actual situation through *total revolution*. Only after the basis has been established in this way, so firmly that it cannot be shaken by any merely economic or political arguments, does the question of the *historical conditions and the bearers* of the revolution arise: the question of the theory of class struggle and the dictatorship of the proletariat. Any critique that only pays attention to this theory, without coming to grips with its real foundation, misses the point.

We shall now look at the *Manuscripts* to see what they contribute to the preparation of a positive theory of revolution and how they treat the real sublation of reification, alienated labor, and private property. We shall once again limit ourselves to the basic state of affairs expressed in the economic and political facts. What also belongs to this positive theory of revolution is—as we shall show—an investigation of the origin of reification: an investigation of the historical conditions and emergence of private property. Two main questions must therefore be answered. How does Marx describe the accomplished sublation of private property, that is, the state of the human essence after the total revolution? How does Marx handle the problem of the origin of private property or the emergence and development of reification? Marx himself explicitly asked both these questions; the answer is given mainly on pages 90–91 [115–17] and 114–21 [135–42].

The total estrangement of man and his loss of reality was traced back to the alienation of labor. In the analysis, *private property* was revealed as the manner in which alienated labor "must express and present itself in real life"[96] and as the "realization of alienation"[97] (we shall return to the close connection between alienated labor and private property below). The sublation of alienation, if it is to be a genuine sublation (and not merely "abstract" or theoretical) must sublate the real form of alienation (its "realization"); and so "the entire revolutionary movement necessarily finds both its empirical and its theoretical basis in the movement of private property—more precisely, in that of the economy."[98]

Through this connection with alienated labor, private property is already *more* than a specific economic category. This extra element in the concept of private property is sharply emphasized by Marx: "Material, immediately sensuous private property is the material, sensuous expression of *estranged human* life. Its movement—production and consumption—is the sensuous revelation of the movement of all production until now, i.e. the realization of the reality of man."[99] Through the explanatory "i.e. the realization . . . of man" that he adds, Marx expressly emphasizes the fact that "production," of which the movement of private property is the "revelation," is not economic production but the self-producing historical occurrence of the whole of human life (as interpreted above). The extent to which private property expresses the movement of estranged human life is more closely described in the following passage: "Just as private property is only the sensuous expression of the fact that man becomes objective for himself and at the same time becomes to himself a foreign and inhuman object; just as it expresses the fact that the expression of his life is the alienation of his life, that his realization in his loss of reality . . . , so the positive sublation of private property" is more than economic sublation; it is the the positive "appropriation" of the whole of human reality.[100] Private property is the real expression of the way in which estranged man objectifies himself, "produces" himself and his objective world, and realizes himself in it. Private property therefore constitutes the realization of an entire form of human *conduct* and not just a given physical "*state*" external to man[101] or "a *merely objective* being" [*gegenständliches Wesen*].[102]

But if an estranged form of behavior that has lost reality is thus realized in private property, then private property itself can only represent an estranged and unreal form of true and essential human behavior. There must therefore be two real "forms" of property: an estranged and a true form, a property that is merely private and a property that is "truly human."[103] There must be a form of "property" belonging to the essence of man and positive communism that, far from meaning the abolition of all property, will be precisely the *restoration* of this truly human form of property.

How can one "define the general nature of private property, as it has arisen as a result of estranged labor, in its relation to *truly human* and *social property*"?[104] The answer to this question must at the same time make clear the meaning and goal of the positive sublation of private property. "The meaning of private property—apart from its estrangement—is the *existence of essential objects* for man, both as objects of gratification and as objects of activity."[105]

This is the most general positive determination of true property: the availability and usability of all the objects that man needs for the free realization of his essence. This availability and usability is realized as *property*—which is by no means self-evident, but is based on the idea that man never simply and directly has what he needs, but only really possesses objects when he has appropriated them. Thus the purpose of labor is to give to man as his own possessions objects that he has transformed and to make them into a world through which he can freely engage in activity and realize his potentialities. The essence of property consists in "appropriation;" a particular manner of appropriation and realization through appropriation is the basis of property and not merely having and possessing. We must now more closely define this new concept of appropriation and property that underlies Marx's analysis.

We have seen how private property consists in an untrue mode of having and possessing objects. In conditions of private property an object is "property" when it can be "used." This use consists either in immediate consumption or in the capacity of the property to be turned into capital. "Life-activity" stands in the service of property instead of property standing in the service of free life-activity; it is not the "reality" of man that is appropriated but objects as things (goods and commodities) and even this kind of appropriation is "one-sided;" it is limited to the physical conduct of man and to objects that can immediately "gratify" or be turned into capital. In contrast to this, "true human property" is now described in its true appropriation: "the sensuous appropriation for and by man of the human essence and of human life, of objective man, of human achievements—should not be conceived merely in the sense of *possession*, of *having*. Man appropriates his total essence in a total manner, that is to say, as a whole man."[106] This total appropriation is then described more closely: "Each of his human relations to the world—seeing, hearing, smelling, tasting, feeling, thinking, observing experiencing, wanting, acting, loving—in short, all the organs of his individual being . . . are in their objective orientation or in their orientation to the object, the appropriation of that object."[107]

Beyond all economic and legal relations, appropriation as the basis of property thus becomes a category that grasps the universal and free relationship of man to the objective world. The relationship to the object that is becoming one's own is "total"—it "emancipates" *all* the human senses. The *whole* man is at home in the *whole* objective world that is "his work and his reality." The *economic and legal* sublation of private property is not the end, but only the *beginning* of the communist revolution. This universal and free appropriation is *labor*, for as we saw, the specifically human relationship to the object is one of creating, positing, forming. But in this case labor would no longer be an estranged and reified activity, but all-around self-realization and self-expression.

The inhumanity represented by reification is thus abolished at the point where it was most deeply rooted and dangerous: in the concept of property. Man no longer "loses" himself in the objective world, and his objectification is no longer reification, if objects are no longer had and possessed in a "one-sided" way and if they remain the work and reality of the one who "produced" or realized them and himself in them. It is not, however, the isolated individual or an abstract plurality of individuals that has been realized in them, but *social* man, man *as* a social being. Man's return to his true property is a return to his social essence; it is the liberation of society.

5

"Man is not lost in his object only when the object becomes for him a *human* object or objective man. This is possible only when the object becomes for him a *social* object, he himself for himself a social being, just as society becomes a being for him in this object."[108] There are thus two conditions for breaking through reification as outlined above: the objective relations must become human—that is, social—relations and they must be recognized and consciously preserved as such. These two conditions are fundamentally interrelated, for the objective relations can only become human and social if man himself is conscious of them *as such*, that is, in his *knowledge* of both himself and object. Thus we again encounter the central role that a particular kind of insight (man's "coming-to-be-for himself") plays in the foundation of Marx's theory. To what extent can knowledge, the knowledge of objectification as something social, become the real impulse for the abolition of all reification?

We know that objectification is essentially a social activity and that it is precisely in his objects and in his labor on them that man recognizes himself as a social being. The insight into objectification, which breaks through reification, is the insight into society as the subject of objectification. For there is no such thing as "society" as a subject outside the individual. Marx explicitly warns against playing off society as an independent entity against the individual: "Above all we must avoid postulating 'society' again as an abstraction vis-à-vis the individual. The individual *is* the *social* being. His life, even if it may not appear in the direct form of communal life in association with others, *is* therefore an expression and confirmation of social life."[109]

Knowledge of objectification thus means knowledge of how and through what man and his objective world as *social relations* have become what they are. It means insight into the historical-social situation of man. This knowledge is no mere theoretical knowing or arbitrary, passive perceiving, but "*praxis*:" the sublation of what exists, making it a "means" for free self-realization.

This also means that the knowledge that defines this task is by no means available to everyone. It can only be known by those who are actually *entrusted with this task* by their historical-social situation (we cannot pursue the way in which the proletariat becomes the bearer of this insight in the situation analyzed by Marx; its content is presented at the close of Marx's *Introduction to the Critique of Hegel's Philosophy of Right*). It is not a matter of "the" task for "man," but of a particular historical task in a particular historical situation. It is therefore necessary that "the sublation of estrangement always proceeds from that form of estrangement which is the dominant power."[110] Because it is dependent on the conditions preestablished by history, the praxis of sublation must, in order to be genuine sublation, reveal these conditions and appropriate them. Knowledge of objectification as knowledge of the historical and social situation of man reveals the historical conditions of this situation and so achieves the *practical force and concrete form* through which it can become the lever of the revolution. We can now also understand how far questions concerning the *origin* of estrangement and insight into the *origin* of private property must be an integrating element in a positive theory of revolution.

Marx's handling of the question of the origins of private property shows the pathbreaking new "method" of his theory. Marx is fundamentally convinced that when man is conscious of his history he cannot fall into a situation that he has not himself created and that only he himself can liberate himself from any situation. This basic conviction already finds its expression in the concept of freedom in the *Manuscripts*. The phrase that the liberation of the working class can only be the work of the working class itself resonates clearly through all the economic explanations; it only enters into "contradiction" with historical materialism if the latter is falsified and turned into a vulgar materialism. If the relations of production have become a "fetter" and an alien force determining man, then this is only because man himself has at some stage alienated himself from his power over the relations of production. This is also true if one sees the relations of production as being determined primarily by the given "natural" forces of production (e.g., climatic or geographical conditions, the condition of the land, the distribution of raw materials) and ignores the fact that all these physical data have always existed in a form historically handed down and have formed a part of particular human and social "forms of intercourse." For the situation of man that exists through such preexisting forces of production only becomes a historical and social situation through the fact that man "reacts" to what he finds preexisting, that is, through the manner in which he appropriates it. In truth these relations of production that have been reified into alien, dominating forces are always objectifications of particular social relations, and the abolition of the estrangement expressed in these relations of production can only be total and real if it can account for economic revolution in terms of these human relations. Thus the question of the origin of private property becomes a question of the activity through which man *alienated* property *from himself*: "How, we now ask, does *man* come to *alienate*, to estrange his *labor*? How is this estrangement rooted in the nature of human development?" Being aware of the crucial importance of this new way of formulating the question, Marx adds: "We have already gone a long way toward the solution of this problem by *transforming* the question of the *origin of private property* into the question of the relation of *alienated labor* to the course of humanity's development. For when one speaks of private property, one thinks of dealing with something external to man. When one speaks of labor, one is directly dealing with man himself. This new formulation of the question already contains its solution."[111]

The answer to this question is not contained in the *Economic and Philosophical Manuscripts*; it is worked out in his later critiques of political economy. The *Economic and Philosophical Manuscripts* do, however, contain a proof within the determination of man's essence that objectification always carries within it a tendency toward reification and labor a tendency toward alienation, so that reification and alienation are not merely chance historical facts. In connection with this it is also shown how the worker through his alienation even "engenders" the nonworker and thus the domination of private property[112] and how he therefore has his fate in his own hands at the origin of estrangement and not just after liberation.

Marx gives his determination of estrangement as self-estrangement in a reference to the real achievement of Hegel's *Phenomenology*: "The real, active orientation of man to himself as a species being . . . is only possible through the *utilization* of all the powers he has in himself and which he has as belonging to a species. . . . [He] treat[s] . . . these generic powers as objects and this, to begin with, is again *only possible in the form of estrangement*.[113]

We fail to find an explanation here as to *why* this is, to begin with, only possible in the form of estrangement; it is, strictly speaking, impossible to give one, for we are confronted with a state of affairs that has its roots in man—as an "objective" being—and that can only be revealed as such. It is man's "neediness"—as already interpreted above—for objects alien to him, "overpowering" and "not part of his being," to which he must relate *as* to external objects, although they only become real objects through and for him. Objects first confront him *directly* in an external and alien form and only become *human* objects, objectifications of man, through conscious historical and social appropriation. The externalization of man thus first tends toward alienation and his objectification toward reification, so that he can only attain a universal and free reality through "the negation of negation:" through the *sublation* of his alienation and the *return* out of his estrangement.

After the possibility of alienated labor has been shown to have its roots in the essence of man, the limits of philosophical description have been reached and the discovery of the real origin of alienation becomes a matter of economic and historical analysis. We know that for Marx the starting point for this analysis is the *division of labor* (see, for example, p. 139 [159]); we cannot go into this further here and shall only look quickly at the way Marx shows that already with the alienation of labor the worker "engenders" the domination of the capitalist and thereby of private property. At the head of this analysis there stands the sentence: "Every self-estrangement of man, from himself and from nature, appears in the relation in which he places himself and nature to *men other than* and differentiated from himself."[114] We are already acquainted with the context of this sentence: the relation of man to the object on which he works is directly his relation to other men with whom he shares this object and himself as something social. Thus, if the worker in the self-alienation of his labor possesses the object as something alien, overpowering, and not belonging to him, this object nowhere confronts him as an isolated thing, belonging to no one and, as it were, outside humanity. The situation is rather this: "If the product of labor does not belong to the worker, if it confronts him as an alien power, then this can only be because it belongs to some *other man than the worker*."[115] With the alienation of labor the worker immediately stands as a "servant" in the service of a "master." "Thus, if the product of his labor . . . is for him an alien . . . object . . . then his position towards it is such that someone else is master of this object, someone who is alien. . . . If he is related to his own activity as to an unfree activity, then he is related to it as an activity performed in the service, under the dominion, the coercion, and the yoke of another man."[116]

It is not a case of a "master" existing first, subordinating someone else to himself, alienating him from his labor, and making him into a mere worker and himself into a nonworker. Nor is it a case of the relationship between domination and servitude being the simple consequence of the alienation of labor. The alienation of labor, as estrangement from his own activity and from its object, already *is* in itself the relationship between worker and nonworker and between domination and servitude.

These distinctions seem to be of only secondary importance, and they do in fact disappear into the background again in the later, purely economic analysis. Nevertheless they must be expressly emphasized in the context of the *Manuscripts*, if only because they are relevant to Marx's crucial reaction to Hegel. Domination and servitude are here not concepts for particular (pre- or early capitalist) formations, relations of production, etc. They give a general description of the social condition of man in a situation of estranged labor. In this sense they point back to the ontological categories of "domination and servitude" developed by Hegel in his *Phenomenology*.[117] We cannot discuss here Marx's further description of the relation between domination and servitude, but we shall select one important point: "everything which appears in the worker as an *activity* of alienation, of estrangement, appears in the non-worker as a *state* of alienation, of estrangement."[118]

We know that the sublation of estrangement (a state in which both master *and* servant find themselves, although not in the same way) can only be based on the destruction of reification, that is, on the practical insight into the activity of objectification in its historical and social situation. Since it is only in *labor* and in the objects *of his labor* that man can really come to understand himself, others, and the objective world in their historical and social situation, the master, as a *non*worker, cannot come to this insight. Since what is actually a specific human activity appears to him as a material and objective state of affairs, the worker has an (as it were) irreducible advantage over him. He is the real factor of transformation; the destruction of reification can only be *his* work. The master can only come to this revolutionary insight if he becomes a worker, which, however, would mean sublating his own essence.

From every point of approach and in all directions, this theory, arising out of the philosophical critique and foundation of political economy, proves itself to be a *practical theory*, a theory whose immanent meaning (required by the nature of its object) is particular praxis; only particular praxis can solve the problems peculiar to this theory. "We see how the resolution of the *theoretical* antitheses is *only* possible in a *practical* way, by virtue of the practical energy of man. Their resolution is therefore by no means merely a problem of understanding, but a *real* problem of life, which *philosophy* could not solve precisely because it conceived this problem as *merely* a theoretical one."[119] We could add to this sentence: but philosophy can solve this problem, if it grasps it as a *practical* problem, that is, if it transcends itself as "only theoretical" philosophy, which in turns means, if it really "realizes" itself as philosophy for the first time.

Marx calls the practical theory that solves this problem, insofar as it puts man as a historical and social being in the center, "real humanism" and identifies it with "naturalism" to the extent that it, if carried through, grasps the unity of man and nature: the "naturalness of man" and the "humanity of nature." If the real humanism outlined here by Marx as the basis of his theory does not correspond to what is commonly understood as Marx's "materialism," such a contradiction is entirely in accordance with Marx's intentions: "here we see how consistent naturalism and humanism distinguishes itself both from idealism and materialism, constituting at the same time the unifying truth of both."[120]

6

Finally we need to examine briefly Marx's critique of Hegel, which was envisaged as the conclusion of the whole *Manuscripts*. We can make the discussion brief because we have already gone into Marx's elaboration of the positive foundations of a critique of Hegel (the determination of man as an "objective," historical and social, practical being) in the context of our interpretation of the critique of political economy.

Marx begins by pointing out the necessity of discussing a question that has still not been adequately answered: "How do we now stand as regards the Hegelian dialectic?"[121] This question, coming at the conclusion of his positive critique of political economy and the foundation of revolutionary theory, shows how much Marx was aware that he was working in an area opened up by Hegel and how he experienced this fact—in contrast to almost all the Hegelians and almost all his later followers—as a scientific-philosophical obligation toward Hegel. After briefly dispatching Bruno Bauer, Strauss, etc., whose "critical critique" makes the need to come to terms with Hegel anything but superfluous, Marx immediately gives his support to Feuerbach: "the only one who has a serious, critical attitude to the Hegelian dialectic and who has made genuine discoveries in this field."[122] Marx mentions three such "discoveries." Feuerbach 1) recognized philosophy (i.e., the purely speculative philosophy of Hegel) as a "form and manner of existence of the estrangement of the essence of man," 2) he established "true materialism" by making "the social relationship 'of man to man' the basic principle of his theory," and 3) precisely through this principle opposed Hegel's mere "negation of negation," which does not go beyond negativity, with a "self-supporting positive, positively based on itself."[123] With this enumeration, Marx simultaneously articulated the three main directions of his own critique of Hegel, and it is to these that we now turn.

"One must begin with Hegel's *Phenomenology*, the true point of origin and the secret of the Hegelian philosophy."[124] From the beginning Marx tackles Hegel's philosophy where its origin is still visible in an unconcealed form: in the *Phenomenology*. If at the beginning of the critique it may still have looked as if it was really only a critique of what one is accustomed to regarding as Hegel's "dialectic," we now see that what Marx criticizes as the dialectic is the foundation and actual "content" of Hegel's philosophy—not its (supposed) "method." And while Marx criticizes, he simultaneously extracts the positive aspects, the great discoveries made by Hegel—that is, only because for Marx there are genuinely positive discoveries in Hegel, on the basis of which he can and must do further work, on the basis of which Hegel's philosophy can and must become for him the subject of a critique. We shall begin with the negative part of his critique—Marx's collation of Hegel's "mistakes"—so that we can then extract the positive aspects from these negative ones and show that the mistakes are really only mistaken interpretations of genuine and true states of affairs.

In the *Phenomenology* Hegel gives "speculative expression" to the movement of the history of the "human essence," but not of its real history, only its "genetic history."[125] That is, he gives the history of the human essence, in which man first becomes what he is and that has, as it were, always already taken place when the real history of man occurs. Even with this general characterization, Marx has grasped the meaning of the *Phenomenology* more profoundly and accurately than most interpreters of Hegel. He then proceeds to a critique of the core of Hegel's own problematic. Hegel's philosophical description of the history of the human essence fails at the start, because Hegel grasps it from the outset only as abstract "self-consciousness" ("thought," "mind") and thus overlooks its true concrete fullness: "Hegel equates the essence of man, man himself, with self-consciousness"[126]; the history of the human essence runs its course purely as the history of self-consciousness or even as history within self-consciousness. What Marx had shown to be crucial for the determination of man's essence and what he had put at the center of his conceptual structure— the "objectivity" of man, his "essential objectification"—is, fatefully, precisely what is given a different meaning and inverted by Hegel. The object (i.e., objectivity as such) is in Hegel only an object *for consciousness* in the emphatic sense that consciousness is the "truth" of the object and that the latter is only the negative side of consciousness. Having been "posited" (created, engendered) by consciousness as its alienation and estrangement, it must also be "sublated" by consciousness again, or "taken back" into consciousness. The object is thus, by the nature of its existence, a purely negative thing, a "nullity"[127]; it is merely an object of abstract thought, for Hegel reduces self-consciousness to abstract thought. "The main point is that the object of consciousness is nothing else but self-consciousness, or that the object is only objectified self-consciousness— self-consciousness as an object. . . . The issue, therefore, is to surmount the object of consciousness. Objectivity as such is regarded as an estranged human relationship which does not correspond to the essence of man."[128] For Marx, however, objectivity was precisely the human relationship in which alone man could come to self-realization and self-activity; it was "real" objectivity, the "work" of human labor, and certainly not the object of abstract consciousness. From this standpoint Marx can say that Hegel fixes man as "a non-objective, spiritual being."[129] This being never exists with genuine objects but always only with the self-posited negativity of itself. It is actually always "at home with itself" in its "otherness as such."[130] It is thus ultimately "non-objective," and "a non-objective being is a . . . *nonbeing.*"[131]

This also constitutes a critique of the *Phenomenology* insofar as it claims to present the movement of the history of man's essential being. If this being whose history is taking place is a "nonbeing," then this history must also be "inessential" in the full sense of the word. Marx perceives Hegel's discovery of the movement of human history in the movement of "self-objectification as self-alienation and self-estrangement"[132] and in the "sublation" of this estrangement as it recurs in many forms throughout the *Phenomenology*. But the objectification is only apparent, "abstract and formal," since the object only has "the semblance of an object" and the self-objectifying consciousness remains "at home with itself" in this seeming alienation.[133] Like estrangement itself, its sublation is only a semblance; alienation remains. The forms of estranged human existence that Hegel cites are not forms of estranged real life but only of consciousness and knowledge [*Wissen*]. What Hegel deals with and sublates are not "real religion, the real state, or real nature, but religion as a subject of knowledge, that is, dogmatics; the same holds true for jurisprudence, political science and natural science."[134] Because alienation is thus only sublated in the mind and not in reality, that is, because "this sublation of thought leaves its object standing in reality," Marx can say that the whole *Phenomenology*—and indeed the whole of Hegel's system, insofar as it is based on the *Phenomenology*—remains within estrangement. This comes out in Hegel's system as a whole in the fact, for example, that "nature" is not grasped as the "self-expression of man's senses," in its ontological unity with man or its "humanity," but is taken as externality "in the sense of alienation, of a mistake, a defect, which ought not to be"—a "nothing."[135]

We shall not go into the other features of the negative critique here. They are already familiar from the *Critique of Hegel's Philosophy of Right*; for example, the conversion of mind into an absolute, the hypostatization of an absolute subject as the bearer of the historical process, the inversion of subject and predicate,[136] etc. What must be borne in mind is that Marx regards all these "inadequacies" as "inadequacies" of a real state of affairs. If Hegel posits the human essence as a "nonbeing," then it is the nonbeing of a real being and thus a real nonbeing; if he has "only found the abstract, logical, speculative expression for the movement of history,"[137] then this is still an expression for the movement of real history; if he has described objectification and estrangement in their abstract forms, then he has still seen objectification and estrangement as essential movements of human history. The emphasis of Marx's critique of Hegel is definitely on the *positive* part, to which we now proceed.

"The outstanding achievement of Hegel's *Phenomenology* and of its final outcome, the dialectic of negativity as the moving and generating principle, is thus first that Hegel conceives the self-creation of man as a process, conceives objectification as loss of the object, as alienation and as sublation of this alienation; that he grasps the essence of *labor* and comprehends objective man . . . as the outcome of man's own labor."[138] The full significance of the interpretation of the *Phenomenology* given here by Marx could only be grasped if we unfolded the central problematic of Hegel's work, which we obviously cannot do here. It would also only then become apparent with what unheard-of sureness Marx sees through all the mystifying and misleading interpretations (which begin even within Hegel's work) and gets back to the bedrock of the problems that were raised, for the first time in modern philosophy, in the *Phenomenology*.

In the sentence quoted above Marx has brought together all the discoveries of Hegel that he recognizes as crucial. In what follows we want briefly to explain these, for Marx, "positive moments of the Hegelian dialectic."

The *Phenomenology* presents the "self-creation of man," which means, after what has already been said, the process in which man (as an organic, living being) becomes what he is according to his essence—that is, human essence. It thus gives the "genetic history"[139] of the human essence or man's essential history. Man's "act of creation" is an "act of self-genesis,"[140] that is, man gives his essence to himself. He must first make himself what he is, "posit" himself and "produce" himself (we have already gone into the meaning of this concept). This history that is given into man's own hands is grasped by Hegel as a "process" characterized by alienation and its sublation. The process as a whole stands under the title of "objectification." The history of man thus occurs and fulfills itself as objectification. The reality of man consists of creating real objects out of all his "species powers," or "establishing a real, objective world."[141] It is this establishing of an objective world that Hegel treats merely as the alienation of "consciousness" or knowledge [*Wissen*], or as the relation of abstract thought to "thinghood," while Marx grasps it as the "practical" realization of the whole of man in historical and social labor.[142]

Hegel defines the relation of knowledge [*Wissen*] to the objective world in such a way that this objectification is simultaneously the loss of the object, that is, the loss of reality or estrangement, so that, "to begin with, [objectification] is again only possible in the form of estrangement."[143] In other words, knowledge [*Wissen*], in the process of becoming objective, initially *loses* itself in its objects. They confront it as something alien and other, in the form of an external world of things and matters that have lost their inner connection to the consciousness that has expressed itself in them and now continue as a power independent of consciousness. In the *Phenomenology*, for example, morality and right, the power of the state and wealth, appear as estranged objective worlds only as "worlds of thought" and not as real worlds,[144] since for Hegel they are externalizations [*Entäusserungen*] of "mind" only and not of real, total human existence.

Although objectification consists initially in the loss of the object or estrangement, it is precisely this estrangement that in Hegel becomes the recovery of true being. "Hegel conceives man's self-estrangement, the alienation of man's essence, man's loss of objectivity and reality as self-discovery, change of his nature, objectification and realization."[145] The human essence—always conceived in Hegel as exclusively knowledge [*Wissen*]—is such that to be able to discover itself it must not only express but alienate itself, not only objectify itself but lose its object. Only if it has really lost itself can it come to itself, only in its "otherness" can it become what it is "for itself." This is the "positive meaning" of negation, "the dialectic of negativity as the moving and generating principle."[146] We should have to go into the foundations of Hegel's ontology to justify and clarify this assertion; here we need only show how Marx interprets this discovery by Hegel.

Through the positive concept of negation just referred to, Hegel conceives "labor as man's act of self-genesis"[147]; "he grasps labor as the essence of man—as man's essence in the act of proving itself."[148] With reference to this Marx goes so far as to say: "Hegel's standpoint is that of modern political economy"[149]— a seemingly paradoxical statement in which, however, Marx summarizes the colossal, almost revolutionary concreteness of Hegel's *Phenomenology*. If labor is here defined as man's essence in the act of proving itself this obviously refers to labor not purely as an economic, but as an "ontological" category, as Marx defines it in this very passage: "Labor is man's coming-to-be for himself within alienation, or as alienated man."[150] How does it come about that Marx should take precisely the category of labor to interpret Hegel's concept of objectification as self-discovery in estrangement and of realization in alienation?

It is not only because Hegel uses labor to reveal the objectification of the human essence and its estrangement, or because he depicts the relation of the laboring "servant" to his world as the first "sublation" of estranged objectivity.[151] It is not only because of this; although the fact that this is viewed as the real beginning of human history in the *Phenomenology* is neither a coincidence nor the result of a purely arbitrary decision, but expresses the innermost direction of the entire work. Marx has thereby—albeit in an exaggerated form—discovered the original meaning of the history of the human essence as it is elaborated in the *Phenomenology* in the form of the history of self-consciousness. It is praxis, free self-realization, always appropriating, sublating, and revolutionizing preestablished "immediate" facticity. It has already been pointed out that Marx holds Hegel's real mistake to be the substitution of "mind" for the subject of praxis. Hence for Marx, "the only labor which Hegel knows and recognizes is abstract mental labor."[152] But this does not alter the fact that Hegel grasped labor as man's essence in the act of proving itself—a fact that retains its vital importance. Despite the "spiritualization" [*Vergeistigung*] of history in the *Phenomenology*, the actual leading concept through which the history of man is explicated is tranforming "doing" [*Tun*].[153]

If the inner meaning of objectification and its sublation is thus praxis, then the various forms of estrangement and their sublation must also be more than mere "examples" taken out of real history and put alongside each other with no necessary connection. They must have their roots in human praxis and be an integral part of man's history. Marx expresses this insight in the sentence that Hegel has found "speculative expression for the movement of history"[154]—a sentence that (as already stated) must be understood positively just as much as negatively and critically. And if the forms of estrangement are rooted as historical forms in human praxis itself, they cannot be regarded simply as abstract theoretical forms of the objectivity of consciousness; under this logical-speculative "disguise" they must have ineluctable practical consequences, they must of necessity be effectively sublated and "revolutionized." A critique must lie hidden already in the *Phenomenology*: "critique" in the revolutionary sense that Marx gave this concept. "The *Phenomenology* is, therefore, an occult critique—still to itself obscure and mystifying: but inasmuch as it keeps steadily in view man's estrangement . . . there lie concealed in it all the elements of the critique already *prepared and elaborated* in a manner often rising far above the Hegelian standpoint."[155] In its separate sections it contains "the critical elements of whole spheres such as religion, the state, civil life, etc.—but still in an estranged form" (ibid.).

Thereby Marx has expressed in all clarity the inner connection between revolutionary theory and Hegel's philosophy. What seems amazing, as measured by this critique—which is the result of a *philosophical* debate—is the decline of later interpretations of Marx (even—*sit venia verbo*—that of Engels!) by people who believed they could reduce Marx's relationship to Hegel to the familiar transformation of Hegel's "dialectic," which they also completely emptied of content.

These suggestions will have to suffice; above all we cannot go into the question if and how the "mistakes" with which Marx charges Hegel can really be attributed to him. It has perhaps become clear through this paper that the discussion really starts at the center of Hegel's problematic. Marx's critique of Hegel is not an appendage of the preceding critique and foundation of political economy, for his examination of political economy is itself a continuous confrontation with Hegel.

On the Philosophical Foundations
of the Concept of Labor in Economics

It has seemed superfluous to attempt a fundamental determination of the concept of labor ever since the tacit agreement was made in economic theory to avoid a "definitional" determination of labor as such and to conceive of labor only as economic activity, as praxis within the economic dimension.[1] "The general concept 'labor' has received such an indeterminate content through its ordinary use that it is hardly possible to demarcate it as an unequivocal concept. It is precisely this situation that gives the representatives of economics the right to utilize a specific economic concept of 'labor' that is not derived from a general concept of 'labor' but, rather, through another procedure."[2] A concept of labor so limited does not appear to prejudice decisions concerning the place, meaning, and function of labor in the totality of human Dasein; the economically relevant differentiations of labor (for example, the distinctions between supervisory and supervised, free and unfree labor, and the types of labor in various branches of production) can all be subsumed under this economic concept of labor. Thus, the elaboration of a "general" concept of labor does seem to be required by economic theory itself.

Yet, this economic concept of labor (which is "definitional" and not derived from or guaranteed by a "general" concept of labor) immediately turns up in the *center* of economic theory: "The concept of labor has entered political economy [*Nationalökonomie*] in three basic groups of problems: in the theory of value and prices, the theory of factors of production, and the theory of costs."[3] Furthermore, in all three groups of problems, labor is a *fundamental* concept and the actual basis of the whole problematic: the theory of the factors of production as well as the theories of value, price, and costs all culminate in labor as an "ultimate," or at least one of the "ultimate" factors. At this point, the lack of a definitional determination of a general concept of labor becomes obvious.

The problem is further complicated by the fact that the economic concept of labor has also had a decisive influence on the interpretation of the essence of labor in general—including labor outside the economic sphere. It has shaped the understanding of the essence and meaning of labor as such in a very definite way, so that labor in the primary, authentic sense means *economic* activity, while the activity of politicians, artists, researchers, and priests, for example, is characterized as labor only in a metaphorical and somewhat uncertain sense and is, in any case, seen in fundamental opposition to economic activity. But the narrowing of the concept of labor has gone even further, and this within economic theory itself. Here the concept of labor is increasingly limited in its application to supervised, unfree activity (whose conceptual model is the labor of the wage laborer)—even when the economic concept of labor is defined explicitly in the context of the basic concepts of the discipline. For example, Max Weber wants to deal with labor only as "oriented to the instructions of a managerial agency" (and not "managerial" [*disponierende*] activity).[4] Gottl formulates his concept of labor from the outset as the counterconcept to any "formative enterprise" (e.g., the entrepeneur's), as "an activity that simply fills time, which anyone is capable of doing" whose "results are measurable in terms of time,"[5] and as the "everyday form" of human action whose quintessential type is "occupational" action.[6]

Hence, the economic concept of labor, which seemed so unambiguous at first, has been fragmented. But this fragmentation and the various concepts of labor (i.e., labor as a factor of production in general, labor as a basic concept of the theory of value and cost, labor as supervised, direction-oriented activity, etc.) that have resulted from it have not been understood in terms of the context in which they arose, nor have they been derived from the concept of labor on which they are based. Is it justified to claim that economic activity is labor in the proper sense? How is economic activity related to other activities in the totality of human Dasein? Why is it that within the various economic activities precisely supervised, direction-oriented activity is seen as labor in the proper sense? It could be that economic theory's limiting of itself to economic labor already presupposes a very specific concept of labor expressing a very specific *mode* of practicing economics that contains a very specific conception of the essence and meaning of economic being in the totality of human Dasein and that, therefore, the apparent obviousness of the economic concept of labor is already highly prejudiced by certain presuppositions. In our opinion, all these questions can only be clarified by a fundamental philosophical discussion of the concept of labor—a discussion that seeks to outline reliably the place and significance of labor within human Dasein. It is precisely the "indeterminate content" that the general concept of labor has acquired that makes it our duty to concern ourselves with this concept again. Perhaps this discussion (which we will only attempt to introduce here) will also shed some light on the immanent [*sachlich*] relations between philosophy and political economy—relations whose significance Marx was the last to recognize and that have since been lost from view.

Recently it has become widely recognized again that it is necessary to reexamine the immanent connection between philosophy and political economy. Over thirty years ago, Max Scheler programmatically demanded a philosophical discussion of basic economic concepts as a means of reaching this goal, and he himself began with a philosophical discussion of the concept of labor.[7] In a completely different context and from a completely different perspective Max Weber reduced the economic systems of various periods to the "ethic" on which they were based. In this way he brought economic theory into the theological-philosophical sphere, precisely by using the concept of labor as his guiding thread.

The modern *science of labor* seeks to do justice to the problem of labor in its full complexity. However, it undertakes this task on a natural scientific-biological basis (whenever it goes beyond the economic-technical dimension). The science of labor views the problem, insofar as it transcends the economic-technical dimension, essentially as a psychological problem. But psychology (especially if founded on the biological-natural sciences) cannot adequately deal with the problem of labor since (as the following investigation hopes to make clear) labor is an ontological concept, that is, a concept that grasps the being of human Dasein itself and as such. The basic characteristics of labor are obscured from the outset if labor is treated as a psychological phenomenon (we shall come back to this in regard to the burdensome character of labor). Because he misunderstands, or completely overlooks, the basis of labor in this way, Giese's *Philosophy of Labor* fails to accomplish what the book's title promises. Giese discusses a great number of possible problems and groups of problems "occasioned" by the concept of labor, but their immanent and necessary interrelatedness never becomes clear. The obscurity of his concepts, which are drawn from a wide variety of disparate sciences and doctrines, is apparent already in his basic determination of the concept of labor as "an epochal phenomenon . . . that corresponds to a purposive activity of individuals and community directed toward occupationally determined cultural goals and that arises on the basis of biological and technological energetics, but that follows teleological directives."[8]

Within economic theory itself, the provocative philosophical underpinnings of the concept of labor are addressed for the most part only when "ethical" questions related to labor are raised, usually in connection with the division of labor and its effects on the laborer's entire existence. Most attempts to elaborate the fundamental significance of "labor" for the totality of human Dasein never get beyond the beginning stages (we are speaking here only of contemporary economic theory!); examples will be mentioned in the notes. We will examine Gottl's treatment of the problem of labor later.

Within philosophy, we find in the work of Hegel the last radical reflection on the essence of labor and an elaboration of it that reaches into the concrete spheres of historical Dasein. It was taken up and further developed on the broadest basis by Marx, especially in the writings of 1844–45. It is integrated into the social theory of Lorenz von Stein, whose description of the social order begins with an inquiry into "the essence of labor." In the following investigation of the concept of labor we will take these three inquiries as our point of departure, but first let us briefly describe the concept of labor in economics, for purposes of comparison.

2

In his essay "What is Labor?," Karl Elster has brought together typical definitions (from textbooks, etc.) of the concept of labor as generally used in economic theory.[9] For our purposes, it is sufficient to point to the examples collected there. However diverse the definitions may sound in their details, they all agree that labor is a definite human "activity," to which then is added, in various ways, the goal, object, and success of the activity. Nothing appears more obvious and unburdened by theoretical presuppositions than the statement that labor is a definite human activity. Are not the demarcations of the phenomenon of labor made by directly contrasting labor with inactivity of all sorts and with "pseudo" activity such as play, distraction, and so on? But if we contrast these definitions with the philosophically founded concepts of labor that have been formulated in the history of the problem most recently, the doubtfulness of the concept of labor in economics becomes clear at once. Nowhere in the philosophical discussion is there any discussion of labor as a specific activity. Hegel conceived of labor as doing [*Tun*] (not activity [*Tätigkeit*];[10] we will discuss this essential distinction shortly), in which "the pure being-for-itself of consciousness . . . steps outside of itself into the element of permanence" and "comes to itself" in this element by giving itself to the object of labor as a "substance."[11] Lorenz von Stein says: "Labor is . . . in every way the ac-tualization of one's infinite determinations through the self-positing of the individual personality," in which the personality "makes the content of the external world its own and in this way forces it to become a part of its own internal world."[12] In the context of his efforts to establish a new foundation for political economy, Marx adopts the Hegelian concept of labor with all its essential characteristics: "Labor is the becoming-for-itself of man within alienation or as alienated man;"[13] it is the "self-creating or self-objectifying act of man."[14] Of course, in contrast to the concrete analyses of the "labor process" in *Capital*, this is only an "abstract" determination of labor, that is in no way sufficient for economic theory. But it remains the foundation for all concrete concepts of labor in Marx and is explicitly operative in *Capital*: "As the creator of use-values, as useful labor, labor is therefore a condition of human existence independent of all social forms; it is an eternal natural necessity that mediates the material exchange between man and nature, and thus human life."[15] Labor as "mediation," "objectification," transition from the "form of unrest" into the "form of being," and so on—these are philosophical moments of the concept of labor that Hegel elaborated.[16]

We have introduced Hegel's philosophically founded concept of labor only to the extent necessary to outline his starting point. Its essential difference from the concept of labor in economics is this: in Hegel's concept labor appears as a fundamental happening of human Dasein, as a happening that constantly and continually penetrates the entirety of man's *being*, during which something also happens to man's "world."[17] Here labor is precisely *not* a specific human "activity" (for no single activity seizes and penetrates the totality of human Dasein; every activity affects only particular regions of this totality and happens only in particular regions of its world); rather, it is that on which every single activity is based and to which each activity always returns: a *doing* [*Tun*]. It is precisely the doing of man as his mode of being-in-the-world, through which he first becomes "for-himself" what he is, comes to his self, acquires the "form" of his Da-sein, his "permanence" and at the same time makes the world his own. Conceived in this way, labor is not determined by the nature of its objects, nor by its goal, content, result, etc., but by what happens to human Dasein itself in labor.

We want to pursue the course suggested by this interpretation of the concept of labor and try to obtain a clear view of this happening itself: labor as the specific *praxis* of human Dasein in the world. We already have a further possibility for delimiting this praxis: through the relation between labor and the objective world [*Gegenständlichkeit*] that is always emphasized in the philosophically founded concept of labor. In labor something happens to man and to the objective world, such that the "result" is an essential unity of man and the objective world: man "objectifies" himself and the object becomes "his," a human object. And this relation between doing and objectification does not just mean, for example, that in every act of labor some sort of object is always there to be worked on. It should also designate a constitutive moment for the whole praxis of human Dasein, a "task" posed for human Dasein as such. It is given this task of "mediating" and "appropriating" the objective world. Only by fulfilling this task can human Dasein become "for-itself" and come to itself. (It is precisely this threefold unity of doing, objectification, and given task that is implicit in the meaning of the word "labor," as Grimm's dictionary indicates; in all of its meanings it aims at a threefold phenomenon: laboring [*Arbeiten*], the object of labor [*Gearbeitete*], and the goal of labor [*zu-Arbeitende*].) Thus, in consideration of the phenomenon of labor, we must always keep all three moments in view. In our examination of labor as doing we must focus simultaneously on what happens to the objective world and on the task that human Dasein takes upon itself in this doing.

3

An obvious way to delimit the concept of labor is by means of another human doing that is often used as a counterconcept to labor: *play*.[18] In what follows, we will briefly summarize the characteristics of play, which will make possible at least a preliminary definition of the term, with a view to our ensuing examination of the character of labor.

Play can (but need not) also involve objects—a person can occupy himself with objects when playing. But in this instance the object has a completely different meaning and a completely different function than in labor. When playing, a person does not orient himself toward the objects, toward their immanent lawfulness (determined by the specific nature of the object), nor toward the demands of their "objective content" [*Sachhaltigkeit*] (the way that labor must orient itself to the objective content of its object in the treatment, use, and formation of it). Rather, play negates as far as possible this "objective" content and lawfulness of the object and puts in its place another lawfulness, created by man himself, to which the player adheres of his own free will: the "rules of the game" (in the broadest sense; those who play alone also follow rules; game rules need not be explicit and can be used *ad hoc* for single cases). In play it is as if the "objectivity"[19] of objects and their effects and the reality of the objective world, which one is normally forced constantly to recognize and interact with, had been temporarily suspended. For once, one does entirely as one pleases with objects; one places oneself above them and becomes "free" from them. This is what is decisive: in placing oneself above the objective world one comes precisely to *oneself*, into the dimension of one's *freedom* that one is denied in labor. In a single toss of a ball, the player achieves an infinitely greater triumph of human freedom over the objective world than in the most massive accomplishment of technical labor.

In regard to the meaning and goal of play, a person is, in playing, with oneself and not with objects (which are other than himself): one expresses one's freedom by acting on the objects, going along with or playing around with them.[20] If we want to express in everyday language the function of play in human life, we refer to specific modes of the happening of the self and not to objects: we speak of distracting oneself, relaxing oneself, forgetting oneself, and recuperating oneself.

With this we already have a further characteristic of play that points directly to labor as its counterphenomenon. Within the totality of human Dasein, play has no duration or permanence. It happens essentially in "intervals," "between" the times of other doings [*Tuns*] that continually dominate human Dasein. But the way that life happens in play is not a happening that is completed in and through itself: it is essentially dependent and points inherently to another doing. Play is self-distraction, self-relaxation, self-recuperation *from* regimentation, tension, toil, intense self-awareness, etc. It is self-distraction, self-relaxation, self-recuperation *for the purpose* of a new concentration, tension, etc. Thus play is in its totality necessarily related to an other from which it comes and at which it is aimed, and this other is already preconceived as *labor* through the characteristics of regimentation, tension, toil, etc.

On the foundation of ethnological studies, Karl Bücher has claimed that play is older than labor: "Technology develops in play, and makes the transition from entertainment to usefulness only very gradually. . . . Art is older than production for use. Even among more highly developed primitive peoples . . . dance still precedes all-important labor or follows it."[21] It is Bücher's great contribution to have demonstrated clearly that labor has in no way exclusively or even primarily arisen only from "economic" motives and that it is not originally located in the economic dimension. However, his formulations of the relationship between play and labor can give rise to dangerous misunderstandings. In the structural sense, within the totality of human Dasein, labor is necessarily and eternally "earlier" than play. It is the starting point, basis, and principle of play insofar as play is precisely a break *from* labor and recuperation *for* labor. Definitive insights into the relationship between play and labor can be found in concentrated form in the philosophy of Aristotle: all play is not inherently telos, but is ἀναπαύσεως χάριν [for the purpose of repose]; thus, according to its telos, it necessarily belongs and is related to ἀσχολία (absence of leisure—labor in the broadest sense). Παίξειν οπως σπουδάξη [to play in order to be busy]: reduced to a formula, this is the essential foundational interrelationship between play and labor.[22]

From the standpoint of play, laboring doing can be characterized preliminarily by three moments: its essential duration, its essential permanence, and its essentially burdensome character. Furthermore, all three moments point beyond the individual process of labor (as an individual "purposeful activity") to laboring doing as such, and to its meaning and function in the totality of human Dasein. In other words, duration, permanence, and burden do not characterize the particular laboring processes, but rather the human doing that is at their basis, is expressed in them, and that enables them to take shape.

Understood in this way, the *duration* of labor means that the task that labor poses for human Dasein can never be fulfilled in one or in many individual labor processes. Thus, this task corresponds to an enduring being-at and being-in-work, and an orientation and concentration of the whole human Dasein toward labor (which is also the case when a life fulfills itself in only a single labor process or a single deed, for the continual orientation of one's Dasein to labor must not be mistaken for continual activity!) Play, on the other hand, is essentially particular, without duration. It happens only temporarily, from time to time. Regarding the happening of human life, one can speak of "life as labor" but not "life as play."

The permanence of labor can be provisionally defined as follows: something should "come out of" labor that, in its meaning or function, is more enduring than the single process of labor and that is part of a "universal" process. What is worked on or procured by labor will be worked into the "world" of the laborer, just as it has been worked out of this very same "world." Either it should be something "permanent" that, after the conclusion of the particular labor process, is still there itself and is also there for others—an "object" (in the widest, still to be clarified, sense). Or it should endow the laborer himself with permanence—by providing and maintaining a foundation for him in his world. In the history of the problem, this aspect of labor has been treated under the heading of "objectification." Labor is objectifying doing; in labor, human Dasein objectifies itself. It becomes actual, existing, historical "objectivity" [*Objektivität*]; it acquires an objective form in the happening of the "world."

The burdensome character of labor is the most susceptible to misunderstanding. [23] One misses the point from the beginning if one attempts to attribute it to specific conditions in the performance of labor, to the social-technical structuring of labor, to the resistance of the materials, etc. Nor is it a question of a "feeling of displeasure" that appears in certain kinds of labor and that can be eliminated or arrested with technological or psychological remedies. Rather, labor as such is already experienced as a "burden" *prior* to all such problems due to the modes and organization of labor insofar as it places human doing under an alien, imposed law: under the law of the "thing" that is to be done (and which still remains a "thing," something other than life itself, even after one has given his own labor). In labor it is always first a question of the thing itself and not of the laborer—even when a complete separation between labor and the "product of labor" has not yet taken place. In labor man is always taken away from his self-being and toward something else: he is always with an other and for an other.

It will be the task of the following investigation to develop and derive these characteristics of labor out of the specific doing of humans, out of human praxis. This should also make clear that labor is by no means primordially [24] an economic phenomenon, but is actually rooted in the happening of human Dasein itself, and that precisely through the concept of labor, economics leads back into deeper spheres that provide its foundation. Thus, any fundamental treatment of the concept of labor by economics demands a return to these spheres, which are the basis of economics, but which transcend it as well.

4

The characteristics of labor that have become visible thus far lead the question of the meaning and function of laboring doing back to the mode of human happening in the world. We must now attempt to bring this happening itself, as *doing*, praxis, into focus (since it is precisely this doing that was first brought to light by the philosophical analysis of the concept of labor).

Human life happens as praxis in the eminent sense that man must make [*Tun*] his Dasein himself, in such a way that he has to seize it and fulfill it as a task. Man's happening is a continual *making*-happen (while the happening of animal Dasein is a mere *letting*-happen: the animal lets its Dasein happen immediately, even when it "does" something; for example, when it builds a nest, protects itself from attack, seeks nourishment. For animals, all this doing is, in Wexberg's apt expression, "biologically sanctioned." The animal does not "have" its Dasein as a given task that it has to fulfill through its modes of being). Man constantly finds himself and his world in a situation that is not immediately his own, so that he cannot simply let his Dasein happen in this immediacy. Instead, he must first make every situation his own, by "mediating" it with himself. This process of mediation is designated by the concepts of "*production and reproduction*" (after Marx, these concepts were deprived of their original essential meaning and relegated to the economic dimension). Production and reproduction by no means refer simply to the happening of "material Dasein" in economic doing, but rather to the mode of making-happen of human Dasein as a whole: appropriation, sublation, transformation, and development of human Dasein in all spheres of life. This applies to both the immediate situation of the "world" and to Dasein within it. This process is a bringing-before-oneself and, as having-brought-before-oneself ("represented"), a creation and development of Dasein and its world in all regions (including "material," "vital" as well as "intellectual" [*geistig*] being). For humans, this doing is essentially a knowing [*wissendes*] doing,[25] which keeps its goal (producing and developing Dasein and its world in an ever more appropriate and suitable way) in sight and that uses this "purpose" as a guide—purposeful doing.

Labor is grounded in this mediating-knowing doing [*vermittelnd-wissenden Tun*] and in the continual production and reproduction of human Dasein (as opposed to the immediate letting-happen process of animal Dasein). All the characteristics cited in the previous analysis of labor are present in this mode of happening. Furthermore, in this, its most universal meaning relating to the happening of human Dasein in the world, one encounters the concept of labor everywhere, whenever something is said about the essence of labor: from the passage in Genesis (which Augustine heavily emphasized in his commentaries) and the Pauline letters all the way up to Hegel. This brings us already to a point where a shift in meaning of the concept of labor and its relegation to the economic sphere begin. One poses the question *why* after all is the happening of human Dasein essentially "mediation," production, and reproduction? Why is man, by his very essence, prevented from letting his Dasein happen immediately? One answers by pointing to the quasi-"natural" situation of man in the world. The happening of human Dasein is labor because the world, as it is, can never satisfy his "needs." Thus he must occupy himself constantly in order to live in the world at all (procuring clothing, nourishment, housing, tools, etc.).

This primordial "lack" in man's natural situation makes "*need*" the driving force of his doing. The first and necessary goal of this doing is the "satisfaction of needs"—and here we are already in the sphere of the traditional definitions of economy and labor as economic doing. Here are three randomly chosen examples. "The object of research in political economy is the activity of man directed toward the satisfaction of his needs."[26] "The goal of every economy is the satisfaction of human needs. Thus, economy is an activity that aims at making possible such a satisfaction of needs."[27] In economic terms, labor is "characterized by the goal . . . of creating means for the satisfaction of needs."[28] These types of definitions do not change essentially when the concept of need and the concept of the activity undertaken to satisfy needs are determined more closely.

All these definitions rest on a foundation that is unable to support a genuine comprehension of the essence of labor. This will be elaborated briefly.

Every theory that starts from "need" as the stimulus of activity takes man primarily as an *organic* being, as organic "life" in the biological sense; for being organically based and conditioned is an essential characteristic of need. Only an organism, a natural-organic unity, has needs. This is not altered by distinguishing human from animal needs through conscious, mastering, or guiding aim-orientation, the freedom of conduct, etc.[29] These things by no means extricate needs from the natural-organic sphere.

But positing man as a natural-organic being is inadequate if the specific mode of his being in the world, if the praxis of his Dasein itself, is in question (as in our hypothesis concerning the concept of labor). Such a procedure would absolutize a definite "dimension" of human being from the beginning (quite apart from whether human being is divisible into "dimensions" at all) and therefore could consider the other dimensions only as superstructures or adjoining structures: this absolutized dimension would be precisely where the satisfaction of needs takes place—the world of the means for the satisfaction of needs or the "world of goods."

This is not the place to investigate whether economics can legitimately take as its starting point a concept of man as a natural organic being [*Wesen*] (as it explicitly or implicitly does by using need as a foundational concept) or whether man performing economic activities does so with his whole being, as it were, and not only as an organism satisfying his needs. In any case, it is certain that a definition of *labor* based on and located in the realm of need satisfaction has already tailored its meaning to a very specific dimension (the material "world of goods"). Indeed, such a definition actually roots the meaning of labor in this dimension so that all other noneconomic aspects of labor are seen primarily from this standpoint.

If, however, human being should not be posited primarily as natural organic being when defining of the concept of labor, how should it be posited? How is human being posited by the philosophically founded concept of labor? We want to speak of it preliminarily as *historical* being. The following considerations should allow labor to emerge as a category of historical being.

Economic theory has not always failed to realize that perhaps the traditional interpretation of the concept of labor is not adequate to account for the full phenomenon of labor. At the very beginning of his book *Work and Rhythm*, Karl Bücher indicates that labor has always been considered only "as an absolute economic category," whereas all other activities, which are ends in themselves, are not seen as labor. Yet, he continues, it is highly doubtful "that such a distinction between labor and other activity can be made at all stages of human development." Bücher, however, does not develop this fruitful insight any further, nor does Thomas Brauer, who, through his consideration of the problem of labor, is forced explicitly to revise the concept of need. Brauer replaces the satisfaction of needs with "procuring what is lacking" [*Bedarfsversorgung*], which is no longer directed primarily toward "mere Dasein," but rather toward "a specific type of being."[30] In principle, this would have made it possible to treat man differently in economics—not merely as a subject of "the world of needs," but in his full being. "Securing and expanding one's existence," which Bücher identifies as the goal of economic activity, is intended to refer to man's "qualitative Dasein" in contrast to his "mere Dasein"—it aims at the *totality* of human praxis. But Bücher does not stick to these insights through the course of his investigation. He falls back quickly on the explanation of economic action through "drives."

More radically, Friedrich von Gottl has recently attempted to place the question of the determination of economic doing on new ground. Here we need to treat his theory only insofar as it relates directly to grasping the concept of labor.

According to Gottl, the economy is driven not primarily by the satisfaction of needs, but by "providing what is lacking." Roughly speaking, this approach is intended to break through the one-sided absolutization of the economic dimension as a "world of goods" and to initiate a consideration of "economics as life" that considers human being in its totality. Lack is not primarily related to individual economic subjects (as mere economic individuals as it were), but rather to the "structures" of the economy as themselves already organized forms of life. Secondly, lack always refers to a totality of demands that in the final analysis aims at nothing less than a determinate "affirmation" and "promotion" of life itself. The "interaction of lack and provision" always leads in the end to an "affirmation of life; that is, it inherently tends toward the promotion of life." "This means that the economy does not aim for any quantitative maximum; it aims explicitly for an overall optimum."[31]

Decisive here is the incipient reestablishment of the link between economic activity and the happening of human Dasein itself. For Gottl is concerned not with goods as a means of satisfying needs, nor with "performance" in the service of the production of goods (Elster), etc. Rather, it is a question of the ability of human Dasein to happen in the plenitude of its possibilities. The significance of this thesis for our inquiry becomes clearer when we see how Gottl determines the immanent telos, the authentic "task," of this happening. It is the synthesis of happening "in a unity of reality," such "that it appears as happening ordered in terms of *duration* and, as unity, in terms of *permanence*."[32] "Whenever life is actualized as a living process there is also an active unity whose duration it has effected itself. This is a unity with internal permanence that has been *brought about by labor* and that has always been adjusted to its surroundings as well."[33] Economic doing must also be seen from this perspective, and "therefore all exchange and production is always a contribution to bringing all happening together in the form of a unity of duration and permanence."[34]

For the problem of labor this implies that economic labor (which is, after all, the only kind at stake in economics) itself has, inherently, a duty and a goal that is itself *no longer economic* (in the sense of satisfying needs within the world of goods). It has the task—essential to human Dasein as such—of self-effectuation [*Selbsterwirkung*], of creating forms with duration and permanence. In fact, the first and final purpose of labor in general is to bring about the being of Dasein itself, in order to "secure" its duration and permanence. Individual lack of all kinds is ultimately grounded in this primordial and constant lack of Dasein in itself—the incomplete process of its self-effectuation in duration and permanence.

With this conceptualization Gottl seeks to move beyond the economic dimension, to the being of man, and to the specific mode of human praxis in the world. And precisely in this being itself is where labor appears, as constant and enduring self-effectuation. Gottl explicitly stresses the "foundational" character of his conceptualizations, which reveals itself in, among other things, the theoretical and actual impossibility of ever providing for everything that is lacking. The primordial lack of human Dasein in which economic doing is ultimately grounded is not the lack of "goods" of any sort, but a lack in human Dasein itself that can never be "satisfied": Gottl calls this the *exigency of life*. "The fundamental nature of the exigency of life asserts itself in the fact that it is possible to imagine providing for all that is lacking, but that in the end something always remains lacking."[35]

Thus, economic theory itself has led us back to the foundation we had already attempted to outline roughly. The "exigency of life" refers to an "onto-logical" condition: it is grounded in the structure of human being, which can never simply let itself happen immediately, but must constantly "effectuate" and "make" [*Tun*] itself. Even the very praxis of human Dasein, as knowing and mediating itself, requires "labor" as its mode of happening.

We have attempted to show that insofar as they take the concept of "needs" and their satisfaction in the world of goods as the starting point, all economic theories fail to recognize labor in its entirety. At best, these theories can explain labor as "material" production and reproduction; in fact, they do not even explain that! Imagine a society that has succeeded in procuring all the economic goods it needs and that this condition was guaranteed for the foreseeable future. The interaction between human Dasein and its world would continue to happen as "labor," even if all economic motives and compulsions disappeared. Then this happening would for the most part shift from the economic dimension to other dimensions of human Dasein and its world (and thus the place, form, and function of the economy in the totality of human life would also change completely: in such a society economic labor could certainly no longer serve as a "model" for labor in general). The essential aspect of labor is not grounded in the scarcity of goods, nor in a lag between the supply of goods present and utilizable at any particular time and human needs; on the contrary, it is rooted in an essential excess of human Dasein beyond every possible situation in which it finds itself and its world. Human being is always *more* than its Dasein at any given time. It transcends every possible situation and for this very reason there is always a discrepancy between it and its immediate existence. This is a discrepancy that demands constant labor for its overcoming, even though human Dasein can never rest in possession of itself and its world.

This essential excess of being over Dasein constitutes the fundamental and irremovable "exigency of life" (Gottl). This is also the source of man's inherent neediness, whose appeasement is the final meaning of labor. Man is constantly in need of enduring self-fulfillment, in need of the reality of his own existence in all its possibilities—a task in whose service the economy also ultimately stands. Further pursuing this train of thought would lead necessarily to an ontology[36] of man, and only on this basis could the concrete character of labor be elaborated. This is of course impossible within the limits of this essay. In order to give greater concreteness to the concept of labor, and especially in order to determine the meaning of its use in economics, we must proceed otherwise. We will take the aforementioned fundamental characteristics of laboring doing (whose basis in the happening of human Dasein has now been outlined, if only roughly) as our point of departure, and then proceed to a consideration of the relation between labor and the objective world [*Gegenständlichkeit*] and the objectification [*Vergegenständlichung*] of life in labor. By proceeding in this way we will develop our insight into the "objectivity" [*Sachlichkeit*] of labor that became apparent during our first examination of the phenomenon of labor.

5

The claim that all labor is essentially related to the objective world appears doubtful at first, if one thinks, for example, of "intellectual" labor, political activity, social service work (such as the activity of doctors, teachers, etc.). In the context of our investigation, being-an-object is the counterconcept to being-a-self. The objective world means, first and foremost, only what is other than the self. For the self all be-ing[37] outside of it is part of the objective world—this includes even other men and one's own body. Although in different ways, works of art, science, etc., belong to the objective world, as do works of technology, nature, objects of use, etc.

The self *is* only in the context of its "world"—in and with the objective world. But in regard to the happening of the self, this particular world as a whole and everything in it happen in a way "other" than the self; they have their own "history" that never coincides with the history of the self. When the self begins to make its Dasein happen, it finds itself confronted with a world that is the world of another Dasein: a world filled and formed by a human animating power that is not its own, that is always already past and is yet present and real. This is a world of public institutions, organizations of a political, social, and economic nature, means of production and objects of consumption, things of use, works of art, etc. It is also a world of the universal division and organization of space and time that, as a whole, remains the work of past Dasein, even in every new creation. Which Dasein it was that gave a particular world its time and which was responsible for the shaping and filling of a particular life-space can only be determined on the basis of the respective historical situation. Depending on the stage of historical development reached, the "subject" of "world-formation" appears as the family, the tribe, the estate, the class, etc. But regardless of how the world has been formed, it is always encountered as the reality of a *past* Dasein, as a past that is still present. And just as the objective world is the reality of Dasein already past, so it also carries the future of this past life in it: it is the actuality of its provisions and plans, its discoveries and mistakes, its alliances and enemies. Thus, it is not a closed "state" [*Zustand*], nor is it a static preexisting multiplicity of disposable beings, but is rather through and through unfinished and open—through and through movement, *happening*. The happening of the objective world with which Dasein is always already confronted, and which extends from the past into the present and anticipates the future, is a happening with its own temporal and spatial dimensions that proceeds alongside the happening of Dasein; it has its own immanent dynamic and its own immanent laws, which even enable it to "take on a life of its own" and to elude the control of Dasein.

Dasein, in order to happen at all, must first let this objective world happen; it must preserve it, take care of it, develop it, and work on it. This is the first decisive experience that laboring doing has. Now we can already say that the process of "mediation," of production and reproduction, begins with the sublation of the past currently present. In order for Dasein to generate its own situation, to appropriate and shape its own world, it must interact with this happening past, which presents itself as an objective process making certain demands on Dasein's happening. The countryside, once it is opened to commerce; the field, once it is cultivated; the mine, once it is dug; the factory, once it begins operations; the law, once it is promulgated; the constitution, once it is implemented; the work of art or science, once it is offered to the public—*they* all have their own "history" that never coincides with the history of any particular Dasein and that can never be deduced from any such history. They all have their own laws of happening. For Dasein to keep happening at all, all of these elements of the objective world must, each in their own way, be cared for, maintained, secured, expanded, and preserved. This labor is by no means determined solely by the needs of contemporary Dasein; it must take into consideration what is lacking in these various elements of the objective world; it must address the necessities that the immediate Dasein of the preformed and prefilled "world" brings with it. [38]

To these demands posed by the objective world, human doing responds by consciously adapting itself to its object and by binding itself to its immanent laws—both of these responses are expressed in every single act of labor and both together are what give the "mediation" between man and the objective world the character of a relation among things and what makes the object into a thing (to be treated as such). Whether explicitly or not, willingly or not, labor is always concerned with the thing itself [*die Sache selbst*]. In laboring, the laborer is always "with the thing": whether one stands by a machine, draws technical plans, is concerned with organizational measures, researches scientific problems, instructs people, etc. In this doing he allows himself to be directed by the thing, subjects and binds himself to its laws, even when he masters his object, handles it, guides it, and lets it go. In each case he is not "with himself," does not let his own Dasein happen. On the contrary, he places himself in the service of something "other than himself," and he is with something "other than himself"—even when this doing fulfills his own freely assumed life. This alienation and estrangement of Dasein, this taking-on-oneself the law of the thing rather than letting one's own Dasein happen is fundamentally inevitable (although it can disappear to the point of being completely forgotten during and after labor). This phenomenon is by no means identical with the resistance of the "material" [*Stoff*] and it does not stop with the termination of a particular process of labor. Dasein is in and of itself subject to this objectivity [*Sachlichkeit*].

We can now attempt to formulate the essential objectivity of labor in its genuine "negativity" and thereby at least allude to the fundamental significance of the burdensome character of labor. The process of human being in the world is "self-actualization" [*Selbsttäterschaft*] from beginning to end, making one's own Dasein happen, being-oneself in every Dasein, but this being-oneself is possible by letting the *objective world* happen, by being with and for an *other*. This is why laboring on the objective world is essentially burdensome, independent of any burden implicit in any particular process of labor. In the end, the burdensome character of labor expresses nothing other than the negativity rooted in the essence of human Dasein. Man can come to his own being only by passing through his other and through "alienation" and "estrangement."

6

By demonstrating the interconnection among the burdensome character of labor, its essential objectivity, and the primordial negativity of laboring doing, only a small part of the relation between labor and the objective world has been revealed. We must pursue this course further and ask: through labor what happens to the objective world and what happens to the laborer?

We approach the problem backwards, as it were, in order to show how the object looks that has already been worked on or already brought forth, that is, how it looks as a finished "product" of labor. One can see that its mode of being-objective has become totally different. Roughly put, if it was previously raw material, matter, a thing, etc., now it is a disposable and utilizable object (a "good"). It now stands in a particular concrete relation to human Dasein and its history; it has been "animated" [*verlebendigt*] in a peculiar way. Its being and happening are no longer a "natural" happening. Its essence is no longer materiality, thinghood, and the like. Its motility[39] can no longer be grasped through the concepts and laws of physics of any kind. What happens to objects worked on and obtained through labor does not take place in the dimension of "nature," "materiality," etc., but in the dimension of human history. Yet, this objective happening is other than that of human Dasein itself. What happens to produced commodities—the functioning factory and the cultivated landscape—happens in the space and time of a historical life; it is a historical happening [*geschichtliches Geschehen*].

This seemingly trivial state of affairs acquires its full significance only when it is developed into the insight that the animation and historicity of the objects is not just a point of view, from which theory sees things, but instead precisely what constitutes the "substantiality" of objects. Through labor the object has become real and generates further effects. Man's objective world is the reality of objectified life. The labor of human lives has been solidified and realized in objects of use, enjoyment, decoration, etc.—in home, city, and country, in all the institutions and organizations that surround us daily. Life that has been objectified in these ways makes demands on, rules, and determines man at every moment (without his necessarily ever becoming conscious of it). Human activity must constantly interact with the historical life that has realized itself in its objects.[40]

By merely encountering the object of labor in a world formed in a certain way man is forced to submit to the particular historicity of this world; in this way the object of labor also makes the historicity of the laborer itself real.[41] By working, man actually places himself in the concrete situation of history, is forced to confront its presence, takes its past on himself, and works on its future. This "practical" becoming historical of man extends through the entire laboring process, from the very specific preexistence of the object as "material" (which is already itself, in regard to selection and form, historically transmitted) to methodology, spatial and temporal organization, and even in the meaning and goal of labor.

It is first and only through labor that man becomes real as a historical being and acquires his determinate position in the historical process. Whoever stands behind a machine, digs coal in a mine, serves behind a counter, functions as an official in a bureaucratic apparatus, or teaches as a scientist has in each case stepped out of his own personal sphere in order to occupy a well-determined place in an already organized and differentiated setting that is divided into various corporations, occupations, classes, etc. He has found his specific place as a part in one of these larger settings. It is first through this preexisting arrangement of labor that the individual is rooted in a unique and noninterchangeable "position" [*Stand*] within the historical world and its happening. The possibilities he has to appropriate and to change his situation are determined by this position. Before and outside of labor, that is, before and outside of praxis in the service of production and reproduction, human Dasein can project many possibilities but it can realize none. Through labor it has entered into a definite realm of possibilities: its Dasein has acquired historical permanence. The laborer *is* now a factory worker, an employee, a civil servant, a businessman, an intellectual, and so on (these titles serve here as examples of actual historical positions) and thereby he has taken over all the concrete relations, conditions, and possibilities of these "positions." The laborer has now become a real historical force or he has become powerless. He is part of a social stratum, a class, a group, etc. and is exposed to the power or powerlessness of these groups.

Man becomes "actu-" historical through labor—precisely this is expressed in the objectification of labor. By working himself into the object of his labor, as it were, the laborer becomes in this object, which he has worked on and brought forth, something persevering, present, "objectively" real and influential within the historical domain and in historically lived time. Marx has sharply emphasized this state of affairs in his description of the labor process: "Labor has bound itself up with its object. It is objectified and the object has been worked upon. What appeared in the form of unrest from the standpoint of the laborer, now appears, from the standpoint of the product, as a static property in the form of being." "During the labor process, labor is constantly converted from the form of unrest into that of being: from the form of movement into that of an object."[42]

By now it has perhaps become clear the extent to which labor is a specifically *historical* category, a category of human Dasein *as* historical Dasein. Labor presupposes a well-determined *relation to time* that thoroughly penetrates Dasein and guides its praxis. We have already mentioned several modes of this relation to time. Human praxis is labor on and in the present through the transformative "sublation" of the past with anticipatory care for the future. The laborer continually maintains himself in his own temporality and in that of the objective world, and this is expressed in many ways: in creating, handling, and evaluating the material of labor, in distributing and administering the means of labor, and especially in partitioning time according to a general rule,[43] to which all laborers are more or less subjected (within individual labor processes, in the division of Dasein into labor and "free time," in the regulation of the length of the working day, etc.). Only within very narrow boundaries is the individual free to organize his own time. The true "subjects" of lived time are various historical communities (more precisely, those "groups" that have established themselves in historical communities as the "dominating class").[44]

From this standpoint, one can shed some light on the question of the role of labor in the life of so-called primitives. It has always been emphasized that labor seems to have an essentially different meaning for primitive people than it has for so-called civilized people[45]—indeed, one cannot speak of labor in the strict sense at all in relation to primitive people at a certain stage of development. For these people labor is not a "regular doing"; in providing what is lacking they do not go beyond "what is necessary at the moment" (even when they know very well that in the future, for example, in the winter, they will suffer from shortages). The time dedicated to labor stands in striking "incongruity" to time devoted to play, dance, production of decorations, etc. These facts directly evoke the interconnection between Dasein's relation to time (historicity) and labor as a mode of Dasein's praxis. Primitives do not have that relation to time that makes human existence historical and constitutes labor as Dasein's praxis. Their existence is essentially *pre*historical, even when we encounter them "in" our history, or even in our present. (The boundary between historical and prehistorical existence cannot be marked with a precise date in our historical chronology: it is an "essential boundary" that separates various modes of Dasein.)

Here we cannot explore the question of whether the commencement of the historical relation to time and with it the transition to labor as Dasein's praxis can be explained through the growing neediness of Dasein resulting from decreasing availability of disposable goods. Economic theory itself seems generally to give a negative answer to this question (at least according to the authors just mentioned here). It holds that the progression from a "preeconomic" to an "economic condition" cannot be explained through "purely economic motives" (Gurewitsch).

7

Now we can venture an attempt to outline, at least in broad strokes, the "place" of labor in the totality of human Dasein. In its broadest and most original sense, labor is grounded in the mode of human being as a historical being: in making one's own Dasein happen through the knowing-mediating praxis of production and reproduction. This praxis (as the praxis of a historical Dasein) is always faced with a preexisting objective world that has already been divided, formed, and filled in a particular way. In its particular position, Dasein must interact with this world and in so doing its labor unfolds in a temporal and spatial multiplicity of individual labor processes with various objects, modes, and goals. The individual labor processes take place in various dimensions of Dasein, depending on the historical situation of the worker and his world: in "material" or in "intellectual" production and reproduction; in the praxis of what is only necessary for human Dasein or in the praxis concerned with what lies beyond these necessities. All of these individual labor processes—not, to be sure, as individual labor processes, but as labor in general—are directed to the final intention of giving human being real duration, permanence, and plenitude in its Dasein.

From this standpoint, it should also be clear that labor as such is not an "end-in-itself," is not self-contained, and is not its own "goal." For it is in and of itself lacking [*mangelhaft*], negative; it is directed toward something that is not yet there, that it is supposed to provide, and that is not already present in it. The genuine fulfillment of this lack [*Mangel*], the goal and end of labor, is precisely that real plenitude of Dasein in its duration and permanence. But when one says that the goal of labor lies outside of it, this "outside of" is dangerously ambiguous. Since the goal of labor is the full reality of Dasein itself, "outside of" cannot mean something beyond Dasein, such as any kind of goal transcending Dasein, or any sort of objectivity whatsoever. The goal of labor is Dasein itself and not something outside of it. But if one speaks of "outside of" in regard to the essential objectivity of labor, the expression is justified. All labor, by its very essence, transcends every particular labor process and all "otherness," through which it passes, on the way to the Dasein of the laborer himself.

In spite of the essential universality and continuity of labor in Dasein, in spite of the determination of Dasein *as* labor, every human doing is not necessarily labor. Indeed, even that doing widely described and glorified as "labor" may not be labor. Each time one merely occupies oneself, or "does something or other," that has no relation to "self-actualization," to making Dasein happen, it cannot be counted as labor. The universal concept of labor outlined here spans the spectrum between two poles; both fall within the concept of labor. On the one side, there is the doing in the service of "material" production and reproduction, that is, providing, procuring, and maintaining Dasein's basic necessities. (One should note that what is important here is not what the worker produces—for an other—but what "comes out" of this labor for the worker himself. In the commodity-producing society the final product of the labor process is no longer part of the production and reproduction of laboring Dasein itself—even a factory worker producing luxury items works for the basic necessities of his existence.) On the other side, there is all the labor that goes beyond these necessities and that is and remains tied to making Dasein happen. We shall now briefly consider the difference, essential for the meaning of labor, between both forms of praxis.

We have already suggested that the world of historical Dasein is divided into two regions: what must necessarily be present and disposable, so that Dasein can happen at all, and what is not merely necessary but in itself complete and fulfilled (we know of no better general designation for these regions than the Aristotelian concepts of ἀναγκαία [necessity] and καλά [beautiful things]).[46] The necessary is not already in itself καλόν [beautiful thing] and does not immediately contain καλόν; as we have seen, it is itself a lack, incomplete in relation to the totality of Dasein, and it is not an "end-in-itself." It compels Dasein first to procure and secure that in which and with which Dasein can happen in the truth and plenitude of its own possibilities. Roughly speaking, the region of ἀναγκαία [necessity] can be equated with the region of material production and reproduction. An appropriate term is lacking for the region beyond material production and reproduction, for that which transcends mere "necessities." Marx described this sphere as the "realm of freedom." We will accept this designation both because it captures well precisely what is at stake here for us, namely, the specific mode of Dasein's praxis beyond material production and reproduction, and because it also expresses the fundamental relationship between the two spheres. As that which provides for Dasein's first and most immediate necessities, material production and reproduction are the condition of all plenitude and fulfillment of Dasein. Only when freed *from* this necessity can Dasein become free *for* its own possibilities. Even beyond necessities, the happening of human Dasein remains praxis: even here there is labor to be done, but its character has changed. It no longer serves the purpose of making mere Dasein happen; it is no longer a constant effort to establish and secure life-space. Its course has altered as it were. Labor no longer aims at the formation and fulfillment of Dasein as something that it first has to bring about and secure; instead, it proceeds *from* the form and plenitude of Dasein as its realization. Thus, this praxis contains its goal and end in itself; it is no longer *at the mercy* [*Ausgeliefertsein*] of an "alien" objective world, is no longer constantly bound to an *imposed* happening, to which it must submit itself in order to exist at all. What Dasein takes on itself and makes happen here is its own authentic self. It discloses the truth and plenitude of its being and maintains itself in this disclosed truth and plenitude—to be, in the final sense, what it *can* be. Thus, praxis in the "realm of freedom" is authentic praxis and that to which all other labor is directed as its "end": the free unfolding of Dasein in its true possibilities.

In principle, every mode of praxis can become "free" according to the possibility and power of the Dasein that realizes itself in it. But because "authentic" human Dasein is not an arbitrary function of an individual or group of individuals, Dasein itself demands the idea of a "hierarchical order" of the modes of praxis based on the immanent truth and plenitude of Dasein. For the Greeks, who were the first in the West to formulate such a "hierarchical order" (which still influences us today), the highest mode of praxis was "theory." We are inclined (although no longer with a such good conscience!) to maintain this hierarchical order and to place "intellectual labor" in art, science, etc., above other modes of praxis. We cannot go into the question of the justification of such a hierarchy here.

With this, we believe we have outlined the universal concept of labor well enough to demonstrate the dimension of it that transcends economics—a dimension that, despite this transcendence, constantly protrudes into economics. For its part, economic theory would not need to concern itself with the philosophical character of the concept of labor if it were methodologically possible to conceive of the economic dimension as a self-enclosed field of objects for scientific research, which did not have as one of its topics human praxis as such (e.g., a model of a pure "world of goods," corresponding approximately to the model of "nature" in modern science as field of objects comprehensible in terms of mathematics). But this possibility is precluded precisely because economic theory constitutes a dimension of human praxis—a dimension whose being and happening are constituted through the being and happening of historical, human Dasein, through its "ontological location" within the totality of being. The meaning of labor, which is grounded in this ontological location of man and is the constitutive element for all human praxis, cannot be excluded from any dimension of the latter.[47] Hence, every genuine economic theory is explicitly or implicitly connected with an ontology of man that transcends it. This ontology provides at least a rough idea of historical human Dasein as such, which guides the economic theory.[48]

8

In order to understand how the concept of labor has been reduced and limited to the economic dimension, and the change in its meaning this has entailed, we need to examine a fact to which we have already alluded several times: the *division of labor*.

The expression "division of labor" is misleading insofar as labor has historically never existed as a unity and totality that at some later point in time was divided. On the contrary, historical labor is always already divided—it is itself partial and must not first be divided. The praxis of every Dasein as it unfolds in individual labor processes always deals only with specific objects in specific dimensions of human Dasein and its world. What individual Dasein needs (in the broad sense, as necessities related to the totality of life) in order to happen comes from others and from a past that is not his own; it also ends with others in a future that is not his own. Dasein happens in a space shaped by others and in a time brought forth [*gezeitigt*] by others. From his position, every individual Dasein contributes his part to this shaping of space and time. This essential particularity "terminates" only with the various historical communities (family, tribe, city, state, etc.) that are the true "subject" of their respective worlds. Only they "have" the totality of all that Dasein needs in order to happen. The praxis of procuring, shaping, securing, and taking care of the objective world always happens within the boundaries of the living space and living time of these particular communities. Through labor, individual Dasein takes what he needs from this world and replaces it as well. The happening of individual Dasein is in itself a happening with others, among others, and for others. Within the totality of the historical community, Dasein's praxis is partial.

The divisions of labor traditionally distinguished as "natural" and "social" obtain only within this particularity. By "natural division of labor," what is understood is the division of labor according to, or under consideration of, sex, constitution, talent, etc. This division of labor arose in the family as the first historical community but, within certain limitations, it is still operative at every stage of historical development. Its prototype is "sexual" division of labor between man and woman. The social division of labor concerns the division of labor according to positions, classes, occupations, etc. and the socially determined ascription of certain kinds of labor to certain groups—beginning with the process of "material" production and reproduction and eventually encompassing all dimensions of Dasein. Here, we need to concern ourselves with both types of the division of labor only insofar as it is necessary to explain the social and economic manifestations of labor and their ascription to a specific mode of Dasein.

Despite all the differences in the causes and principles that determine them, the natural and social divisions of labor coincide in that the division of labor manifests itself based on the opposition between *dominating and dominated* labor ("directing" and "directed" labor). This opposition as such (considered *prior* to its realization and crystalization in socio-economic relations) lies in the very essence of labor as the praxis of historical Dasein. Laboring as knowing doing demands that one maintain and conduct oneself with a view to one's own possibilities and one's objectivity. It also demands a certain circumspection and foresight regarding what is supposed to happen in and through labor, as well as self-assurance about what "is to be done" with objects and with Dasein. And since all labor is partial labor in a common living space and time, this circumspection and foresight always encompasses the Dasein and the labor of others as well: it implies reckoning with other Dasein, with their possibilities and necessities. The first guarantee for the establishment, securing, and further development of Dasein lies in the depth, breadth, and force of this circumspection and foresight, within the conditions of the "natural" and socio-economic situation of Dasein. Since praxis always confronts a noninterchangeable, unique situation of Dasein, a unique and noninterchangeable set of possibilities and necessities, this circumspection and foresight is also, from the very beginning, already "divided" differently. This does not mean, however, that this original difference, which is rooted in the always situated historicity of Dasein, already implies either socio-economically determined difference in terms of "status groups" [*Stände*], "classes," etc., or socio-economically determined appropriation of labor. Instead, the power of Dasein, which is a function of the degree of his circumspection and foresight, could determine its "standing" in the world, without being determined by mere socio-economic ascription.

But the social division of labor and the respective "relations of production" in these societies decisively oppose every "essential" (i.e., directed toward the most authentic possibilities of human Dasein) division of labor.[49] In what follows we must refer to states of affairs [*Sachverhalte*] whose basis we cannot elaborate. But we will make reference to them only to a limited extent and in such a general way that they would be accepted by any theory as a basis for further discussion.

Every historical community [*Gemeinschaft*] (every "political" collectivity that is relatively independent and has its own socio-economic foundation and developed socio-economic structures and that can be described as the "subject" of its own historical space and time) is constituted by the basic relationship of domination and servitude [*Herrschaft und Knechtschaft*]. Each is constituted in a (political, economic, or social) struggle that results in the conquering party maintaining the conquered in a state of servitude under its domination.[50]

The concepts of domination and servitude, used by Hegel as categories of historical Dasein, designate here a universal historical condition: servitude means the praxis of Dasein in its entirety is enduringly and constantly bound to material production and reproduction and placed in the service and under the direction of another Dasein (indeed, the one that "dominates") and its needs. The historical community becomes the "subject" of this process [*Geschehen*] only when domination is secure and enduring and, correspondingly, servitude has the duration and permanence of a total mode of Dasein. The meaning and goal of an historical community is attained only in an order that encompasses the totality of Dasein, which prescribes the separation and satisfaction of its needs. This order is always a specific division of labor since it is precisely in labor that the duration, permanence, and plenitude of Dasein is realized and guaranteed.

The realization of the division of labor in the relation of domination and servitude, which has been constructed and secured socio-economically, is the fundamental condition of every further division—among status groups, classes, occupations, etc.—related to the socio-economic appropriation of labor. Initially, the praxis of the subjugated Dasein is limited and bound to providing for mere common necessities (through what means and in what way cannot be investigated here). Material production and reproduction establishes itself as a mode of being (servitude) that dominates Dasein as a whole.

We saw that all labor demands a certain measure of knowing circumspection and foresight. Praxis in the realm of freedom beyond material production and reproduction demands a circumspection and foresight that is only possible on the basis of a very specific position of Dasein within the world: a position in which Dasein has already procured what is necessary and has attained a certain distance from the most necessary and immediate things. Only in such a situation, beyond what is immediately present and what must be necessarily provided, can the totality and plenitude of be-ing become apparent to Dasein, which must be in possession of this insight in order really to happen freely. One of Hegel's and Marx's most profound insights is that binding Dasein in its totality to material production and reproduction reifies Dasein and prevents it from stepping over into the dimension of free praxis. Human labor as a mode of human being cannot be separated from man—nor can its "product." When the object of labor becomes independent and is separated from the being of the worker, the latter is itself also necessarily objectified. The worker's Dasein is alienated and estranged and confronts him as an alien objective power divorced from his own freedom. Whomever's Dasein is placed in the service of "things," those things become chains from which he can no longer liberate himself without negating [*aufheben*] his Dasein as such. Dasein's enduring and constant bondage to material production and reproduction cuts off at the roots the growth of conscious foresight and circumspection corresponding to its authentic possibilities. "Status" [*Stand*] and the ascription of labor to it are no longer determined by the power of Dasein, grounded in foresight and circumspection; they become socio-economic bonds, into which the individual is born or forced.

Labor is in its very essence and meaning related to the happening of Dasein in its totality, that is, to praxis in both dimensions (necessity and freedom). But it is transferred and becomes limited to the economic dimension—the dimension of production and reproduction of necessities—as soon as the two-dimensionality of necessity and freedom *within* the totality of Dasein becomes a two-dimensionality of *different* totalities of Dasein: different modes of Dasein founded and transmitted in the socio-economic sphere. Now, for the first time, the entire burden and toil of labor falls (insofar as it is grounded in the objectivity of labor) into the dimension of material production and reproduction, into praxis related to necessity, while at the same time the dimension of freedom is disburdened of and separated from this praxis.[51] The socio-economic division of labor, expressed in the fundamental relationship of domination and servitude, severs the essential union of both dimensions of human Dasein and both fundamental modes of its praxis. Since only this union can realize the full meaning of labor as making the *totality* of human Dasein happen, severing it also cuts off the labor of material production and reproduction from the positivity through which alone it becomes complete.[52] The real, enduring, and constant process of making Dasein happen is now completely absorbed by the praxis of material production and reproduction, which remains in the hands of specific socio-economic status groups and classes from beginning to end, while praxis in the dimensions beyond this sphere also appear as socio-economic appropriation and is no longer open to *every* Dasein as one's own free possibility that can and must be realized.

This crucial phenomenon of cutting off material production and reproduction from the dimensions of "freedom" that complete and fulfill it has serious repercussions for these very dimensions and praxis in them. Once separated from the spheres that both fulfill and bind it, the disengaged praxis of the "economic dimension" devours the *totality* of Dasein and objectifies its *free* praxis as well. This process is taking place right before our eyes, but we cannot discuss it in more detail here. Labor is losing its authentic meaning beyond material production and reproduction as well. It is no longer essentially connected to the real happening, the real praxis of Dasein. It can no longer fulfill its highest possibility, which is to intervene in the happening of the totality of Dasein in order to give it meaning and purpose. Robbed of its full reality as *praxis*, labor does in fact reach the point where it is no longer *labor* in the final sense; it now only accompanies labor, follows it or precedes it (without solid ground).

The sublation of the established socio-economic division of the totality of Dasein into antagonistic modes of Dasein, and the transformation of material production and reproduction, which has taken on a life of its own and been severed from the dimensions that fulfill it, into a praxis controlled, limited, and completed by these dimensions is the condition of the possibility of authentic labor being returned to Dasein and that labor, freed from estrangement and reification, once again becoming what it essentially is: the free and full realization of the whole man in his historical world. "In fact, the realm of freedom begins only where labor determined by necessity and external exigency ceases. Therefore, it lies according to its nature beyond the sphere of actual material production. . . . Freedom in this realm means that socialized men, that is, the associated producers rationally control their material exchange with nature, bringing it under their common control, instead of being controlled by it as a blind force, performing it with the least expenditure of energy and under conditions most worthy and adequate to their human nature. But it nonetheless still remains a realm of necessity. Beyond it begins the development of human powers that is an end in itself, the true realm of freedom. This, however, can only unfold on the basis of the realm of necessity."[53]

German Philosophy, 1871–1933

Between 1871 and 1933 the German philosophical tradition experienced a dramatic shift: with neo-Kantianism, it began with the attempt to renew philosophy by establishing it as an exact science (following the example of mathematics) and ended with the jettisoning of scientific philosophy by "heroic and racist realism." This transformation coincided almost perfectly with the historical development of the Third Reich from the Second Empire, that is to say, with the passage from a liberalism influenced by feudalism and military aristocracy to the overt dictatorship of monopoly capitalism in the service of a totalitarian state. The tendencies that would spell the end of the particularly bourgeois mentality of the nineteenth century as well as its rationalist philosophy were at work from the beginning. This transition developed in the following manner: the foundations of transcendental idealism reestablished by neo-Kantianism, and also by Edmund Husserl's phenomenology—which we will consider in a moment—were undermined by the antirationalist currents of vitalist philosophy, existentialism, historicism, and intuitionist metaphysics. Some of these philosophical ideas were beginning to move beyond the limits of bourgeois thought in an attempt to envision a rational ordering of human society. But at the same time that the most advanced elements of the bourgeoisie were being suppressed and losing their influence, these ideas, which had been the essence of the bourgeoisie, were losing their critical capacity. Rendered powerless through vulgarization (such was the case with Nietzsche's critique of bourgeois conceptions as well as with Dilthey's discovery of the world of history), they became instead a sanctification of the existing social order.

1. Neo-Kantianism

After the fall of Hegelian philosophy, which reigned practically unchallenged in Germany up until the middle of the nineteenth century, scientific positivism sought to assume the role of philosophy. From the start, however, the power and the technological successes of the methods of the physical sciences proved useless when applied to human society. This "Ignorabimus"[1] had implications that reached beyond metaphysics. In the face of the sterility of social theory and practice, there arose a need to sketch some well-grounded philosophical bases for a conception of the human world. This need became still more urgent in light of cyclical economic crises and as the quality of life for the lower classes, instead of increasing with technological advances, declined steadily. Even though the average living conditions tended to rise during periods of prosperity, the lower classes lost all security. A shift in ideology was certain to come about. Insofar as this transformation was achieved through bourgeois philosophy itself, it consisted of a turn to transcendental philosophy as the basis of bourgeois rationalist theory. Neo-Kantianism represented the first attempt to overcome theoretical anarchy by returning to the Kantian notion of "pure reason" as a domain autonomous from theory and practice. The true founder of neo-Kantianism was Hermann Cohen (1842–1918), professor at Marburg. He began with a new interpretation of Kantian philosophy: *Kants Theorie der Erfahrung* (1871) [Kant's Theory of Experience], *Kants Begründung der Ethik* (1877) [The Foundation of Kant's Ethics], and *Kants Begründung der Aesthetik* (1889) [The Foundation of Kant's Aesthetics]. Cohen's "philosophical system" provided a solid foundation for philosophy as well as for the leading scientific theory of his day: *Logik der reinen Erkenntis* (1902) [The Logic of Pure Knowledge], *Ethik des reinen Willens* (1904) [The Ethic of Pure Will], *Aesthetik des reinen Gefühls* (1912) [The Aesthetic of Pure Emotion]. Cohen's collaborator, Paul Natorp (1854–1924), also a professor at Marburg, completed the philosophical system with respect to social philosophy and psychology: *Sozialpaedagogik* (1899) [Social Pedagogy], *Plato's Philosophy of Ideas* (1903), *Die logischen Grundlagen der exakten Wissenschaften* (1910) [The Logical Basis of the Exact Sciences], *Allgemeine Psychologie* (1912) [General Psychology], and *Vorlesungen über praktische Philosophie* (1925) [Lectures on Practical Philosophy]. Ernst Cassirer firmly established the philosophical and historical foundations of neo-Kantianism. He would later enter into discussion with the modern proponents of transcendental idealism (irrationalism and the philosophy of existence). Among his works the following deserve mention: *Das Erkenntnisproblem in der Philosophie und Wissenschaft der neueren Zeit* (1906–20) [The Problem of Knowledge in Philosophy and Science since the Middle Ages], *Substance and Function* (1910), and *Philosophy of Symbolic Forms* (1923–1929).

In the given context, neo-Kantianism surpassed the *ontonomie*[2] of the physical sciences and aimed instead for a universal aprioristic philosophy, but it is important to keep in mind that it let itself be guided in this direction by the scientific method itself. Even more so than in the case of Kant himself, the methods and instruments of pure logic remained the directives for each part of the system. Neo-Kantianism distinguished itself from Kant's philosophy in two main ways. First of all, the empirical and nonrationalist factors of Kantian philosophy were almost entirely eliminated (for example, the dependence of reason on the immediate givens of the senses, the receptive nature of sensation, and the doctrine of the thing-in-itself). With Cohen, sensation is quantified by the infinitesimal method. Passive sensation becomes the product of spontaneous reason (see Cohen's work on the principle of the infinitesimal method, which appeared in 1883). In this way, pure theory's authority as an absolute guide is preserved, thanks to a system in which empirical facts appear only as the result of reason. In other words, reason becomes a demiurge. It creates the whole of reality. "The contents of reason must be considered as the products of reason itself" (Cohen). Not only theoretical problems but also practical ones are treated in the same manner by this philosophy: culture as well as nature emanates from pure reason. Within the structure of the state itself the self-creation of the ethical person [*Selbsterzeugung der sittlichen Person*] is to be achieved. One perceives here a philosophy of the state according to which socialist ideas that were at first dangerous enter into the construction of the democratic state, of a liberal "*Rechtsstaat.*" Of course, however, these social ideas are only incorporated on the condition that they be mitigated through metaphysical interpretation (Natorp). Second, the difference between Kant and neo-Kantianism consists in a tendency that threatens to destroy the original sense of transcendental philosophy. The fundamental principles of reason no longer possess the character of extratemporal judgment and synthesis, the character, that is to say, of being valid for every time and place. The methods and hypotheses of neo-Kantianism are instead subject to historical change. The eternal truths of bourgeois consciousness are put into question by this conception of the fundamental categories as variable. The certainty with which it was felt that bourgeois ideas were obvious and absolute thus suffered its first blow. The relativism of which I will speak later in the context of Dilthey was already in progress. It would never have gained in force, however, if it were only conceived within the framework of transcendental philosophy; only by concerning itself with rationality's dependence on specific social phenomena would it acquire real influence. In any case, the doctrine of the variability of fundamental categories was symptomatic of a state of crisis in which liberal idealism had already found itself. This symptom became still more noticeable in the subsequent development of neo-Kantianism, represented especially by Natorp's work, *Vorlesungen über praktische Philosophie* [Lectures on Practical Philosophy]. In this work, the rationalist logic of Cohen is transformed into a mystic of the Logos, in other words, a pure metaphysics.

Neo-Kantianism's autodissolution was remarkable. The faith in the creative force of reason, in its autonomy over reality, corresponded to the florescence of liberalism. At this time, the activity of each individual, guided by his autonomous reason, seemed to guarantee the good of society as a whole; the wills of individuals appeared to be harmonized by the ordering power of a superior rationality without necessitating the elaboration of any plan for the normal functioning of economy and society. But the real-world foundations of this faith had for a long time been disappearing. Repeated economic crises compromised these foundations further and further. Philosophy would not continue in the path traced out for it by neo-Kantianism. Even during the time of the early successes of neo-Kantianism, a reaction was beginning to manifest itself; Dilthey's *Introduction to the Human Sciences* had appeared in 1883, and in 1894 Windelband delivered his famous rectoral address "Geschichte und Naturwissenschaft" [History and Natural Science]. These works were an expression of bourgeois philosophy's attempt to conceptualize the historical world and reestablish the contact with the real world that it had lost. From the outset, this attempt was based on the foundations of transcendental idealism itself, and this period was marked by the rise of the Baden School.

Windelband, Rickert, Lask

The efforts made by Windelband (1848–1915) in every domain—*Präludien* (1884)[Preludes], *Die Erneuerung des Hegelianismus* (1910) [The Renaissance of Hegelianism], *Introduction to Philosophy* (1914)—were developed and systematized by Rickert (born in 1863): *Der Gegenstand der Erkenntnis* (1892) [The Object of Knowledge], *The Limits of Concept Formation in Natural Science* (1896), *Die Philosophie des Lebens* (1920) [*The Philosophy of Life*], and *System der Philosophie* (1921) [Systems of Philosophy].

The validity of using mathematical science as a model for concepts of philosophical truth, it was recognized, is limited: the cultural sciences (philosophy included) are constructed independently from them. The philosophers of this school created a fundamental division between two groups of sciences, a division that would remain dominant for decades to come. The physical sciences are "nomothetic," while the cultural sciences are "idiographic." The former study general laws, while the latter study concrete historical particulars. The concrete historical particulars, however, are only considered in relation to the general and perpetual values of culture. History thus loses its realist character and is moved instead to a purely spiritual and idealistic sphere; it is only a matter of eternal values whose realization is abetted or impeded by historical events. This alone seems to give history a meaning that it does not possess in reality. According Rickert, one cannot speak of the laws of history in the same way one speaks of the laws of science; in fact, history appears much too superior to be explained by laws. It is easy to see that this philosophy is directly opposed to historical materialism, and one might easily speculate that one of the reasons for the success of this philosophy was the desire of certain circles of intellectuals to oppose an idealist philosophy of history to the tradition of Marxism that was beginning to gain ground. Reality is transformed into a system of values. To judge, it then follows, is to take a position vis-à-vis values, and the truth is a value that one must accept. True knowledge goes beyond facticity to grasp eternal values that do not "exist" but "valuate" in an eternal domain of meaning. Acutely aware that this new domain of history and meaning would break open the traditional forms of transcendental philosophy, Emil Lask (1875–1915) sought to create a new logic of philosophy: *Die Logik der Philosophie und die Kategorienlehre* (1911) [The Logic of Philosophy and the Doctrine of Categories], and *Die Lehre vom Urteil* (1912) [The Theory of Judgment]. If transcendental philosophy aims to understand itself correctly, it must jettison the categories of traditional logic, because these categories correspond only to the existence of reality; they are incapable of understanding the existence of values. Whereas Lask proposed to create a new system of categories to replace the traditional system, the historicity of concepts appeared to be the culmination of philosophy, moving philosophy in the direction of a relativity of all systems of categories. Lask, who died in the Great War, was not able to pursue his radical insights.

Despite its transcendental moving of history into the philosophy of values, the Baden School's way of conceiving history had an enormous influence. German bourgeois sociology owes to this school its most important methodological innovations. Its main representative, Max Weber (1864–1920), remained influenced by Rickert until his death; the same holds true for the cultural philosophy and the social history of Ernst Troeltsch (1865–1923). The influence of the Baden School spread even beyond the circles of bourgeois sociology. At the center of this school, one finds researchers such as Georg Lukács, who opposed to the objective and neutral science of Max Weber a Marxist sociology conceived of as a motor of revolutionary practice.

The Renaissance of the New Hegelianism

The path that led from the renaissance of Kant to that of Hegel was marked by two principal tendencies: the reaction against the autonomous subjectivity of pure reason and a certain manner of conceiving the historical world. The neo-Hegelianism inaugurated by Windelband himself never produced any original works. Its merits reside instead in the domains of the history of idealist philosophy and Hegelian philology. Richard Kroner's study, *Von Kant bis Hegel* (1921–24) [From Kant to Hegel], is without a doubt one of the best analyses of the development of German idealism from the point of view of idealist philosophy. We are indebted to Georg Lasson for the new and comprehensive critical edition of Hegel's works, which appeared in 1911 and contains numerous texts never published, completed and refined using Hegel's manuscripts. The comprehensive monographs on Hegel by Nicolai Hartmann (1929) and Theodor Haering (1929) provide us with an understanding of Hegel still more profound than that of the old Hegelian School. The attempts at a new elaboration of Hegelian thought (for example, in the cultural philosophy of Kroner and Hans Freyer) demonstrate that the most fertile ground for a true Hegelian renaissance was not, in fact, provided by bourgeois philosophy. The real results of Hegelian philosophy are only preserved today in Marxist theory. Georg Lukács, in his famous work *History and Class Consciousness* (1923), draws out the most extreme implications of Hegelian philosophy from a Marxist point of view. (In philosophy, everything that is extreme takes on an idealist character rather than a materialist one.) I might add that in France, Hegel is considered first and foremost as the philosopher who divinized the state, but I hold this view to be too narrow. Hegel, it is true, said that the rational state that reflects the idea of philosophy, in other words, the community that confers justice in the interest of all, is God on earth. It is possible that he made an error with regard to the Prussian state of his time—this is without a shadow of a doubt— which he interpreted in much too positive of a light. This was not the fault of Hegel as dialectician, however, but Hegel as a Prussian citizen.

2. Phenomenology

Everything we understand today by the term "phenomenology" is nothing but a mixture of disparate philosophical tendencies that no longer have anything in common with the philosophy of Husserl, the founder of the phenomenological school. Since the year 1900, phenomenology has undergone a considerable transformation. Because divergent tendencies have dominated within the school, phenomenology's influence in the domain of ideology has by no means been uniform. The principal stages of phenomenology's development are marked by the publication dates of Husserl's various works (born in 1859): *Logical Investigations* (1900–1901 [first edition]), "Philosophy as Rigorous Science" (1913 [revised version]), *Ideas: General Introduction to Pure Phenomenology* (1913), *Formal and Transcendental Logic* (1929), and *Cartesian Meditations* (1931).

At the outset, phenomenology figured in the general reaction against positivism. In the *Logical Investigations* Husserl attacked the introduction of "psychologism" in logic by establishing the crucial distinction between the psychic experience that accompanies all judgments and the signification imposed by these judgments. Pure logic only deals with the latter significations, which form an ideal sphere of meanings and relationships between meanings, unaffected by time, and in which legitimacy manifests itself everywhere a priori. The decisive innovation of Husserl's *Logical Investigations* lies in its theory of intuition. Up to this point philosophy only recognized sensory intuition (pure, empirical sensation); Husserl enlarged the domain of intuition by recognizing "nonsensory" intuition as well, the intuition of ideal significations and their relationships. Through "nonsensory" or "eidetic intuition," one perceives clearly the categories and the categorical laws of being in itself, independent of empirical determination; in other words, the universal ideas of concrete facts. This theory, known as the "intuition of essences," would later become one of the most discussed aspects of phenomenology. In its original intention, it bore no relationship either with a mystical theory of knowledge or with the speculation of a metaphysical domain of ideas.

Phenomenology became one of the most influential currents in German philosophy. Its new pathos issued from its strict pretension to penetrate to the things themselves, to jettison all false theories in favor of the facts as they present themselves, as simple phenomena. Phenomenology permitted one to interrogate these phenomena as to what they said about their Logos ("phenomen"-"ology"). The massive influence of the *Logical Investigations* came only with the second edition (1913), at a time when Husserl himself had already transformed phenomenology into a transcendental science of essences (*Ideas*). To the world of facts, Husserl systematically added a world of essences, the study of which constituted the foundation of pure phenomenology considered as the fundamental a priori science of all other sciences. Simultaneously, this science of essences found its direction and its transcendental justification through the "phenomenological reduction." This reduction, which recalls the Cartesian method of the *Meditations*, is the suspension of the everyday habits involved in the perception and comprehension of the world, the suspension of faith in the existence of reality. The bracketing of reality opens the path toward the only absolutely certain foundation of philosophy: the transcendental subjectivity of "pure ego" in which the world constitutes itself as it is. The two principal trajectories, briefly stated, in which phenomenology developed are: the transcendental strain and the objective-metaphysical strain. These trajectories played very different roles in the preparation of the new ideology of monopoly capitalism.

1. Transcendental phenomenology had hardly been developed by Husserl himself when he transformed it into a "constitutive" phenomenology. This phenomenology went well beyond the transcendental philosophy of Kant and aimed to bring to light nothing less than the origins of the world along with the a priori structures of being. In so far as it maintains a universal justification of all theory based on the pure reason of consciousness in general, it continues to work today against the subordination of theory to extrarational suppositions. Though now fractured, this philosophy is still connected to progressive moments of liberal consciousness and belongs properly to the preracist era.

2. The case of objective-metaphysical phenomenology is completely different. The exploitation of the intuition of essences in the service of an intuitionist metaphysics suppresses the critical and rationalist tendencies of phenomenology. The total subordination of reason to metaphysical reality (essentially emotive and irrational) prepares the way for racist ideology.

Max Scheler

Max Scheler (1873–1928) began as a disciple of R. Eucken (*Die transzendentale und die psychologische Methode* (1900)[3] [The Transcendental and Psychological Method]). Then, relatively independently of Husserl, Scheler moved in the direction of phenomenology (*Formalism of Ethics and Non-Formal Ethics of Values* [1913–14]). He next developed a system of philosophy founded on the general bases of sociology, psychology, and biology: *Vom Umsturz der Werte* (1919) [The Revolution of Values], *On the Eternal in Man* (1921), *The Nature of Sympathy* (1923), *Die Wissenformen und die Gesellschaft* (1926) [The Forms of Knowledge and Society], *Man's Place in Nature* (1928), and *Schriften aus dem Nachlaß* [Posthumous Works]. Scheler led the most energetic philosophical attack against the "ratio": he privileged the emotional dimensions of human being (feelings and values) over the "ratio" as the real foundations of knowledge. These values are grouped in a complete system, distinct from man, in a fixed hierarchy. Scheler's metaphysics, however, is often interrupted and suspended by sociological and anthropological forays. The introduction of the historical world, to which Scheler's philosophy remained open (Scheler is one of the richest and most lively influences in contemporary German philosophy), rendered the system mutable. Scheler arrived at an understanding of mind in its reciprocal relationships with the vital, political, and economic spheres. In his anthropology, mind is, in the end, only a thin, superior layer of vital and organic being. But nowhere was the philosophical concretion achieved by Scheler extended to the real and material history of man; it remained within the framework of a metaphysics of man in general.

As Scheler's successor, Nicolai Hartmann constructed an ethics of values (*Ethics* [1926]). Hartmann, who began as a neo-Kantian, moved quickly in the direction of an objective ontology (*Grundzüge einer Metaphysik der Erkenntnis* [1921] [Metaphysics of Knowledge]), which he sought to link up to a critical idealism. His alleged independence from all previous suppositions (he rejected idealism, realism, metaphysics, and transcendental philosophy) was never more than a superficial realism (*Das Problem des geistigen Seins* (1933) [The Problem of Spiritual Reality]).

Martin Heidegger

In Heidegger's philosophy, phenomenology aims, through a sudden turnabout, to regain true human facticity. Philosophy was supposed to become part of human praxis again. It should be noted that phenomenology's radical move into the realm of facticity would, on the one hand, soon be redirected toward the transcendental and, on the other hand, lead immediately to the political ideology of racist Germany. Already in Heidegger's principal work, *Being and Time* (1927), the radical motifs are submerged beneath the transcendental currents. In his more recent works, pure metaphysics absorbs all other problems:

The Essence of Reasons (1929), *Kant and the Problem of Metaphysics* (1929), and "What is Metaphysics?" (1929). In his most recent publications, Heidegger places himself firmly in the camp of "political existentialism"; he has become a spokesman for the Third Reich.

For Heidegger, metaphysics, in its ancient form of ontology, that is to say, as a theory of being in itself and in its entirety, is the first and ultimate task of philosophy. However (and here Heidgger follows in the direction first delineated by Husserl), being exists only in the understanding of man. Thus, before performing ontology, it is first necessary to analyze human being. Grasping human being, for Heidegger, is not a matter of pure consciousness of the transcendental "ego" as in Husserl, but one of concrete man in his facticity. Therefore, it is not the "ego cogito"—the pure abstraction that dominated philosophy from Descartes until Hegel—that serves as the foundation for philosophy, but real human existence such as it is found in its real history. Here Heidegger distinguishes himself from Husserl; phenomenology becomes a "hermeneutic" of human existence known as "existential analytics." What Heidegger proposed as a concrete analysis of human existence and its modes of being constitutes one of the most fertile avenues of the new philosophy. It is here that the influence of Dilthey's philosophical research is manifestly present.

Here I will say a few words about the work of Wilhem Dilthey (1833–1911). His works became available in the period from 1883 to 1910 but their true worth was not recognized until after the war (*Gesammelte Schriften* (1914) [Complete Works]). Dilthey's philosophy represents the highest point that bourgeois thought was able to reach in terms of the nature and structures of history. Dilthey employed his insightful analyses of man and the historical world to combat positivistic and dogmatic metaphysics. He recognized clearly the dangers inherent in transcendental philosophy: its propensity for turning the philosophy of concrete man away from man's real affairs and concerns. If, in his later works, he undertook a reconstruction of philosophy based on the foundations of concrete life, this reinterpretation of philosophy should in no way be identified with irrationalist misconceptions. Dilthey's conception of life is precisely the critical weapon he uses against absolute and eternal categories. He undermines these categories and ossified systems by revealing their true functions in history.

Heidegger sought to develop Dilthey's project. The new direction signaled by Heidegger's ontology is his attempt at a universal interpretation of being *in time.* Here we witness a decisive abandonment of the traditional categories of bourgeois thought. Up to this point, the entirety of metaphysics sought to explain being conceptually and within the Logos (as the end result in Hegel's philosophy, ontology becomes logic). According to Heidegger, it is not the Logos but time that constitutes the original horizon in which one finds and understands being. Heidegger aims to renew onto*logie* as onto*chronie*. In the same vein, he interprets human being in its temporal structures, in its relationships with time. The real temporality of human being is its historicity. Heidegger understands man as essentially historical; he considers the actual possibilities of the human being and the conditions of his realization as determined by history. However, opposed to this tendency toward historicity in his philosophy there is also a transcendental trajectory necessitated by the very idea of phenomenology and ontology. Heidegger's "existential" analytic distorts concrete man and orients itself toward human existence *in general*, in the neutrality of its ontological essence. Heidegger's philosophy is wedded to the idea of an authentic existence that is realized through a firm willingness to die for one's own possibilities. It is here that Heidegger's existential analytic is transformed into a politics of heroic, racist realism. Pure *consciousness* as a residue of the destruction of the world in Husserl becomes, with Heidegger, pure human *existence*, human existence in its transcendental purity. The original inclination toward historicity is paralyzed; history is transported into human existence, it even becomes identical with real existence. In the end, man has no other choice but to accept and appropriate the historical situation in which he finds himself. Since the material sphere remains entirely outside of this philosophy and can in no case serve as a criteria for real existence, man, isolated within himself, becomes easy prey for any real power, that, by referring to the actual situation as the true historical situation, demands of man total submission to its domination. The characteristics of authentic existence—the resoluteness toward death, the decision, the risking of life, and the acceptance of destiny—are severed from all relations to the real misery and the real happiness of mankind and from all relations to the reasonable ends of humanity. In this abstract form, these characteristics become the fundamental categories of the racist worldview.

3. The Dissolution of Bourgeois Philosophy into Heroic, Racist Realism

The transformation of contemporary German philosophy began with the restitution of philosophy as an exact science, following the example of mathematics, in other words, with an extreme rationalism. But the more the faith in liberalism adjoined to this conception was undermined, the more the irrationalist and naturalistic currents within it came to the fore. As was the case for *society as a whole*, the progressive forces and groups within this movement backed down in the face of monopoly capitalism in its dictatorial phase. Thus, the development of philosophy did not lead to the renaissance of *philosophy*, but to its further submission to economic and social forces. The destruction of the absolute ratio and the suspension of the traditional categories of bourgeois thought were not achieved through the progression toward the nature and structures of history, but through the return to the prehistoric domain of organic nature (life, race, blood, spirit). The forces of this reactionary irrationalism are multiple. "The philosophy of life" (that, with Nietzsche and particularly with Bergson, incorporated a critique of contemporary society) now wages an attack against all critical and progressive tendencies. Ludwig Klages (*Der Geist als Widersacher der Seele* (1929–33) [Spirit as Antagonist of the Soul]) interprets spirit as the deterioration of life as a whole that, in the obscurity of blood and instincts, possesses its own truth. Oswald Spengler, who, in his *Decline of the West* (1918–22), had already derationalized the categories of Hegel's philosophy of history, has become in his more recent works (*Man and Technics* [1931] and *The Hour of Decision* [1933]) the prophet of brutal heroism and the enemy of progress and culture. Power for power's sake, movement for movement's sake, war for war's sake—with such phrases as these he legitimates the politics of social and economic imperialism.

Thus has the principal trajectory in German philosophy undergone a complete change of tack: the ratio abandoned its pretense to guide and now aligns itself with extrarational forces. "Reality does not let itself be known [*connaître*], it only lets itself be acknowledged [*reconnaître*]." In this phrase, which signals not only the abandonment of philosophy but all theory as well, the new ideology is powerfully present (Heinrich Forsthoff, *Das Ende der humanistischen Illusion* [1933] [The End of the Humanist Illusion]). The truth of thought and action is rendered dependent on conditions not previously subject to the social practices of man (race, blood, soil, nationality, etc.). The result is a total destruction of the dialectical relationships between theory and practice: theory enters into the service of a practice predestined to transfigure or conceal it. The discovery of existential analysis that the actions and dispositions, simultaneously heroic and humble, of the spirit are the authentic realization of human being is now given a fixed social meaning. The resoluteness, sacrifice, and humility necessary in order to maintain an inhuman social practice and to deny an authentic human practice can be advocated by the dominant classes only as attitudes without aim or value. The human being becomes a simple means whose end is secondary; "on the edge of absurdity" man finds his true reality (Ernst Jünger, *Der Arbeiter* (1932) [The Worker]).

Insofar as philosophy has yet to be fully converted into an ideology of monopoly capitalism, there remains only one possibility (apart from Marxist tendencies): the return to the interiority of man and his isolation, as well as a return to "communication" among isolated individuals. This is the path followed in the philosophy of Karl Jaspers. The price paid for this return, in Jaspers's philosophy, is a blindness to the real forces and sorrows of our time. At best he offers us an aristocratic psychology of a delicate and profound mind (*Philosophy*, 1932).

We will now move on to a brief summary of the main currents of this new philosophy-turned-politics that designates itself as "heroic-racist realism." The chairs of the German universities have been turned over to them almost without exception. Its main advocates are Ernst Krieck (first at Frankfurt and now as successor to Rickert at Heidelberg) and Alfred Bäumler (Berlin).

1. In anthropology, an irrational "homo animal politicum" has re-placed the rational "homo animal": a being who acts politically and for whom the goal is rational, but the question of "why," the purpose of his actions is secondary (Bäumler [*Männerbund und Wissenschaft* (Masculine Association and Science)] (1934), pp. 108 and 118). In place of the preracist value systems of Scheler and Hartmann, we now find a hierarchy of imperialistic values in which heroism, power, demonism, and sacrifice are deemed superior.

Ernst Jünger and Alfred Rosenberg

2. In epistemology and metaphysics we find on the primary agenda, on the one hand, a rejection of German idealism (from Kant through Hegel) as a rational humanist philosophy and, on the other hand, a rejection of materialism as a Marxist degeneration of the true values of life. The supposed realism that results is actually a mysticism of certain natural and national powers in which race, nation, blood, and soil appear as though they were handed down by God, as if they were eternal and sacred facts (Ernst Krieck in his review ["Volk in Werden" ("Volk in Development")]).

3. In the philosophy of the state and the philosophy of right, the liberal doctrine of the state of the rule of law and reason is replaced by the doctrine of the total state. Considered as an ensemble of existential relations, the state is placed above all rational critique and above all legal norms. It is authorized to mobilize constantly, for its own ends, the entire citizenry and to accept their sacrifices, even though it itself does not offer a reciprocal "terrestre."[4] The founder of this doctrine is the famous state jurist Carl Schmitt. (Already before him, in 1931, the writer Ernst Jünger had proposed the term "total mobilization." He advocated a constant mobilization of the civilian population akin to military mobilization and preparation.) Law is understood as the expression of natural forces and the particularities of the people, and it is, consequently, limited to a racist and nationalistic point of view.

4. In psychology, "Gestalt" theory—which, in contrast to mechanistic theory, teaches that the perceived world is constructed through indivisible, primordial forms (Wolfgang Köhler and Max Wertheimer)—is utilized in order to forestall all critical and historical analysis. As a result, static forms are constructed that, abstracted from the flux and reflux of movement, are not subject to historical change. A fixed historical form is extracted from its developmental course and sanctioned in its extant state (Jünger, *Der Arbeiter* [The Worker]).

Heidegger's Politics

An Interview

Frederick Olafson: Professor Marcuse, you are very widely known as a social philosopher and a Marxist; but I think there are relatively few who know that Martin Heidegger and his philosophy played a considerable role in your intellectual career. Perhaps we could begin by just laying out the basic facts about that contact with Heidegger and with his philosophy.

Herbert Marcuse: Here are the basic facts—I read *Sein und Zeit* when it came out in 1927 and after having read it I decided to go back to Freiburg (where I had received my PhD in 1922) in order to work with Heidegger. I stayed in Freiburg and worked with Heidegger until December 1932, when I left Germany a few days before Hitler's ascent to power, and that ended the personal relationship. I saw Heidegger again after the war, I think in 1946–47, in the Black Forest where he has his little house. We had a talk, which was not exactly very friendly and very positive, there was an exchange of letters, and since that time there has not been any communication between us.

Olafson: Would it be fair to say that during the time you were in Freiburg you accepted the principle theses of *Being and Time* and that you were, in some sense, at that time, a Heideggerian? Or were there major qualifications and reservations even then?

Marcuse: I must say frankly that during this time, let's say from 1928 to 1932, there were relatively few reservations and relatively few criticisms on my part. I would rather say on *our* part, because Heidegger at that time was not a personal problem, not even philosophically, but a problem of a large part of the generation that studied in Germany after the first World War. We saw in Heidegger what we had first seen in Husserl, a new beginning, the first radical attempt to put philosophy on really concrete foundations—philosophy concerned with human existence, the human condition, and not with merely abstract ideas and principles. That certainly I shared with a relatively large number of my generation, and needless to say, the disappointment with this philosophy eventually came—I think it began in the early thirties. But we re-examined Heidegger thoroughly only after his association with Nazism had become known.

Olafson: What did you make at that stage of the social aspect of Heidegger's philosophy—its implications for political and social life and action? Were you yourself interested in those at that stage, did you perceive them in Heidegger's thought?

Marcuse: I was very much interested in it during that stage, at the same time I wrote articles of Marxist analysis for the theoretical organ of the German Socialists, *Die Gesellschaft.* So I certainly was interested, and I first, like all the others, believed there could be some combination between existentialism and Marxism, precisely because of their insistence on concrete analysis of actual human existence, human beings, and their world. But I soon realized that Heidegger's concreteness was to a great extent a phony, a false concreteness, and that in fact his philosophy was just as abstract and just as removed from reality, even avoiding reality, as the philosophies which at that time had dominated German universities, namely a rather dry brand of neo-Kantianism, neo-Hegelianism, neo-Idealism, but also positivism.

Olafson: How did he respond to the hopes that you had for some kind of fruitful integration of his philosophy with, let us say, a Marxist social philosophy?

Marcuse: He didn't respond. You know as far as I can say, it is today still open to question whether Heidegger ever really read Marx, whether Heidegger ever read Lukács, as Lucien Goldmann maintains. I tend not to believe it. He may have had a look at Marx after or during the Second World War, but I don't think that he in any way studied Marx.

Olafson: There are some positive remarks about Marx in Heidegger's writing, indicating that he was not at all . . .

Marcuse: That's interesting. I know of only one: the *Letter on Humanism.*

Olafson: Yes.

Marcuse: Where he says that Marx's view of history exceeds all other views. That is the only remark. I know the *Letter* was written under the French occupation after the World War, one didn't know yet how things would go, so I don't give much weight to this remark.

Olafson: More generally, how do you view the importance of phenomenological and ontological analyses of the kind that Heidegger offered in *Being and Time*, their importance I mean, for purposes of social analysis? You've made it clear that Heidegger himself was not interested in developing them in that direction. Do you think that they might have had uses beyond those that he was interested in?

Marcuse: In my first article ("Contribution[s] to a Phenomenology of Historical Materialism," 1928), I myself tried to combine existentialism and Marxism. Sartre's *Being and Nothingness* is such an attempt on a much larger scale. But to the degree to which Sartre turned to Marxism, he surpassed his existentialist writings and finally dissociated himself from them. Even he did not succeed in reconciling Marx and Heidegger. As to Heidegger himself, he seems to use his existential analysis to get away from the social reality rather than into it.

Olafson: You see these pretty much dropping out of the work of people who have perhaps begun with ontology and phenomenology, but have gone on to . . .

Marcuse: Yes.

Olafson: To Marxism. You don't see a continuing role for that kind of . . .

Marcuse: I don't think so. You see, I said at the beginning, I spoke about the false concreteness of Heidegger. If you look at his principle concepts (I will use German terms because I am still not familiar with the English translation), *Dasein, das Man, Sein, Seiendes, Existenz*, they are "bad" abstracts in the sense that they are not conceptual vehicles to comprehend the real concreteness in the apparent one. They lead away. For example, *Dasein* is for Heidegger a sociologically and even biologically "neutral" category (sex differences don't exist!); the *Frage nach dem Sein* remains the ever unanswered but ever repeated question; the distinction between fear and anxiety tends to transform very real fear into pervasive and vague anxiety. Even his at first glance most concrete existential category, death, is recognized as the most inexorable brute fact only to be made into an insurpassable *possibility*. Heidegger's existentialism is indeed a transcendental idealism compared with which Husserl's last writings (and even his *Logical Investigations*) seem saturated with historical concreteness.

Olafson: Does that leave social theorists then with materialism or behaviorism as some kind of working theory of human nature? I take it that both Heidegger and Sartre have been attempting to resist philosophies of that kind. Does the dropping out of phenomenological and ontological elements in social theory mean an acceptance, de facto, of behaviorism?

Marcuse: No, it does not. It depends entirely on what is meant by ontology. If there is an ontology which, in spite of its stress on historicity, neglects history, throws out history, and returns to static transcendental concepts, I would say this philosophy cannot provide a conceptual basis for social and political theory.

Olafson: Let me take you up on that reference to history. This is one of the things that Heidegger interested himself in quite considerably and there are at least two chapters in *Being and Time* that deal with history. Here of course the treatment is in terms of what Heidegger called historicity, or historicality, which means that the theme is treated in terms of a certain structure of individual (primarily individual) human existence, that is to say the individual's relationship to his own past, the way he places himself in a tradition, the way he modifies that tradition at the same time as he takes it over. Does that work seem to you to have, a lasting value, to have an element of concreteness?

Marcuse: I would see in his concept of historicity the same false or fake concreteness because actually none of the concrete material and cultural, none of the concrete social and political, conditions which make history have any place in *Being and Time*. History too is subjected to neutralization. He makes it into an existential category which is rather immune against the specific material and mental conditions which make up the course of history. There may be one exception: Heidegger's late concern (one might say: preoccupation) with technology and technics. The *Frage nach dem Sein* recedes before the *Frage nach der Technik*. I admit that much of these writings I do not understand. More than before, it sounds as if our world can only be comprehended in the German language (though a strange and torturous one). I have the impression that Heidegger's concepts of technology and technics are the last in the long series of neutralizations: they are treated as "forces in-themselves," removed from the context of power relations in which they are constituted and which determine their use and their function. They are reified, hypostatized as Fate.

Olafson: Might he not have used the notion of historicity as a structure of personal existence in a different way? Isn't it important for a social theory to show how an individual situates himself in a certain society, in a certain tradition? Isn't it important that there be a characterization of that situation that is not just given at the level of relatively impersonal forces and tendencies, but that shows how the individual ties into those forces and tendencies?

Marcuse: There most certainly is a need for such an analysis, but that is precisely where the concrete conditions of history come in. How does the individual situate himself and see himself in capitalism—at a certain stage of capitalism, under socialism, as a member of this or that class, and so on? This entire dimension is absent. To be sure, *Dasein* is constituted in historicity, but Heidegger focuses on individuals purged of the hidden and not so hidden injuries of their class, their work, their recreation, purged of the injuries they suffer from their society. There is no trace of the daily rebellion, of the striving for liberation. The *Man* (the anonymous anyone) is no substitute for the social reality.

Olafson: Heidegger sees individual human beings as concerned above all with the prospect of their individual death, and this supersedes all the kinds of concrete social considerations that you have mentioned. Do you think that that emphasis and that lack of interest in the concrete and the social comes out of his theological training or bent of mind?

Marcuse: It may well be that his very thorough theological training has something to do with it. In any case, it is very good that you bring up the tremendous importance the notion of death has in his philosophy, because I believe that is a very good starting point for at least briefly discussing the famous question of whether Heidegger's Nazism was already noticeable in his philosophy prior to 1933. Now, from personal experience I can tell you that neither in his lectures, nor in his seminars, nor personally, was there any hint of his sympathies for Nazism. In fact, politics were never discussed—and to the very end he spoke very highly of the two Jews to whom he dedicated his books, Edmund Husserl and Max Scheler. So his openly declared Nazism came as a complete surprise to us. From that point on, of course, we asked ourselves the question; did we overlook indications and anticipations in *Being and Time* and the related writings? And we made one interesting observation, ex-post (I want to stress that, ex-post, it is easy to make this observation): If you look at his view of human existence, of being-in-the-world, you will find a highly repressive, highly oppressive interpretation. I have just today gone again through the table of contents of *Being and Time*, and had a look at the main categories in which he sees the essential characteristics of existence or *Dasein*. I can just read them to you and you will see what I mean: "idle talk, curiosity, ambiguity, falling and being-thrown into, concern, being-toward-death, anxiety, dread, boredom" and so on. Now this gives a picture which plays well on the fears and frustrations of men and women in a repressive society—a joyless existence: overshadowed by death and anxiety; human material for the authoritarian personality. It is for example highly characteristic that love is absent from *Being and Time*—the only place where it appears is in a footnote in a theological context together with faith, sin, and remorse. I see now in this philosophy, ex-post, a very powerful devaluation of life, a derogation of joy, of sensuousness, fulfillment. And we may have had the feeling of it at that time, but it became clear only after Heidegger's association to Nazism became known.

Olafson: Do you think that Heidegger as a man was simply politically naive? Do you think he understood the implications of his collaboration with the Nazi Party as Rector of the University of Freiburg?

Marcuse: Well, I can speak rather authoritatively because I discussed it with him after the war. In order to prepare my answer, let me first read the statement which he made, I quote literally: "Let not principles and ideas rule your being. Today, and in the future, only the *Führer* himself is German reality and its law." These were Heidegger's own words in November 1933. This is a man who professed that he was the heir of the great tradition of Western philosophy of Kant, Hegel, and so on—all this is now discarded, norms, principles, ideas are obsolete when the *Führer* lays down the law and defines reality—the German reality. I talked with him about that several times and he admitted it was an "error"; he misjudged Hitler and Nazism—to which I want to add two things, first, that is one of the errors a philosopher is not allowed to commit. He certainly can and does commit many, many mistakes but this is not an error and this is not a mistake, this is actually the betrayal of philosophy as such, and of everything philosophy stands for. Secondly, he admitted, as I said, it was a mistake—but there he left the matter. He refused (and I think that somehow I find this rather sympathetic), he refused any attempt to deny it or to declare it an aberration, or I don't know what, because he did not want to be in the same category, as he said, with all those of his colleagues who suddenly didn't remember any more that they taught under the Nazis, that they ever supported the Nazis, and declared that actually they had always been non-Nazi. Now, in the case of Heidegger, as far as I know, he gave up any open identification with Nazism I think in 1935 or 1936. He was not Rector of the University any more. In other words, from that time on he withdrew, but to me this in no way simply cancels the statement he made. In my view, it is irrelevant when and why he withdrew his enthusiastic support of the Nazi regime—decisive and relevant is the brute fact that he made the statement just quoted, that he idolized Hitler, and that he exhorted his students to do the same. If, "today and in the future," only the *Führer* himself is "German reality and its law," then the only philosophy that remains is the philosophy of abdication, surrender.

Olafson: In his discussions with you did he give any indication of his reasons for withdrawing, or what he believed the "mistake" of Nazism to be? I'm wondering in particular if it was motivated by anything that one would call a moral consideration, or . . .

Marcuse: In fact, I remember he never did. No, he never did. It certainly wasn't anti-Semitism. That I remember. But he never did, you are quite right. I think I do understand now why he turned against the pre-Hitler democracy of the Weimar Republic—because life under the Weimar Republic certainly in no way conformed to his existential categories: the struggle between capitalism and socialism, waged almost daily on the streets, at the work place, with violence and with the intellect, the outburst of a radically rebellious literature and art— this entire world, "existential" throughout, lies outside his existentialism.

Olafson: There's one important concept in *Being and Time* which we haven't alluded to, and that is the concept of authenticity or *Eigentlichkeit*, a concept that has known a wide popularity, I guess, both before and after Heidegger, implying a certain false relationship to oneself, and thereby a certain false relationship to one's fellow men and I suppose to one's society. Does this strike you as a concept, in Heidegger's development of it, that has any continuing utility?

Marcuse: It is an interesting concept. Again, if I remember how he actually defines authenticity, the same categories come to my mind, which I would call rather oppressive and repressive categories. What is authenticity? Mainly, if I remember correctly, and please correct me if I don't, the withdrawal from the entire world of the others, *Das Man*, I don't know what the English translation is . . .

Olafson: The anonymous anyone.

Marcuse: Authenticity would then mean the return to oneself, to one's inner-most freedom, and, out of this inwardness, to decide, to determine every phase, every situation, every moment of one's existence. And the very real obstacles to this autonomy? The content, the aim, the What of the decision? Here too, the methodical "neutralization": the social, empirical context of the decision and of its consequences is "bracketed." The main thing is to decide and to act according to your decision. Whether or not the decision is in itself, and in its goals morally and humanly positive or not, is of minor importance.

Olafson: There is another side to the concept—I agree with what you have been saying about this side of it—but there's another side in which Heidegger treats inauthenticity as a kind of deep attempt that human beings make to present themselves to themselves in a form that suppresses or blocks out the element of decision, the element of responsibility for themselves, that incorporates them into some kind of larger, whether it be physical or social, entity, and thus relieves them of the necessity for decision. Now that bears (it seems to me, perhaps I am wrong) some analogy to things that you have had to say about tendencies in modern technological society.

Marcuse: Yes, I certainly wouldn't deny that authenticity, in a less oppressive sense, is becoming increasingly difficult in the advanced society of today, but it seems to me that even in the positive sense, authenticity is overshadowed by death, by the entire interpretation of existence as being toward death, and the incorporation of death into every hour and every minute of your life. This again I see as a highly oppressive notion, which somehow serves well to justify the emphasis of facism and nazism on sacrifice, sacrifice *per se*, as an end-in-itself. I think there is a famous phrase by Ernst Jünger, the Nazi writer, who speaks of the necessity of sacrifice *"am Rande des Nichts oder am Rande des Abgrunds"*—"on the edge of the abyss, or on the edge of nothingness." In other words a sacrifice that is good because it is a sacrifice, and because it is freely chosen, or allegedly freely chosen, by the individual. Heidegger's notion recalls the battle cry of the fascist Futurists: *Eviva la Muerte*.

Olafson: You mentioned Sartre's name a while ago, and I'd like to turn now, if I may, to the relationship between Heidegger and Sartre. As you yourself have pointed out, I think, on occasion—Sartre's *Being and Nothingness* is very heavily dependent upon Heidegger's *Being and Time* as, of course, it is upon other works in the German tradition, like *The Phenomenology of Mind*. Heidegger, on the other hand, has from the standpoint of his latter thought, repudiated any suggestion of common ground between these two philosophies, or these two statements. And that, of course, has been contested by others. How do you see this problem of the relationship between Heidegger and Sartre, and the relationship of Heidegger to the whole wider phenomenon of existentialism in the post-war period?

Marcuse: Well, it is a large question and I can only answer a small part of it. I believe there is a common ground between Sartre's early work and Heidegger, namely the existential analysis, but there the common ground ends. I would do injustice to Sartre if I would prolong it beyond that point. Even *L'Etre et le Néant* is already much more concrete than Heidegger ever was. Erotic relationships, love, hatred, all this—the body, not simply as abstract phenomenological object but the body as it is sensuously experienced, plays a considerable role in Sartre—all this is miles away from Heidegger's own analysis, and, as Sartre developed his philosophy, he surpassed the elements that still linked him to existentialism and worked out a Marxist philosophy and analysis.

Olafson: Doesn't the *Critique of Dialectical Reason* still strike you as a very idiosyncratic version of Marxism still marked importantly by the earlier thought?

Marcuse: It is important, and again it contains elements of truth, but I don't know whether you can really incorporate them into his earlier work, and his later work I just haven't followed adequately, so I wouldn't know.

Olafson: The interesting question that arises of course in connection with that is what Heidegger's place would be in the history of Western philosophy so conceived, because it has seemed, as you were saying, to many that *Being and Time* was a final turn on the transcendental screw, as it were, and that he would stand then in the same tradition as the people that he seems to be criticizing so trenchantly.

Marcuse: In the specific context of the history of philosophy, this may be true. In the larger political context, one may say that German Idealism comes to an end with the construction of the Nazi state. To quote Carl Schmitt: "On January 30, 1933, Hegel died."

Olafson: And yet Heidegger's philosophy enjoyed enormous prestige in Germany in the post-war period. I think that is beginning to slack off a bit . . .

Marcuse: True.

Olafson: . . . or has been for the last decade, and I suppose it was more the later philosophy than the philosophy of *Being and Time* that formed the basis for that renaissance of interest in Heidegger. Do you have any impressions of his influence on German intellectual life in the post-war period?

Marcuse: I only know, as you said, that by now it has been reduced considerably. There was a great interest in Heidegger for quite some time after the war, and I think you are right, it was mainly the late work and not the early work.

Olafson: Theodor Adorno, a former colleague of yours, has characterized that influence in highly critical terms.

Marcuse: Yes.

Olafson: As a glorification of the principle of heteronomy, which I take to mean essentially the principle of external authority of some kind. If that is true then there is a kind of paradox in the fact that a philosophy of will and self-assertion, of authenticity, has turned around into an ideological basis for an essentially heteronomous and authoritarian social orientation.

Marcuse: Yes, but as we discussed, I think the roots of this authoritarianism you can find (again ex-post) in *Being and Time*, and the heteronomy may not only be that of outside authorities and powers, but also, for example, the heteronomy exercised by death over life. I think that Adorno has this too in mind when he speaks of it.

Olafson: Do you think that Hegel is dead, that classical German philosophy is effectively at an end? Can there be continuators, more successful, perhaps, than Heidegger?

Marcuse: You mean the tradition of German Idealism?

Olafson: I mean, is it still possible for living philosophies to be built on the great classical authors, Hegel and Kant, whether through revision, or however? Are these still living sources of philosophical inspiration?

Marcuse: I would definitely say yes. And I would definitely say that one of the proofs is the continued existence and development of Marxist theory. Because Marx and Engels themselves never failed to emphasize to what extent they considered themselves as the heirs of German Idealism. It is, of course, a greatly modified idealism, but elements of it remain in social and political theory.

Olafson: I think you've already characterized, in general terms, what permanent effect Heidegger's philosophy, his teaching, had upon your own thought, upon your own philosophical work. Is there anything that you want to add to that? On balance, does the encounter with Heidegger seem to you to have enriched your own philosophical thinking, or is it something that you essentially had to see through and overcome?

Marcuse: I would say more. There was, as I said, the mere fact that at least a certain type and kind of thinking I learned from him, and at least the fact—which again today should be stressed in the age of structuralism—that after all the text has an authority of its own and even if you violate the text, you have to do justice to it. These are elements which I think continue to be valid to this very day.

Olafson: The analysis of the situation of the individual human being, the conscious human being—is this susceptible, do you think, of continuing treatment?

Marcuse: No. As far as I am concerned, the existential analysis *à la* Heidegger today, I don't think there is anything in it I could say yes to, except in a very different social and intellectual context.

Olafson: Could you give us any indication of what the nature of that context might be?

Marcuse: That is very difficult. It would open up a completely new topic. The entire dimension that has been neglected in Marxian theory, for example, how social institutions reproduce themselves in the individuals, and how the individuals, by virtue of their reproducing their own society act on it. There is room for what may be called an existential analysis, but only within this framework.

Olafson: Well, thank you very much.

Marcuse: You're welcome.

Postscript: My Disillusionment with Heidegger

Being and Time appeared during the phase of the Weimar Republic's final collapse: the impending catastrophe—the advent of the Nazi regime—was generally sensed. But the dominant philosophical trends didn't reflect this situation. To me and my friends, Heidegger's work appeared as a new beginning: we experienced his book (and his lectures, whose transcripts we obtained) as, at long last, a *concrete* philosophy: here there was talk of existence [*Existenz*], of *our* existence, of fear [*Angst*] and care and boredom, and so forth. We also experienced an "academic" emancipation: Heidegger's interpretation of Greek philosophy and of German idealism, which offered us new insights into antiquated, fossilized texts.

Only gradually did we begin to observe that the concreteness of Heidegger's philosophy was to a large extent deceptive—that we were once again confronted with a variant of transcendental philosophy (on a higher plane), in which existential categories had lost their sharpness, been neutralized, and in the end were dissipated amid greater abstractions. That remained the case later on when the "question of Being" was replaced by the "question of technology": merely another instance in which apparent concreteness was subsumed by abstraction—bad abstraction, in which the concrete was not genuinely superseded but instead merely squandered.

I left Freiburg in January 1933. Prior to 1933 neither I nor my friends had observed or known anything about Heidegger's connection to Nazism. Only later did we attempt to reconstruct the affinity between his philosophy and his politics. Today it seems inexcusable to me to dismiss Heidegger's support of the Hitler regime as a (brief) mistake or error. I believe that a philosopher cannot make such a "mistake" without thereby disavowing his own, authentic philosophy.

Glossary

John Abromeit

Aufhebung/aufheben: sublate. Rather than attempt to distinguish which of the three meanings of the German verb "*aufheben*" ("lift up," "negate," or "preserve") was predominant in each particular usage, as some translators have done, we have opted to translate the term with "sublate" throughout, and leave it up to the reader's discretion to decided which meaning(s) are intended.

Bestimmung/Bestimmtheit/Definition: determination/determinacy/defi-nition. We have translated "*Bestimmung*" and "*Bestimmtheit*" as "determina-tion" and "determinacy" to preserve the distinction among the three terms, which is crucial in the dialectical tradition, particularly since Hegel. Marcuse's frequent use of the concept of *Bestimmung* in is line with this tradition, insofar as he shares Hegel's rejection of the possibility of fixing the meaning of concepts once and for all in a static "definition." Accordingly, *Bestimmtheit* implies that which exists in the immediacy of the present, that which is merely a moment in a larger underlying process.

Bewegtheit: motility. We have followed Seyla Benhabib's translation of this term as "motility"[1] in order to preserve the crucial distinction between "*Be-wegtheit*" and "*Bewegung*" ("movement"; see the entry below for *Geschehen*). Along with "happening" and "historicity," "motility" is one of the most impor-tant concepts Marcuse appropriates from Heidegger at this time. It signifies the uniquely and ontologically historical existence of authentic Dasein. Most importantly, it signifies a particular relationship to time. In *Being and Time* Heidegger goes to great lengths to demonstrate that human Dasein is primarily a temporal, not a spatial, being. He argues that the Cartesian understanding of time is based on an abstract and quantitatively measurable conception of space as *res extensa*.[2] The dominant concept of time in modernity is based on the quantitatively measurable *movement* of an object through this abstract space. But this understanding obscures the more fundamental temporality and *motility* of Dasein. Heidegger traces this fatefully reductionist interpretation of time all the way back to Aristotle's physics and metaphysics, in which time is also interpreted on a model of quantifiably measurable movement in space—what Heidegger calls *Jetzt-Zeit* (literally, "now-time"). Heidegger writes:

> Ever since Aristotle all discussions of the concept of time have clung *in principle* to the Aristotelian definition; that is, in taking time as their theme, they have taken it as it shows itself in circumspective concern. Time is what is "counted"; that is to say, it is what is expressed and what we have in view, even if unthematically, when the *travelling* pointer (or the shadow) is made present. When one makes present that which is moved in its movement, one says "now here, now here, and so on." These "nows" are what get counted. . . . The world-time which is "sighted" in this manner in the use of clocks, we call the "*now-time.*"[3]

When Dasein's complex relationship to time and history is construed in this manner, as quantifiable movement through abstract space, its unique ability to act resolutely based on its highest possibilities and to project these possibilities into the future is fundamentally lost; in other words, its historically mediated and self-reflexive *motility* is reduced to the passive *movement* of a mere thing. Marcuse was well aware of parallel analyses in the Marxist tradition of the rise of an abstract conception of time, and its link to the problems of alienation and reification[4] but no one in the Marxist tradition had yet attempted, in the manner of Heidegger's existential analytic or his analysis of historicity, to provide a detailed, positive demonstration of what a nonreified relationship to time and history would look like at the level of the concrete individual. Marcuse believed that Heidegger had, on this particular point, moved beyond the abstract concept of subjectivity that dominated both bourgeois and Marxist discussions at that time. Heidegger's attempts to extend his analysis of subjectivity to a collective level, on the other hand, remained "pseudoconcrete," in Marcuse's eyes.

Dasein: Dasein. We have decided to leave this concept untranslated in order to distinguish it from other closely related concepts, such as *Existenz* and *Mensch*. But the reader should not automatically assume that Marcuse always uses this concept in its emphatic Heideggerian sense. "Dasein" is a familiar term in Hegel's lexicon and it is also not uncommon in standard spoken German. By not translating the term, we leave it up to the discretion of the reader to decide if Marcuse is using it in the Heideggerian, Hegelian, or merely standard nonphilosophical sense.

Erbe: inheritance. We have opted to break with MacQuarrie and Robinson's translation of this term as "heritage," because Marcuse's Marxist appropriation of the term has a more concrete, materialist inflection. Marcuse speaks often of the "historical inheritance" that provides the more or less favorable conditions for the development of each successive generation. The problem is not just that "historical heritage" is redundant; "heritage" also has stronger traditional and cultural connotations that fail to capture Marcuse intentions. Although Marcuse does not subscribe to Engels's ontological materialism, he does emphasis that the "historical inheritance" is a dialectical unity of material and cultural or intellectual elements. Marcuse and Heidegger both insist that each generation must *disavow* or *negate* its historical inheritance, but for Heidegger this negation is a means of repeating past possibilities that have been obscured by inauthentic forms of existence, while for Marcuse the negation of the present also involves the preservation of those material and intellectual elements that will make possible the emergence of *qualitatively new* and more emancipated forms of life.

Entäußerung/Entfremdung: alienation/estrangement. Although "*Entäußerung*" is sometimes translated as "externalization" (in which case "*Entfremdung*" is then usually translated as "alienation") to capture Hegel's more neutral use of the term, in his *Economic and Philosophic Manuscripts of 1844*, Marx's use of the concept is clearly negative and critical. In the last two essays in this volume, which is where the terms appear, Marcuse uses them primarily in the latter sense. In the few cases when Marcuse uses the term in the more neutral, Hegelian sense, we have translated it as "externalization" and included the original in brackets.

Erkenntnis/Erkennen/Wissen: The translation of these three terms poses virtually insurmountable problems. While there are not any good solutions, the least misleading in this context is to use "knowledge" as the standard translation of both "*Erkenntis*" and "*Wissen*" and "knowing" for "Erkennen." The difficulty arises because Marcuse uses "*Erkennen*" and "*Erkenntnis*" to mean both 1) "cognizing" and "cognition" in the technical sense of the term in the tradition of Kantian and neo-Kantian epistemological [*erkenntnistheoretische*] reflection (which stresses the split between an actively cognizing subject that provides the basic structuring categories of knowledge and a passively cognized object that provides the unformed material of knowledge) and 2) "knowing" and "knowledge" in the more standard sense of the term, which implicitly or explicitly stresses the unity of the knowing subject and the known object, as is the case in Heidegger's phenomenology, which views the dualistic approach to knowledge of *Erkenntnistheorie* as artificial and derivative.[5] As a dialectical thinker, Marcuse agrees with Heidegger on this point. He believes that this is one of Heidegger's arguments that can contribute to recovering some of the most important insights of the Hegelian-Marxist tradition. Accordingly, when Marcuse uses "*Erkenntnis*" or "*Erkennen*" in the first sense, it is always critical. An example of Marcuse using the term in the former way to stress the limitations of the Kantian and neo-Kantian epistemology, is the following passage from the essay on the dialectic: "In the true sense of the word only human Dasein can be called historical, because knowledge [*Wissen*] of one's own existence and a knowing [*wissendes*] (not merely cognizing [*erkennendes*]) relation to reality belong to authentic being-historical."[6] The problem, however, is that Marcuse uses the term more often in the second, more neutral sense. For example, in a discussion of Plato's philosophy in the same essay, Marcuse states that, "the dialectic belongs to the highest level of human knowledge [*Erkenntnis*]."[7] In a discussion of Marx in "Contributions to a Phenomenology of Historical Materialism" he also states, "all genuine knowledge is, in the most profound sense, 'practical' knowledge, in that it brings a human Dasein 'into the truth.'"[8]

If one were to translate "*Erkenntis*" and "*Erkennen*" consistently as "cognition" and "cognizing," this would greatly distort Marcuse's intentions in cases like these—and many others—in which "knowledge" does not refer critically to the modern, dualistic epistemological tradition. Nonetheless, we have included the original in brackets wherever "knowledge" is used to translate "*Wissen*" in order to preserve the distinction between it and "*Erkenntnis*." Also, in just a few instances, when Marcuse contrasts *Erkenntis* or *Erkennen* directly with *Wissen*, we have translated the former as "cognition" and "cognizing" and included the original in brackets. In any case, the distinction between a negatively construed, epistemological *Erkenntnis* and a more positively construed concept of *Wissen* (as a necessary moment in self-reflexive, historically mediated praxis) figures prominently only in the essay on the dialectic. But even in that essay, this distinction is secondary to the main thrust of Marcuse's argument, which is to overcome the passive, spectatorial conception of subjectivity that resulted from a one-sided or abstract privileging of knowledge—a position that dominated contemporary debates from neo-Kantianism to historicism to Social Democratic orthodoxy. Marcuse saw Heidegger's concepts of motility, happening, and historicity as an important, if ultimately unsatisfying attempt to recover a more active and concrete concept of subjectivity. He used Heidegger's concepts as a springboard for attempting to recover the genuinely concrete concept of subjectivity in Hegel and Marx's conception of the dialectic. He would present this argument in the most detail in the *Habilitationsschrift* he wrote under Heidegger's direction, *Hegel's Ontology and the Theory of Historicity*, in which he traced the competing tendencies in Hegel's thought between a critical, ontological conception of being as *life*, and an affirmative, epistemological concept of being as *absolute knowledge*. He argued that the latter tendency gained the upper hand in Hegel's *Logic* and remained dominant in his later work, but that the former tendency, which served as the basis of his early writings, was still present in the *Phenomenology of Spirit*.[9] Thus it was not a coincidence, as Marcuse points out in his essay on the *Philosophic and Economic Manuscripts of 1844*, that Marx considered the *Phenomenology* "the true point of origin and the secret of the Hegelian philosophy,"[10] and that it served as the point of departure for his own dialectical theory.

Existential/existentiell: In the few cases when Marcuse has used "existential" in its emphatic Heideggerian sense, we have either left it untranslated or included the original in brackets. In all other cases we have translated both "existential" and "existentiell" as "existential," because the latter term appears only in the second essay, "On Concrete Philosophy," and Marcuse does not consistently preserve Heidegger's distinction between "existential" and "existentiell."

Geschehen: happening; historical occurrence. With the possible exception of the concept of historicity (see below), to which it is closely related, *Geschehen* was the most prominent and important concept that Marcuse appropriated from Heideggerian phenomenology during this time. *Geschehen* was so crucial for Marcuse because it captured the dynamic, "ontological" historicity unique to human Dasein, which he believed had been lost in recent discussions of Marx's theory. As Marcuse put it in his first published essay, "The truths of Marxism are not truths of knowing, but rather truths of happening."[11] In *Being and Time*, Heidegger defines "*Geschehen*" in the following way:

> The motility [*Bewegtheit*] of existence is not the movement [*Bewegung*] of something present-at-hand. It is definable in terms of the way Dasein stretches along. The specific movement in which Dasein *is stretched along and stretches itself along*, we call its "*happening*." The question of Dasin's "connectedness" is the ontological problem of Dasein's historical occurrence. To lay bare the

structure of happening, and the existential temporal conditions of its possibility, signifies that one has achieved an *ontological* understanding of *historicity.* [12]

For Heidegger, in other words, the way in which human Dasein exists is not merely dynamic, but ontologically *historical.* Thus the *motility* of Dasein differs qualitatively from the mere *movement* of all other physical objects in space and time, which is governed by natural laws. As the only be-ing for whom being itself is an issue, Dasein's existence always involves appropriating past possibilities and projecting them into the future, and a failure to recognize this—to draw one's possible modes of existence solely from the bad immediacy of the present—is to live irresolutely and inauthentically, in the manner of a mere "thing amongst things." But the authentic type of existence, to which *Geschehen* refers, entails a very specific type of historical consciousness for Heidegger. He chooses—carefully, as always—the concept of *Geschehen* due to its etymological kinship with the German word for history, "*Geschichte.*" Heidegger argues that the German term, with its close proximity to "*Geschehen,*" implies a self-reflexive and active relationship to history. He distinguishes "*Geschichte*" from the Latin term "*Historie,*" which implies a passive, spectatorial, inauthentic way of relating to history. He writes,

> *Geschichte* indicates a happening that we ourselves are, and in which we are involved. There is a difference between *Geschichte* and movement, e.g. of the stars. . . . *Geschichte* is formally a certain type of movement. It is the sort of happening that is still there as past, about which we know in a certain way. . . . A rigorous explanation of *Geschichte* would necessitate differentiating it from [mere] movement. . . . Movement is the broader concept, which denotes the phenomenon of change, the transition from-to . . . ; movements take place in the world. *Geschichte* happens to me myself; I am this happening. . . . This happening is not just change or mere transition, but rather as we proceed ahead of ourselves, we are the very happening itself. . . . We are [*Geschichte*], i.e. our own past. Our future lives out of the past. [13]

Heidegger defines "Historie," on the other hand, as "the knowledge [*Erkenntnis*] of a happening. The type of knowledge that makes it possible to inform ourselves about a past event is called 'historical.' " [14] Thus, for Heidegger, the concept of *Geschehen* was intended to move beyond the passive, detached approach to the past implied by "*Historie*" and to capture the active, self-reflexive, and historically conscious existence of authentic human Dasein implied by "*Geschichte.*" It was precisely this attempt to recapture the full meaning of history for human Dasein that seemed so promising to Marcuse as way of overcoming the dualistic and ultimately passive epistemologies not only of bourgeois neo-Kantianism and historicism, but also of the objectivist philosophy of history of Social Democratic orthodoxy.

Geschichtlichkeit: historicity. Along with *Geschehen* (see above), this is the most important concept that Marcuse appropriates from Heidegger in the late 1920s. "*Geschichtlichkeit*" has the same etymological and ontological implications as "*Geschichte*" and "*Geschehen*." In fact, in Heidegger's philosophical lexicon, "*Geschichtlichkeit*" is very closely related to "*Geschehen*." As Heidegger puts it in *Being and Time*: "The question of Dasein's 'connectedness' is the ontological problem of Dasein's happening. To lay bare the *structure of happening*, and the existential-temporal conditions of its possibility, signifies that one has achieved an *ontological* understanding of *historicity*."[15]

The structure of happening is the key to an ontological understanding of historicity, insofar as happening refers to the uniquely two-dimensional character of Dasein's existence. Whereas the historical existence of ordinary beings is merely one-dimensional, in the sense that they always exist in the immediacy of the present, Dasein's historical existence is "ecstatically open," as Heideggger puts it, in the sense that Dasein must, in order to exist authentically, constantly project itself into the future by resolutely appropriating the highest possibilities it has inherited from the past. Dasein's relationship to time and history—its unique *historicity*—is *ontological* in the sense that it is more fundamental than the merely *ontic* relationship of ordinary beings to time and history, which they experience in a merely passive way. But the potential to take a more active, two-dimensional stance toward time and history lies within the very *being* of Dasein and to refuse this potential is tantamount to rejecting the very essence of human being. Marcuse initially believes that Heidegger's analysis of ontological historicity and its loss in inauthentic forms confirms Marx's analysis of alienation and reification, and his belief is strengthened substantially by the publication of Marx's *Economic and Philosophic Manuscripts of 1844*. In contrast to Heidegger, however, Marcuse argues that the cause of the alienation and inauthenticity of contemporary forms of existence is not *Seinsvergessenheit*—a complete inability to even pose the question of the meaning of being—but rather the reified social relations produced by modern industrial capitalism. Marcuse's interpretation is abetted by Heidegger's argument in the fifth chapter of the second division of *Being and Time*, in which he first develops the far-reaching implications of the concept of historicity, that authentic historicity can be attained only collectively.[16] But Marcuse differs with Heidegger once again in his Marxist insistence that the only genuinely historical collective subject in the present would be a self-consciously universal subject, not a particularistic "community of destiny," as Heidegger argued in *Being and Time* and in his defense of National Socialism a few years later.

Mensch/menschlich/Menschheit/Menschlichkeit: We have translated "*menschlich*" as "human" and both "*Menschheit*" and "*Menschlichkeit*" as "humanity" throughout. Despite its sexist overtones, we have opted to follow the conventional translation of *Mensch* as "man" or "men." In the original German "*Mensch*" is gender neutral, and the reader should keep this in mind throughout. We made this decision not only because this was the term that Marcuse himself used when he wrote in English (in *One-Dimensional Man*, for example), but also because it was impossible to develop an alternative that could be used consistently. Neither "humans" nor "human beings" worked in all cases. Furthermore, using "man"/"men" made it possible to preserve the distinction between "*Mensch*" and "*menschliches Sein*" (human being). The concept of *Mensch* is most important in Marcuse's essay on Marx's *Economic and Philosophic Manuscripts*. Marcuse seizes on the anthropological elements in Marx's text, which resonate well with his own appropriation of Heidegger's analysis of the ontological historicity of Dasein.[17] Marcuse believes that both Heidegger and Marx identified certain characteristics that are shared by all "men" and that actually determine the very essence of man, but that these very characteristics are forgotten or repressed in the inauthentic or alienated forms of existence analyzed by Heidegger and Marx. Marcuse believes that Heidegger went further than any other contemporary philosopher, insofar as he recognized the depth of the problem, but he remains ultimately unsatisfied with Heidegger's explanation of its causes. With the publication in 1932 of Marx's *Economic and Philosophic Manuscripts of 1844*, Marcuse believes that the way to a truly concrete explanation of the problem, in terms of the alienation of man's very essence that lies at the heart of capitalist social relations, has been found—as his enthusiastic review of Marx's early work makes clear. For Marcuse, in other words, capitalism is not simply an exploitative system of property relations, but a perversion of the very essence of man. Thus Marcuse affirms the early Marx's interpretation of capitalism as the "prehistory" of mankind, with the implication that "man" will not fully realize his latent potential as a "species being" until a qualitative break is made.

Ontologie/ontologisch: ontology/ontological. The question of why a young, critical Marxist like Marcuse would be attracted to Heidegger's "ontological" philosophy is one that has stymied most interpreters of Marcuse's writings from this period.[18] In order to understand Marcuse's writings between 1928 and 1933 it is crucial to recognize that the concept of ontology he has appropriated from Heidegger differs in many respects from the traditional meaning attributed to it.[19] For Heidegger, and for Marcuse during this time as well, "ontology" does not signify a realm of eternal truths that exist outside of history and are unaffected by the passage of time. In *Being and Time* Heidegger argues that Dasein—and thus, by extension, being in general—are temporal and historical at the most fundamental level; in other words, Heidegger's "ontology" is historical through and through. Marcuse follows Heidegger in this regard; in fact, Heidegger's attempt to establish historicity as the very essence of human being appealed so greatly to Marcuse because he felt that man's unique relationship to history had been lost in contemporary theoretical discussions—both bourgeois and Marxist.[20] For both Heidegger and Marcuse, ontology serves as a counterconcept to epistemology; it is intended to highlight the impossibility of attaining a transcendental position beyond temporality and history.[21] For this reason, the concept of *immanence* also plays an important role in Marcuse's writings during this time. For example, Marcuse argues—in the spirit of Marx's critique of utopian socialism—that emancipatory social change cannot overshoot the *objective* possibilities that exist in a latent but unrealized state in the present historical situation. In this respect, Marcuse moves decisively beyond Heidegger, who dismisses the entire sphere of "ontic" history, and—unlike Hegel and Marx in their *determinate* negations—insists that the *entire* history of the West has been misguided and that the slate needs to be wiped *completely* clean. Marcuse also insists that social change must be firmly anchored in the knowledge and actions of the individual subjects who bring it about and cannot be imposed upon them by some "external" force, for this would represent a violation of the fundamental principle of immanence. Marcuse criticizes the vanguardist implication of Lukacs's concept of class consciousness on this basis.[22] In short, Marcuse was convinced at this time not only that Heidegger's concept of ontology was reconcilable with the thoroughly historical theories of Hegel and Marx, but he also believed it captured their fundamental insights better than most of their contemporary interpreters.[23]

Sein/Seiendes: being/be-ing. The concepts of *Sein* and *Seiendes* and the distinction between them form the foundation of the central problematic that

Heidegger addresses in *Being and Time*.[24] But, as with so many other of Heidegger's concepts, *Sein* and *Seiendes* present the translator with virtually insurmountable problems; several different solutions have been put forth. "*Sein*" has been rendered as "Being" (always capitalized) and "being" and "*Seiendes*" has been translated as "entity," "essents" and "beings," to name only the most widely recognized translations. We have decided to add yet another variation on these terms—and to create an unsightly neologism—by translating "*Sein*" as "being" and "*Seiendes*" as "be-ing." Our decision to translate the terms in this way was not based on a conviction that our solution is necessarily superior to the others, and even less on a Heideggerian faith in the power of neologisms, but rather because it seemed best to capture Marcuse's particular use of the concepts in these essays, which is by no means limited to the Heideggerian idiom. Not only does Hegel's *Logic*—which Marcuse was carefully studying during this time—begin with an analysis of the philosophical import of *Sein*, but it is also virtually impossible to write anything in German without using the term in a wide variety of nontechnical locutions. If we had followed MacQuarrie and Robinson's translation of "*Sein*" as "Being," we would have given the reader the false impression that every time Marcuse uses "*Sein*," it is in the emphatic Heideggerian sense. Nor did we want to take it on ourselves, as Seyla Benhabib did in her translation of *Hegel's Ontology*, to translate the term as "Being" only when Marcuse uses it in the emphatic Heideggerian sense. We have decided to translate "*Sein*" consistently as "being"—capitalizing it only when it appears at the beginning of a sentence—in order to let the reader decide for him or herself how Marcuse is using the term in any given context. This left us with the even more difficult problem of translating "*Seiendes*." Thankfully, this term in particular, and the distinction between "*Sein*" and "*Seiendes*" more generally, are not central to Marcuse's concerns in these essays. In fact, "*Seiendes*" figures prominently only in the essay on the dialectic; the term appears only a handful of times in the other essays. But even in "On the Problem of the Dialectic" Marcuse does not use it consistently in the Heideggerian sense. Once again, then, our primary concern was to render the term in a consistent and recognizable way in order to leave its interpretation to the reader, as much as possible. Translating the term as "beings," as does Benhabib, would have limited us to the plural and would also have given the term a substantialist connotation that it does not always have. MacQuarrie and Robinson's "entity" or "entities" is also overly substantialist (for Marcuse, *Seiendes* are not limited to objects or things that have a concrete existence), and Ralph Mannheim's translation of

"*Seiendes*" as "essent" and "essents" carries essentialist overtones that are also inappropriate for Marcuse's usage of the term. Translating the term as "be-ing" has allowed us not only to retain the close relationship between "*Sein*" and "*Seindes*," but also to preserve Marcuse's distinctions between the singular "be-ing" and the plural "be-ings." Furthermore, drawing attention to the "ing" by setting it apart with a dash in "be-ing" expresses the grammatical relationship between "*Sein*" and "*Seiendes*" in German: the former being the infinitive and the latter the gerund of that infinitive. But "be-ing" does not automatically imply a substantive form either, as do the other translations mentioned above, and we consider this an advantage. The reader should not assume that "be-ing" implies a concrete object in the world; Marcuse uses the term to refer to *both* essence and appearance: it is precisely the task of the dialectic to determine the reality of "be-ings."[25]

   Tun/Tätigkeit: Doing/Activity. This distinction, which figures most prominently in the last essay, "The Philosophical Foundations of the Concept of Labor in Economics," has far-reaching implications for Marcuse's interpretation of Hegel and Marx. As Marcuse argues in the essay, the concept of labor has its basis in a much broader notion of human "doing" that—following Hegel—he is careful to distinguish from "activity." As Marcuse puts it:

> We have introduced Hegel's philosophically founded concept of labor only to the extent necessary to outline his starting point. Its essential difference from the concept of labor in economics is this: in Hegel's concept labor appears as a fundamental happening of human Dasein, as a happening that constantly and continually penetrates the entirety of man's *being*, during which something also happens to man's "world." Here labor is precisely *not* a specific human "activity" (for no single activity seizes and penetrates the totality of human Dasein; every activity affects only particular regions of this totality and happens only in particular regions of its world); rather, it is that on which every single activity is based and to which each activity always returns: a *doing* [*Tun*]. It is precisely the doing of man as his mode of being-in-the-world, through which he first becomes "for-himself" what he is, comes to his self, acquires the "form" of his Da-sein, his "permanence" and at the same time makes the world his own. Conceived in this way, labor is not determined by the nature of its objects, nor by its goal, content, result, etc., but by what happens to human Dasein itself in labor.[26]

For Marcuse, in other words, the transformation and reduction of "doing" to any single activity, or even worse, to an abstract activity such as wage labor, which he observes in both the economic literature of the time and the real world it describes, represents an impoverishment and distortion of the most basic, "ontological" characteristics of human beings: the process by which they, through appropriating the material and intellectual "world" into which they are "thrown," create themselves and at the same time transform that world. Marcuse uses Hegel's distinction between doing and activity, in combination with Heidegger's concepts of Dasein, world, and happening to offer an original interpretation of Marx's notions of alienation and reification. He argues that the key to this problematic is to be found in *philosophical foundations* of Marx's concept of labor. The furthest thing from Marcuse's mind is to confer onto-logical status upon on the *conventional* concept of labor. By highlighting the "ontological" status of "doing," which also includes aesthetic production and even play, Marcuse brings into sharp relief the far-reaching and catastrophic implications of the fact that it has been largely supplanted by abstract wage labor in modern capitalist societies. Marcuse's discussion of the philosophical foundations of Marx's concept of labor goes a long way toward refuting the cur-rently widespread and fundamentally misguided claims that Marx conceived of labor merely as rational-purposive behavior and thus remained trapped within the "production paradigm" or even "wanted to turn the whole world into a giant workhouse."[27]

Ursprünglich: primordial, originary. For the most part, we have followed MacQuarrie and Robinson in translating this Heideggerian concept as "pri-mordial." On some occasions, however, we have opted for "originary," for reasons of readability. No difference in meaning is intended.

Vergegenständlichung/Verdinglichung/Gegenständlichkeit: We have fol-lowed the more or less standard translations of these Marxian terms as "objecti-fication," "reification," and "objectivity." In the few cases in which we translated "*Gegenständlichkeit*" as "objective world" or "*Sachlichkeit*" or "*Objektivität*" as "objectivity," we have included the original in brackets.

Verhalten/ sich verhalten: conduct/to conduct oneself, to relate (oneself) to. This concept, which is particularly important for the early Marx, expresses his conviction that human beings are unique in their ability to consciously relate to their own history. Marcuse recognizes the parallels between Marx's use of this term and Heidegger's arguments about happening, motility, and historicity. Thus "conduct," "conducting oneself," and "relating (oneself) to" always implies a conscious, self-reflexive relationship to history.

Vorhanden/zuhanden: We have followed MacQuarrie and Robinson's translation of Heidegger's concepts as present-at-hand and ready-to-hand.

Wesen: essence, being. We have attempted to translate this concept as "essence" whenever possible, but Marcuse occasionally uses it in such a way—in the essay "New Sources on the Foundation of Historical Materialism" in particular—that it can only be translated as "being." When, for example, Marcuse uses the concept of *Gattungswesen*, in his own writings or in passages quoted from Marx's early writings, we have followed the conventional translation of this term as "species being." In the few other cases when it was necessary to translate *Wesen* as "being" we have included the original in brackets in order to preserve the distinction between it and *Sein*.

Wissenschaft: science. In German, "*Wissenschaft*" refers to all forms of systematic scholarly inquiry. Within this tradition fields that would be placed in the "humanities" in the Anglo-American world, such as philosophy, theater, and literature, can be pursued as a "science." Thus the reader should keep in mind that "science" does not refer solely to the natural and/or social sciences.

Notes

Introduction

The epigraph is from "Zum Geleit," in Antworten auf Herbert Marcuse, *ed. Jürgen Habermas (Frankfurt: Suhrkamp, 1968), 10–11. The translation is mine.*

1. For a good history of the German Revolution, see A. J. Ryder, *The German Revolution of 1918: A Study of German Socialism in War and Revolt* (Cambridge UK: Cambridge University Press, 1967).

2. Marcuse's dissertation has never been translated into English. It is included in volume 1 of Marcuse's *Schriften* (Frankfurt: Suhrkamp, 1978), 7–346. For a discussion of its basic themes, see Douglas Kellner, *Herbert Marcuse and the Crisis of Marxism* (Berkeley and Los Angeles: University of California Press, 1984), 18–32.

3. Marcuse, "Entäuschung," in *Erinnerungen an Martin Heidegger*, ed. Günther Neske (Pfullingen: Neske, 1977), 162.

4. For their testimonies, see Arendt, "Martin Heidegger at Eighty," in *Martin Heidegger and Modern Philosophy: Critical Essays*, ed. Michael Murray (New Haven CT: Yale University Press, 1978), 295–303; Löwith, *My Life in Germany Before and After 1933: A Report*, trans. Elizabeth King (Urbana: University of Illinois Press, 1993); Gadamer, *Philosophical Apprenticeships*, trans. Robert R. Sullivan (Cambridge MA: MIT Press, 1985), 45–54.

5. For an important discussion of German mandarin cultural and political attitudes, see Fritz Ringer, *The Decline of the German Mandarins: The German Academic Community, 1890–1933* (Cambridge MA: Harvard University Press, 1968).

6. Letter to Maximilian Beck, 9 May 1929, cited in Douglas Kellner, *Herbert Marcuse*, 35. During 1920–21, the young Horkheimer studied with Husserl and seems to have been favorably impressed by Heidegger. As he remarks in a letter: "The more I am taken with philosophy, the further I distance myself from what is understood by that at this university. We have to look not for formal laws of knowledge, which are in the end quite unimportant, but for substantive propositions concerning life and its meaning. I know today that Heidegger was one of the most significant persons who spoke to me. . . . Do I agree with him? How could I, as I know only one thing for certain about him: for him the motive of philosophizing springs not from intellectual ambition and some prefabricated theory, but from the everyday, from his own experience"; Horkheimer, *Gesammelte*

Schriften, vol. 15, ed. Alfred Schmidt and Gunzelin Schmid Noerr (Frankfurt: Fischer, 1995), 77. The translation is mine.

7. See Luxemburg's famous pamphlet, "The Russian Revolution," in *Rosa Luxemburg Speaks*, ed. Mary-Alice Waters (New York: Pathfinder, 1970), 498–540.

8. For a good discussion of these themes, see Russell Jacoby, "The Critique of Automatic Marxism: The Politics of Philosophy from Lukács to the Frankfurt School," *Telos* 10 (Winter 1971): 119–46.

9. Marx, *Capital*, vol. 1, in *The Marx-Engels Reader*, ed. Robert C. Tucker (New York: Norton, 1978) 32.

10. Heidegger, *Being and Time*, trans. John MacQuarrie and Edward Robinson (San Francisco: Harper, 1962), 102–4. All further references to the English translation of *Being and Time* are to this edition.

11. "On Concrete Philosophy," ch. 2 of this volume, 42. All further references are to this translation and will be cited by page number in the text.

12. From this standpoint, Marcuse's understanding of Heidegger's methodological importance seems to foreshadow Max Horkheimer's distinction between traditional theory and Critical Theory; see Horkheimer, *Critical Theory: Selected Essays*, trans. Matthew J. O'Connell et al. (New York: Herder and Herder, 1973), 188–243.

13. Marx, "Theses on Feuerbach," in *The Marx-Engels Reader*, 143–45; all further references will be cited by page number in the text. See also Lukács's important gloss on the "Theses" in *History and Class Consciousness: Studies in Marxist Dialectics*, trans. Rodney Livingstone (Cambridge MA: MIT Press, 1971), 186–87, 198.

14. Marcuse, "Contributions to a Phenomenology of Historical Materialism," ch. 1 of this volume, 10–11. All further references are to this translation and will be cited by page number in the text.

15. See Thomas Willey, *Back to Kant: The Revival of Kantianism in German Social and Historical Thought, 1860–1914* (Detroit: Wayne State University Press, 1978).

16. See Wilhelm Dilthey, *Die jugendgeschichte Hegels: und andere Abhandlungen zur Geschichte des deutschen Idealismus* (Stuttgart: B. G. Teubner, 1959) and Michael Ermarth, *Wilhelm Dilthey: The Critique of Historical Reason* (Chicago: University of Chicago Press, 1978).

17. For an indictment of bourgeois thought that was obviously of great inspirational value for Marcuse, see Lukács's discussion of "The Antinomies of Bourgeois Thought," in *History and Class Consciousness*, 110–48.

18. Marcuse, *Hegel's Ontology and the Theory of Historicity*, trans. Seyla Benhabib (Cambridge MA: MIT Press, 1987), 251.

19. In *Herbert Marcuse*, Kellner suggests that Marcuse's attraction to Heidegger in part resulted from the mood of "radical action" that was so widespread on both the left and the right during the 1920s: "The concept of the *radical act* stands at the center of Marcuse's theory. For Marcuse—and here we see for the first time indications of his synthesis between Heidegger and Marx—the radical act is *existential*: it aims at an

alteration of the roots of existence; it intends to bring forth a fundamental change in human existence" (41).

20. For Dilthey's belated influence on Heidegger, which had a monumental influence on the later drafts of *Being and Time*, see Heidegger, *The History of the Concept of Time: Prologomena*, trans. Theodore Kisiel (Bloomington: University of Indiana Press, 1992). In the literature on Heidegger, this text is also known as the Kassel Lectures. For their place in the *Entstehungsgeschichte* of *Being and Time*, see Kisiel, *The Genesis of Heidegger's Being and Time* (Berkeley and Los Angeles: University of California Press, 1997), 311–420. Habermas presents a highly favorable interpretation of Dilthey in *Knowledge and Human Interests*, trans. Jeremy J. Shapiro (Boston: Beacon, 1971), 140–86. For an excellent treatment of the concept of historicity in Dilthey and Heidegger, see Charles Bambach, Dilthey, *Heidegger and the Crisis of Historicism: History and Metaphysics in Heidegger, Dilthey and the Neo-Kantians* (Ithaca NY: Cornell University Press, 1995).

21. Heidegger, *Der Begriff der Zeit* (Tübingen: Niemeyer, 1989), 25.

22. Marcuse, "Heidegger's Politics," in *Marcuse: Critical Theory and the Promise of Utopia*, ed. Robert Pippin et al.(South Hadley MA: Bergin and Garvey, 1988), 96. All further references will be cited by page number in the text.

23. See Victor Farias, *Heidegger and Nazism*, ed. Joseph Margolis and Tom Rockmore, trans. Gabriel R. Ricci (Philadelphia: Temple University Press, 1989) and Hugo Ott, *Martin Heidegger: A Political Life*, trans. Allan Blunden (New York: Basic, 1993).

24. See the accounts in Kellner, *Herbert Marcuse*, 401, n. 1, where Kellner cites Habermas as claiming that Marcuse had told him Heidegger had rejected the habilitation study, and Benhabib, "Translator's Introduction," *Hegel's Ontology*, x–xi.

25. Rolf Wiggershaus, *The Frankfurt School: Its History, Theories, and Political Significance*, trans. Michael Robertson (Cambridge MA: MIT Press, 1994), 104.

26. Whether Heidegger actually provided the letter in question cannot be confirmed: allegedly, much of Klostermann's prewar correspondence was destroyed by bombing during World War II. For a detailed account based on documents in the Marcuse Archive, see Peter-Erwin Jansen, "Marcuses Habiltationsverfahren: Eine Odyssee," in *Befreiung Denken: Ein politischer Imperativ*, ed. Peter-Erwin Jansen (Offenbach: Verlag 2000, 1990), 141–50.

27. Marcuse, "On the Philosophical Foundations of the Concept of Labor in Economics," ch. 5 in this volume, 138. All further references are to this translation and will be cited by page number in the text. Here, the parallels with aspects of Kojève's argument in his *Introduction to the Reading of Hegel* are striking. For Kojève, "desire" is an expression of human lack. Of course, the ultimate source of Marcuse's and Kojève's argument may have been the same: the master-slave section of Hegel's *Phenomenology of Spirit*.

28. See the discussion in Kellner, *Herbert Marcuse*, 33.

29. Friedrich Schiller, *On the Aesthetic Education of Man, in a Series of Letters*, trans. Reginald Snell (New York: Frederick Ungar, 1965), 80.

30. See Marcuse, Jürgen Habermas, Heinz Lubasz, and Tilman Spengler, "Theory and Politics: A Discussion," trans. Leslie Adelson, *Telos* 38 (Winter 1978–79): 126: "At the end of 1932 it was perfectly clear that I would never be able to qualify for a professorship under the Nazi regime." All further references will be cited by page number in the text.

31. "New Sources on the Foundation of Historical Materialism," ch. 4 in this volume, 86. All further references are to this translation and will be cited by page number in the text.

32. In a number of interviews, Jürgen Habermas has claimed that he identified closely with Marcuse's intellectual path "from Heidegger to Horkheimer," since for approximately four years, he had been a "thoroughgoing Heideggerian." Habermas continues: "It was while I was working on the concept of ideology that I came across Marcuse's early articles [on Heidegger]. There you could see the exact breaking-point between an orthodox Heideggerian and a Marxist. I still can show you the lines where Herbert made the substantive, the strategic criticism of Heidegger—namely where he rejects not just the ontological difference but the difference between history and historicity. So I can recognize my own point of departure, so to speak, from Heidegger in these texts of Marcuse" (Habermas, *Autonomy and Solidarity: Interviews*, ed. Peter Dews [New York: Verso, 1986], 194).

33. See, for example, Leszek Kolakowski, *Toward a Marxist Humanism: Essays on the Left Today*, trans. Jane Zielonko Peel (New York: Grove, 1968).

34. For more on phenomenological Marxism, see Paul Piccone, "Phenomenological Marxism," *Telos* 9 (Fall 1971): 3–31 and Pier Aldo Rovatti, "Critical Theory and Phenomenology," trans. Tom Hull, *Telos* 15 (Spring 1973): 25–40. As Rovatti remarks, "Within certain limits thee is a convergence of content in the sense that both the Frankfurt School and phenomenology were on the attack against a model of scientific development and 'bad' rationalization leading both positivism in its new forms as well as idealism to a radical crisis" (25).

35. Karl Löwith, "The Political Implications of Heidegger's Existentialism," trans. Richard Wolin, in *The Heidegger Controversy: A Critical Reader* (Cambridge MA: MIT Press, 1993), 173.

36. For Adorno's critical views on Heidegger, which surfaced as early as 1931 in his Frankfurt University inaugural lecture, see "The Actuality of Philosophy," trans. Benjamin Snow, *Telos* 31 (Spring 1977): 120–33; see also his critical review of Marcuse's *Hegel's Ontology*, in *Zeitschrift für Sozialforschung*, vol. 1 (1932): 409–10. Adorno would continue his polemics against Heideggerianism in the postwar period. See *The Jargon of Authenticity*, trans. Knut Tarnowski and Frederic Will (Evanston IL: Northwestern University Press, 1975) and *Negative Dialectics*, trans. E. B. Ashton (New York: Seabury, 1973), 61–131.

37. Marcuse, "German Philosophy, 1871–1933," ch. 6 in this volume, 160. For more on Marcuse's relation to Heidegger, see Alfred Schmidt, "Existential Ontology and Historical Materialism in the Work of Herbert Marcuse," trans. Anne-Marie and Andrew Feenberg, and Robert Pippin, "Marcuse and Hegel on Historicity" in *Marcuse: Critical*

Theory, 47–67 and 68–94. Also see Seyla Benhabib, xi, *Hegel's Ontology*.

38. The correspondence has been reproduced in *The Heidegger Controversy*, 160–64.

39. For a good account of Marcuse's attitudes toward the New Left, see Kellner, *Herbert Marcuse*, 276–319.

40. Cited by Marcuse in *One-Dimensional Man: Studies in the Ideology of Advanced Industrial Society* (Boston: Beacon Press, 1964), 153–54; Marcuse's translation (for a complete English translation of Heidegger's essay, see "The Question Concerning Technology," in *The Question Concerning Technology and Other Essays*, trans. William Lovitt [New York: Harper and Row, 1977], 3–35). To my knowledge, this is the only time Marcuse ever directly cited Heidegger following the war.

41. See Marcuse, *Technology, War, and Fascism*, ed. Douglas Kellner (New York: Routledge, 1998), 39–66.

42. Marcuse, *An Essay on Liberation* (New York: Penguin, 1969), 19.

1. A Phenomenology of Historical Materialism

All bracketed notes in this essay were written by Eric Oberle except notes 2 and 57, which were cowritten by John Abromeit. The bracketed notes in all the other essays were written by the editors.

1. [This paragraph contains several different versions of the German word *Erkenntnis*, drawing on the philosophical term meaning "knowledge in general" in a way that is broadly evocative of two distinct philosophical traditions. On the one hand, Marcuse's use of *Erkenntnis* in the singular suggests an adherence to Kantian and neo-Kantian traditions that see the establishment of a rigorous *Erkenntnistheorie* (epistemology) as the proper framework for assessing the validity of a judgment. On the other hand, Marcuse's invocation of the term *Erkenntnisse* (acts of knowledge or perception in the plural) draws on the phenomenological tradition of analyzing the immanent structure and content of the different domains of "knowledge" or knowledge-acts (*Bereiche der Erkenntnisse*) according to their structure and type. (Numbers, for example, have a different knowledge structure than, say, religious experience or ready-to-handness.) See the glossary entry for *Erkenntnis/Erkennen/Wissen*.]

2. [In what follows, the German concept of *Tat* has been translated as "act" or "deed." As with the concept of *Lebensraum* (see n. 57 below), Marcuse's reliance on the concept of the radical *Tat* in this essay illustrates the difficulty inherent in his attempt to transform the meaning of some of the key concepts of conservative revolutionary discourse in Weimar Germany.

Popularized by the widely influential writings of the French theorist Georges Sorel (whose *Reflections on Violence* from 1908 advanced an anti-intellectual and antiliberal political ideology), the idea that "the act" served as the foundation for politics and philosophy flourished in the social upheavals following World War I. In the 1920s this ideology won many adherents within both the European radical right and left. Mussolini once claimed that he had learned more from Sorel than any other theorist, while two of the most important right-wing theorists in Weimar Germany, Carl Schmitt, and

Ernst Jünger, had learned their Sorelian lessons as well. One of the most important incubators of conservative revolutionary ideology in the final years of Weimar Republic was a monthly political journal called *Die Tat*. But one of the most important targets of Schmitt, Jünger, and the contributors to *Die Tat* was Marxist theory, and Marcuse's Marxist appropriation of the term can be reasonably distinguished from the irrational voluntarism of Sorel and the Weimar conservative revolutionaries.

In contrast to the *Tat* circle, Marcuse argued that the radical act—like Marx's concept of *praxis*—must be *mediated* socially, theoretically and historically; that is, it must be carried out *collectively* by a universal subject (the self-conscious proletariat), must *follow* theoretical reflection, and must be historically *necessary* (see pp. 5, 32). Marcuse did not, in other words, believe that a radical act could be committed at any time, or by an isolated individual, or in the name of a particularist (e.g., national) group, and he certainly did not celebrate violence as its own end.

Marcuse's objections to Heidegger's understanding of radical action in this essay—that it is not adequately mediated by an analysis of its concrete social and historical conditions (see, for example, p. 15, 24)—anticipate the more substantial critiques of Schmitt, Jünger, and Sorel in his essays after 1933 (his misgivings about this trio are already apparent in his essay on the recent history of German philosophy; see ch. 6 of this volume). Nevertheless, Marcuse's stress on the radical act in this essay verges on calling into question the Marxian notion of the primacy of theory over practice; for example, when he stresses the "*immediate* unity of theory and practice" (see p. 9). In his essays after 1933, when Critical Theory became increasingly isolated, Marcuse would—following Horkheimer—modify, or at least clarify his views on this issue, by explicitly granting greater independence to theory, even viewing it as a mediated form of praxis in and of itself.]

3. [Here and elsewhere, "science" is the translation of the German *Wissenschaft*. See the glossary entry for *Wissenschaft*.]

4. [See the glossary entry for *Erkenntnis/Erkennen/Wissen*.]

5. [See the glossary entry for *Geschehen*.]

6. [Here and elsewhere "historicity" is the translation of the German *Geschichtlichkeit*. See the glossary entry for *Geschichtlichkeit*.]

7. ["Motility" is the translation of the German *Bewegtheit*. See the glossary entry for *Bewegtheit*.]

8. [See the glossary entry for Dasein.]

9. [The German *Aufweisung* has here been translated as "exhibition" and "demonstration." Part of the vocabulary of phenomenology, *aufweisen* is a variant form of the German verb meaning "to point" (*weisen*) that describes the type of knowledge that emerges as a consequence of having made something explicit that was previously implicit. According to the most radical conception of phenomenology, a series of "exhibitions" serves in the place of the traditional notion of "proof" or "demonstration," while the more cautious version of the idea is that only after a phenomenon has been properly "exhibited" does a

framework emerge within which its validity can be established. In Max Scheler's *Essence and Forms of Sympathy*, an "exhibition" (*Aufweisung*) is thus described according to the central trope of the "phenomenological analysis" as a knowledge-act whereby the investigator "allows something to be perceived or known" (*erkennen lassen*). Marcuse, drawing on *Being and Time*'s similar deployment of *aufweisen*, uses the term to describe the recovery of an inherent but obscured relation between the theoretical knowledge under investigation (that of the Marxian fundamental situation) and everyday human existence or practice (historical action). This essay's "exhibitions," then, are meant to intervene in a broken cycle of knowledge: they take an element of existence that has become obscured even as it has remained part of everyday knowledge (*Erkenntnis* in the quotidian sense), and, through analysis, they allow it to be recognized as such (*erkannt als Erkenntnis*) and thus to become part of theoretical knowledge (*Erkenntnis* in the formal sense). See also the glossary entries for *Tat* and *Erkenntnis*, noting the contrast to *Bestand*.]

10. Karl Marx, *Deutsche Ideologie*, in *Marx-Engels-Archiv* 1, ed. D. Rjazanov (Frankfurt: Marx-Engels-Archiv, 1927), 286. [*The German Ideology*, in *The Marx-Engels Reader*, 197 (translation modified).]

11. *Deutsche Ideologie*, 295. [*The Marx-Engels Reader*, 191.]

12. *Deutsche Ideologie*, 251. [*The Marx-Engels Reader*, 160.]

13. Karl Marx, *Die heilige Familie*, in *Aus dem literarischen Nachlaß v. Marx u. Fr. Engels* 2, ed. Franz Mehring (Stuttgart: Dietz, 1920), 132. [Marx, *The Holy Family, or, Critique of Critical Criticism: Against Bruno Bauer and Company*, trans. Richard Dixon and Clemens Dutt (Moscow: Progress Publishers, 1970), 43.]

14. Karl Marx, "Zur Kritik der Hegelschen Rechtsphilosophie," in *Marx-Engels Gesamtausgabe*, half-vol. 1, sect. 1 (Frankfurt: Marx-Engels-Archiv, 1927), 614. ["Contribution to a Critique of Hegel's *Philosophy of Right*: Introduction" in *The Holy Family*, 60.]

15. [See the glossary entry for *existential/existenziell*.]

16. *Deutsche Ideologie*, 229. [Marcuse cites *The German Ideology* as the source of this quote, but it is actually from the "Theses on Feuerbach," in *The Marx-Engels Reader*, 145.]

17. *Deutsche Ideologie*, 228. [Per n. 16 above, the source here is the "Theses on Feuerbach," in *The Marx-Engels Reader*, 144.]

18. Karl Marx, *Archiv* 1, 237. [The cited text appears in a note from the original manuscript of *The German Ideology* (at the end of the very first section on Feuerbach), which Marx subsequently crossed out. In English, one can find the full context of this phrase only in the unabridged version of *The German Ideology*, trans. S. Ryazanskaya (Moscow: Progress Publishers, 1964). The reference here is to a reprint of the 1976 3rd revised edition of the Progress unabridged version (Amherst NY: Prometheus Books, 1998), 34.]

19. *Archiv* 1, 253. [*The German Ideology*, in *The Marx-Engels Reader*, 162.]

20. Karl Marx, "Sankt Max" ["Saint Max"], *Dokumente des Sozialismus* 4 (Stuttgart: Dietz, 1902), 369. [*The German Ideology* (unabridged version), 308 (translation modified).]

21. [See the glossary entry for *Mensch*.]

22. *Deutsche Ideologie*, 237. [*The German Ideology* (unabridged version), 149 (translation modified).]

23. Karl Marx, "Einleitung zur *Kritik politischen Ökonomie*," in *Zur Kritik politischen Ökonomie*, 10th ed., ed. Karl Kautsky (Berlin: Dietz, 1924), xiv. ["Introduction to *A Contribution to the Critique of Political Economy*," in *A Contribution to the Critique of Political Economy*, trans. S. W. Ryazanska (London: Lawrence and Wishart, 1971), 189.]

24. The concept of "reproduction" takes on a different meaning in the subsequent economic analyses of *Capital*.

25. *Deutsche Ideologie*, 245, also 238. [*The German Ideology*, in *The Marx-Engels Reader*, 156, 149.]

26. *Deutsche Ideologie*, 239. [*The German Ideology*, in *The Marx-Engels Reader*, 154 (translation modified).]

27. *Deutsche Ideologie*, 239. [*The German Ideology*, in *The Marx-Engels Reader*, 154 (translation modified).]

28. *Die heilige Familie*, 195. [*The Holy Family*, 110.]

29. *Deutsche Ideologie*, 254. [*The German Ideology*, in *The Marx-Engels Reader*, 172.]

30. [See the glossary entry for *Erbe*.]

31. "Einleitung zur *Kritik politischen Ökonomie*," xxv. ["Introduction to *A Contribution to the Critique of Political Economy*," 190.]

32. *Deutsche Ideolgie*, 255f. [*The German Ideology*, in *The Marx-Engels Reader*, 172.]

33. *Die heilige Familie*, 133. [*The Holy Family*, 44–45 (translation modified).]

34. Karl Marx, *Das Elend der Philosophie*, 5th ed., ed. Friedrich Engels, trans. Eduard Bernstein and Karl Kautsky (Stuttgart: Dietz, 1913), 109. [*The Poverty of Philosophy* (New York: International Publishers, 1963), 126 (translation modified).]

35. Karl Marx, "Thesen über Feuerbach," in *Marx-Engels-Archiv* I, 230 ["Theses on Feuerbach," in *The Marx-Engels Reader*, 145.]

36. In what follows, those thoughts from *Being and Time* that are decisive for our concerns will be presented in extreme brevity.

37. [See the glossary entry for *Sein/Seiendes*.]

38. Martin Heidegger, *Sein und Zeit* (Halle: Niemeyer, 1927), 7. [*Being and Time*, 27 (translation modified). See also the glossary entry for *Sein/Seiendes*.]

39. *Sein und Zeit* , 211. [*Being and Time*, 254.]

40. *Sein und Zeit*, 69. [*Being and Time*, 98. "Ready-to-handness" is the translation of Heidegger's concept of *Zuhandenheit*. See glossary entry for *vorhanden/zuhanden*.]

41. [See the glossary entry for *ursprünglich*.]

42. [Here "making-provision" translates the term *Besorgung*. The term is related to one of the central definitions in *Being and Time*, the positing of *Sorge* ("care" or "concern") as the primary mode of being that Dasein has as *being-in-the-world*. This idea of care is presented by Heidegger as foundational, and thus should not be confused with benevolence, but rather be understood in terms of the whole realm of involvement with things or beings—an involvement which encompasses not simply all the emotive connotations

inherent in the idea of concern (nurturing of, interest in, investigation of, benevolence toward, etc.) but also their opposites (acquisitiveness of, distaste for, ignorance of, fear of, etc.).

The verbal form of the German noun *Sorge* has two different meanings: *besorgen* means both to be concerned about, as in the phrase "Your parents were so concerned about you!", and to acquire or simply "to get," as in the phrase "I went out and got some groceries." The latter meaning can carry appetitive or aggressive connotations, the former rather emotive and sympathetic ones, a duality which MacQuarrie and Robinson attempted to capture by translating *besorgen* in *Being and Time* as "provisioning" or "making-provision." Marcuse, who invokes the idea of *Besorgung* in the potentially explosive language of the "provisioning of life-space" (*Besorgung des Lebensraums*) appears to have done so in a manner that tries to keep an awareness of its full double meaning present at all times. This tension, in turn, is argumentatively tied to his understanding of Marx's notion of the dialectics of economic development.]

43. ["The they" is here a translation of *Being and Time*'s *das Man*, a term which Heidegger uses to refer to Dasein in its inauthenticity. Like the French *on*, the German *man* is used to indicate social conventionality or impersonal directives, as in the English phrase "one simply does not do that." By lending the word *man* a capitalization and a definite article, Heidegger's *das Man* emphasizes the power of "the they" as the voice of inauthentic being.]

44. *Sein und Zeit*, 118. [*Being and Time*, 155 (translation modified).]

45. ["Primordial" and "originary" have both been used to translate Heidegger's concept of *Ursprünglichkeit*. See the glossary entry for *ursprünglich*.]

46. *Sein und Zeit*, 129. [*Being and Time*, 167.]

47. [The German word *Geerbten* is here translated as "inherited," *Erbe* as inheritance. See the glossary.]

48. *Sein und Zeit*, 283. [*Being and Time*, 434 (translation modified).]

49. *Sein und Zeit*, 383. [*Being and Time*, 435 (translation modified).]

50. *Sein und Zeit*, 385–86. [*Being and Time*, 436–37.]

51. *Sein und Zeit*, 384. [*Being and Time*, 436 (translation modified).]

52. *Sein und Zeit*, 385. [*Being and Time*, 436.]

53. [No second part to *Being and Time* was ever published, though *Being and Time*'s projection of a project involving "the historical destruction of the philosophy of history" is often used to describe Heidegger's later work.]

54. *Sein und Zeit*, 117. [*Being and Time*, 153.]

55. [See n. 42 above on *Sorge/Besorgen*.]

56. [See *Being and Time*, 438.]

57. ["Life-space" is the translation of the German term *Lebensraum*. More strikingly than any other concept in Marcuse's first published essay, the repeated use of this fraught term illustrates his problematic proximity to the discourse of conservative revolution in Weimar in the late 1920s. While the term itself would not enter the popular lexicon

in Germany until after the National Socialist seizure of power in 1933, it had been introduced into scholarly discussions around the turn of the century by the Leipzig geographer Friedrich Ratzel, and by the late 1920s it had become an integral part of conservative revolutionary ideology. Variations of it appeared frequently throughout Hitler's *Mein Kampf* (1925), and while Hans Grimm's novel *Volk ohne Raum* [People without a Space](1927) did not employ the term, its mixture of imperialism and pseudoscientific evolutionary doctrine served to popularize the concept.

The question facing readers of Marcuse's 1928 "Contributions" is thus: given that Marcuse must have been aware of the right-wing ideological implications of the concept, why did he appropriate it for his own critical Marxist project? Marcuse's writings in the 1920s were also part of the revolt of vitalism (*Lebensphilosophie*) and phenomenology against positivism and neo-Kantianism that peaked during the Weimar Republic. In his early dissertation on the German artist novel, the concept of life (*Leben*) played an important role, and it was also a crucial concept in his *Habilitationschrift* on Hegel. Like many of his generation, Marcuse was attracted to the philosophical concept of life because it articulated discontent with the rapid and contradictory processes of modernization and rationalization in Central Europe during the second half of the nineteenth and the first decades of the twentieth century. (One thinks here of Max Weber's analysis of rationalization as an "iron cage" or Georg Lukács's rehabilitation of Marx's concept of reification in order to analyze the same phenomenon.)

Similar attempts to recapture the "pure experience" of the "life-world," which had allegedly been lost as a result of societal rationalization and a corresponding rigid objectivism in the sciences, also characterized the phenomenological movement in the first decades of the twentieth century. In this context one thinks, for example, of Heidegger's discussion of Dasein as *being-in-the-world*, or of his critique of abstract Cartesian space (*Raum*) in *Being and Time*. Marcuse uses the concept to refer to space neither in an abstract Cartesian sense nor in the blatantly ideological and pseudobiological sense of Ratzel and the National Socialists, but rather in a sense that is thoroughly infused with the historicity of human Dasein. Marcuse even goes a step further than Heidegger—and in so doing demonstrates his fundamental difference from the discourse of conservative revolution—insofar as he recognizes that life-space is not a monolithic and particularistic "community of destiny" but is rather riven with social contradictions that can be resolved only by a *universal* subject (see, for example, p. 23ff). Marcuse was, nonetheless, not as quick as his future colleague Max Horkheimer to recognize the danger of the discourse of life being placed in the service of conservative, or even conservative revolutionary ends. It was not until *after* 1933—when it became clear that "the struggle against reason" of Heidegger, Carl Schmitt, and other theorists of "political existentialism," as Marcuse refers to them, had "drive[n] [them] blindly into the arms of the powers that be"—that Marcuse reconsidered the critical potential of the rationalist tradition. This reconsideration would culminate in his defense of the critical, negative, and dialectical rationalism of Hegel in his 1941 *Reason and Revolution*.

For a discussion of Marcuse's relationship to the discourse of conservative revolution in Weimar Germany, see Alfons Söllner "Disciples de gauche de la révolution conservatrice: La théorie politique d'Otto Kirchheimer et de Herbert Marcuse dans les dernières années de la République de Weimar," in *Weimar ou l'explosion de la modernité*, ed. Gérard Raulet (Paris: Éditions Anthropos, 1984), 113–30; Gérard Raulet, "Die 'Gemeinschaft' beim jungen Marcuse," in *Intellektuellendiskurse in der Weimarer Republik: Zur Politischen Kultur einer Gemengelage*, ed. Manfred Gangl and Gérard Raulet (Darmstadt: Wissenschaftliche Buchgesellschaft, 1994), 97–110; and John Abromeit "Herbert Marcuse's Critical Encounter with Martin Heidegger, 1927–33," in *Herbert Marcuse: A Critical Reader*, ed. John Abromeit and W. Mark Cobb (London: Routledge, 2004). For Horkheimer's critique of the authoritarian tendencies of vitalism and phenomenology in the late 1920s see his *Gesammelte Schriften*, vol. 10, 317–33 and 377–419. For Marcuse's critique of "political existentialism" after 1933 see "The Struggle Against Liberalism in the Totalitarian View of the State," in *Negations: Essays in Critical Theory*, trans. Jeremy J. Shapiro (Boston: Beacon, 1968), 3–42.]

58. [Wilhelm Dilthey, *The Formation of the Historical World in the Human Sciences*, ed. Rudolf A. Makkreel and Frithjof Rodi, trans. Rudolf A. Makkreel, John Scanlon, and William H. Oman (Princeton NJ: Princeton University Press, 2002).]

59. [Here is Marcuse's first usage of the term "material content," a translation of German *materiale Bestand*. Marcuse uses a variant of an important word in the Heideggerian vocabulary for temporality, *Bestand*. In Heidegger's philosophy as a whole, the term *Bestand* refers to the sum of always already existing objects and entities (*Seiende*) comprising Dasein's environment (*Umwelt*). The word is derived from the common German verb *bestehen*, which, in its first meaning, means "to remain," "to persist," or "to exist over time." This primary set of temporal meanings is in turn allied with its second main meaning, which connotes the artifactual or physical components of things, their status of "consisting of" or "subsisting out of" discrete elements. The most common nominal form of *bestehen* is *Bestand*, which in German means "ongoing existence" (for example of a building or a institution), but also "stock" or "reserve" in the sense of a source of future activity or strength. *Bestand*, finally, often serves as the end element in compound words used to denote the status quo pertaining to a related "set" of things, as in the phrase *Tatbestand* (a factual state of affairs within philosophy) or *Lehrbestand*, the current state of knowledge.

In the vocabulary of *Being and Time*, these interrelated meanings play a modest role in the exposition of how Dasein, in its primary attitude of care and appropriation (*Sorge*) finds itself in its historicity and facticity already engaged with the world and with a concrete set of involvements, and thus with Dasein's *Bestand*. In Heidegger's writings of the 1930s, the term *Bestand*, often translated as "standing reserve," plays a decidedly more significant role, coming to refer to the overall the process whereby the world, nature, and even human existence itself are historically transformed into the "raw material" of technology.

60. Wilhelm Dilthey, *Der Aufbau der geschichtlichen Welt in den Geisteswissenschaften* (Leipzig: Teubner, 1927), 287–88. [*The Formation of the Historical World*, 307 (translation modified).]

61. "Einleitung zur *Kritik politischen Ökonomie*," xliii. ["Introduction to *A Contribution to the Critique of Political Economy*," 212.]

62. Friedrich Engels, *Ludwig Feuerbach und der Ausgang der klassischen Deutschen Philosophie*, ed. Hermann Duncker, Marxistische Bibliothek: Werke Des Marxismus Leninismus, vol. 3 (Wien: Verlag für Literatur und Politik, 1927), 52. [*Ludwig Feuerbach and the Outcome of Classic German Philosophy* (New York: International Publishers, 1941), 44.]

63. Vladimir Lenin, *Sammelband*, in *Der Kampf um die soziale Revolution* (Wien: Verlag für Literatur und Politik, 1925), 623. [The translation here is Eric Oberle's. This is a reference to Plekhanov, who, as Lenin suggests, adopted this phrase from Hegel.]

64. Karl Marx, "Nachwort," in *Das Kapital* (Berlin: Dietz, 1923), xlviii. ["Afterword," in *Capital*, vol. 1, trans. Ben Fowkes (New York: Vintage, 1977), 103.]

65. [See the glossary entry for *Tätigkeit* and *Tun*.]

66. Friedrich Engels, *Dialektik und Natur*, in *Marx-Engels-Archiv* 2 (Frankfurt: Marx-Engels-Archiv, 1927). [*Dialectics of Nature*, ed. and trans. Clemens Dutt (New York: International Publishers, 1960).]

67. [See Wilhelm Dilthey, *Introduction to the Human Sciences*, ed. and trans. Rudolf A. Makkreel and Frithjof Rodi (Princeton NJ: Princeton University Press, 1989).]

68. Karl Liebknecht, *Studien über die Bewegungsgesetze der Gesellschaftlichen Entwicklung* (München: Wolff, 1922), see especially 95ff.

69. *Studien über die Bewegungsgesetze*, 98.

70. [See n. 57, ch. 1.]

71. [See the glossary entry for *Ontologie*.]

72. *Sein und Zeit*, 389. [*Being and Time*, 389 (translation modified).]

73. "Thesen über Feuerbach," in *Archiv* 1, 227. ["Theses on Feuerbach," in *The Marx-Engels Reader*, 143.]

2. On Concrete Philosophy

1. These observations attempt to demonstrate, from the position worked out for phenomenological philosophy by Heidegger's book *Being and Time*, the possibility of a concrete philosophy and its necessity in the present situation. Such a philosophy can only actually prove its value through its accomplishments. The following remarks are not intended to substitute for it; they only attempt to prevent parts of a concrete philosophy, to the extent that they are actually present, from constantly being dismissed as "unphilosophical," or at best as an interlude between episodes of "true" philosophy.

2. [See glossary entries for *Sein* ("being") and *Mensch* ("man").]

3. [See glossary entry for *Erkenntnis/Erkennen/Wissen*.]

4. "Truth" in the following is always used only in the just intimated sense of existentially essential true conditions, in other words, not to refer to mere "accuracies," which never address the being of Dasein and its modes of existence.

5. [For what Heidegger sees as the philosophical significance of the etymological kinship between these two terms, see the discussion of *Geschehen* in the glossary.]

6. [See the glossary entries for *Ontologie* and *Geschichtlichkeit* ("historicity").]

7. On these relationships, see Lukács, *Geschichte und Klassenbewußtsein: Studien über marxistische Dialektik* (Berlin: Malik, 1923), 94ff. [*History and Class Consciousness*, 83ff.]

8. On this topic, see my "Contributions to the Phenomenology of Historical Materialism." [Ch. 1 of this volume.]

9. [See the glossary.]

10. Søren Kierkegaard, *Bogem on Adler*, in *Der Begriff des Auserwählten*, trans. Theodor Haeker (Innsbruck: Brenner, 1926), 94, 101. [*On Authority and Revelation: The Book on Adler, or a Cycle of Ethico-Religious Essays*, trans. Walter Lowrie (Princeton NJ: Princeton University Press, 1966), 63, 66 (translation modified).]

11. See n. 43, ch. 1.

3. On the Problem of the Dialectic

1. Siegfried Marck, *Die Dialektik in der Philosophie der Gegenwart*, half-vol. 1 (Tübingen: Mohr, 1929). [The Dialetic in Contemporary Philosophy.]

2. *Die Dialektik* 1, iii.

3. [See the glossary entry for *Sein* and *Seiendes*.]

4. Julius Stenzel, *Studien zur Entwicklung der Platonischen Dialektik von Sokrates zu Aristoteles* (Breslau: Trewendt and Granier, 1917). [*Plato's Method of Dialectic*, ed. and trans. D. J. Allan (Oxford UK: Clarendon, 1940).]

5. [See the glossary entry for *Bewegtheit*.]

6. [Plato, *Theaetetus*, in *Complete Works*, ed. John Cooper, trans. M. J. Levett, rev. Myles Burnyeat (Hackett: Indianapolis IN, 1997), 152d (translation modified).]

7. [Plato, *Philebus*, in *Complete Works*, trans. Dorothea Frede, 15a.]

8. [Here and elsewhere "determination" has been used to translate the Hegelian concept of *Bestimmung*. See the glossary entry for *Bestimmung/Bestimmtheit/Definition*.]

9. [See the glossary entries for *Erkenntnis/Erkennen/Wissen*.]

10. *Die Dialektik* 1, 23ff.

11. [*Philebus*, 26e-27b.]

12. We need not address the essentially necessary relation of the Platonic dialectic to spoken argument and counterargument as revelation of being because this meaning of the dialectic was completely lost in its further development and can be valid only within the Greek world.

13. [See glossary entry for *Geschichtlichkeit*.]

14. [Marcuse's insertion.]

15. G. W. F. Hegel, *Phänomenologie des Geistes*, vol. 2, in *Sämtliche Werke*, ed. Georg Lasson (Leipzig: Meiner, 1928), 31. [*Hegel's Phenomenology of Spirit*, trans. A. V. Miller (Oxford UK: Clarendon Press, 1977), 27 (translation modified).]

16. *Phänomenologie des Geistes*, 36. [*Phenomenology of Spirit*, 32.]

17. G. W. F. Hegel, *Wissenschaft der Logik*, vols. 3–4, in *Sämtliche Werke*, ed. Georg Lasson (Leipzig: Meiner, 1923), 36. [*Hegel's Science of Logic*, trans. A. V. Miller (London: Allen and Unwin, 1969), 54 (translation modified).]

18. *Wissenschaft der Logik*, 36. [*Science of Logic*, 54 (translation modified.]

19. *Phänomenologie des Geistes*, 20. [*Phenomenology of Spirit*, 17. [Insertion in brackets is Marcuse's.]

20. [See glossary entry for *Geschehen*.]

21. Martin Heidegger, *Vom Wesen des Grundes* (Halle: Niemeyer, 1929); *Kant und das Problem der Metaphysik* (Bonn: Cohn, 1929). [*The Essence of Reasons*, trans. Terrence Malick (Evanston IL: Northwestern University Press, 1969); *Kant and the Problem of Metaphysics*, trans. Richard Taft (Bloomington: Indiana University Press, 1997).]

22. *Die Dialektik* 1, 122ff.

23. *Die Dialektik* 1, 131ff.

24. Siegfried Marck, *Die Dialektik in der Philosophie der Gegenwart*, half-vol. 2 (Tübingen: Mohr, 1931).

25. *Die Dialektik* 2, 89.

26. *Die Dialektik* 2, 88ff.

27. *Die Dialektik* 2, 95.

28. *Die Dialektik* 2, 95ff, 5ff.

29. *Die Dialektik* 2, 91.

30. *Die Dialektik* 2, 91.

31. *Die Dialektik* 2, 95.

32. *Die Dialektik* 2, 94.

33. [See glossary entry for *Vergegenständlichung/Verdinglichung/Gegenständlichkeit*.]

34. [See glossary entry for *Verhalten/sich verhalten*.]

35. G. W. F. Hegel, *Hegels Theologische Jugendschriften*, ed. Herman Nohl (Tübingen: Mohr, 1907), 303. [*Early Theological Writings*, tr. T. M. Knox (Philadelphia: University of Pennsylvania Press, 1971), 254.]

36. *Die Dialektik* 2, 95.

37. *Phänomenologie des Geistes*, vol. 2, in *Sämlitche Werke*, ed. Hermann Glockner (Stuttgart: Frommann, 1927), 134–40. [*Phenomenology of Spirit*, 106–11.]

38. *Die Dialektik* 2, 90.

39. Einleiting zur *Wissenschaft der Logik*. [*Science of Logic*, 50 (translation modified).]

40. *Die Dielektik* 2, 95.

41. *Die Dialektik* 2, 96.

42. *Die Dialektik* 2, 97.

43. Richard Hönigswald, *Die Grundlagen der Denkpsychologie: Studien und Analysen* (München: Reinhardt, 1921).[Foundations of the Psychology of Thinking.]

44. *Die Dialektik* 2, 16.

45. *Die Dialektik* 2, 21.

46. *Die Dialektik* 2, 23.

47. *Die Dialektik* 2, 25. [See glossary entry for *Vergegenständlichung*.]

48. *Die Dialektik* 2, 25.

49. *Die Dialektik* 2, 6.

50. *Die Dialektik* 2, 12.

51. *Die Dialektik* 2, 17.

52. *Die Dialektik* 2, 20.

53. [*Critique of Pure Reason*, trans. Norman Kemp Smith (London: Macmillan, 1961), 300.]

54. *Die Dialektik* 2, iii.

55. *Die Dialektik* 2, ii.

56. Stenzel's article, mentioned in the first part of the essay, and Gadamer's book (particularly the first chapter), *Platos dialektische Ethik: Phänomenologische Interpretationen zum "Philebos"* (Leipzig: Meiner, 1931)[*Plato's Dialetical Ethics: Phenomenological Interpretations relating to the Philebus*, trans. Robert Wallace (New Haven: Yale University Press, 1991] are relevant here.

57. *Wissenschaft der Logik*, 414. [*Science of Logic*, 762 (translation modified).]

58. *Wissenschaft der Logik*, 423. [*Science of Logic*, 769 (translation modified).]

59. *Wissenschaft der Logik*, 425. [*Science of Logic*, 771–72 (translation modified).]

60. *Die Dialektik* 2, 6.

61. *Die Dialektik* 2, 12.

62. G. W. F. Hegel, *Enzyklopädie der philosophischen Wissenschaften im Grundrisse, und Andere Schriften aus der Heidelberger Zeit*, in *Sämtliche Werke*, vol. 6, ed. Hermann Glockner (Stuttgart: Frommann, 1927), 136. [*The Logic of Hegel: Translated from* The Encyclopedia of the Philosophical Sciences, trans. William Wallace (Oxford UK: Clarendon, 1874), 315 (translation modified).]

63. [On Marcuse's appropriation of Hegel's concept of "doing," see the entry for *Tun/Tätigkeit* in the glossary.]

64. *Phänomenologie des Geistes* (Glockner), 305. [*Phenomenology of Spirit*, 245 (translation modified).]

65. *Phänomenologie des Geistes* (Glockner), 314. [*Phenomenology of Spirit*, 253 (translation modified).]

66. [See glossary entry for *aufheben*.]

67. [See n. 2, ch. 1.]

68. *Phänomenologie des Geistes* (Glockner), 148ff. [*Phenomenology of Spirit*, 118–19.]

69. *Phänomenologie des Geistes* (Glockner), 151. [*Phenomenology of Spirit*, 120 (translation modified).]

70. *Phänomenologie des Geistes* (Glockner), 149. [*Phenomenology of Spirit*, 118–19 (translation modified).]

71. *Phänomenologie des Geistes* (Glockner), 149. [*Phenomenology of Spirit*, 118–19 (translation modified).]

72. *Die Dialektik* 2, 170.

73. *Phänomenologie des Geistes* (Glockner), 265; also 267 and 332ff. [*Phenomenology of Spirit*, 212 (translation modified); also 214 and 267.]

74. *Phänomenologie des Geistes* (Glockner), 373ff. [*Phenomenology of Spirit*, 301.]

75. *Phänomenologie des Geistes* (Glockner), 223. [*Phenomenology of Spirit*, 178.]

76. *Phänomenologie des Geistes* (Glockner), 223. [*Phenomenology of Spirit*, 178.]

4. New Sources on Historical Materialism

1. *Ökonomisch-philosophischen Manuskripte von Jahr 1844*, in *Marx-Engels-Gesamtausgabe*, half-vol. 3, sect. 1, ed. D. Rjazanov (Frankfurt: Marx-Engels-Archiv, 1932). It was published almost simultaneously under the title *Nationalökonomie und Philosophie*, in *Der Historische Materialismus: Die Frühschriften*, ed. S. Landshut and J. P. Mayer (Leipzig: Kröner, 1932), 283 ff. In this edition, a piece (which is hardly dispensable for an understanding of the whole) is missing. The missing part is reprinted on pp. 39–94 of the *Gesamtausgabe* as *Erstes Manuskript*.

2. [See glossary entries for *Vergegenständlichung* ("objectification"), *Entäußerung* ("alienation"), and *Aufhebung* ("sublation").]

3. *Ökonomisch-philosophischen Manuskripte*, 153. [*Economic and Philosophic Manuscripts of 1844*, ed., Dirk J. Struik, trans. Martin Milligan (London: International Publishers, 1970), 173.]

4. [See the glossary.]

5. *Ökonomisch-philosophischen Manuskripte*, 34. [*Economic and Philosophic Manuscripts*, 64.]

6. [See the glossary entry for *Wissenschaft*.]

7. [See the glossary entry for *Mensch* ("man"), *Wesen* ("essence") and *Bestimmung* ("determination").]

8. *Ökonomisch-philosophischen Manuskripte*, 114. [*Economic and Philosophic Manuscripts*, 135.]

9. *Ökonomisch-philosophischen Manuskripte*, 109. [*Economic and Philosophic Manuscripts*, 130.]

10. *Ökonomisch-philosophischen Manuskripte*, 81. [*Economic and Philosophic Manuscripts*, 106.]

11. [See glossary entry for *Tätigkeit* ("activity").]

12. *Ökonomisch-philosophischen Manuskripte*, 77. [*Economic and Philosophic Manuscripts*, 102.]

13. *Ökonomisch-philosophischen Manuskripte*, 82. [*Economic and Philosophic Manuscripts*, 107.]

14. *Ökonomisch-philosophischen Manuskripte*, see the table on p. 39. [*Economic and Philosophic Manuscripts*, 7.]

15. *Ökonomisch-philosophischen Manuskripte*, note from Russian publisher, 38.

16. *Ökonomisch-philosophischen Manuskripte*, 91. [*Economic and Philosophic Manuscripts*, 117.]

17. *Ökonomisch-philosophischen Manuskripte*, 91. [*Economic and Philosophic Manuscripts*, 117.]
18. *Ökonomisch-philosophischen Manuskripte*, 117–18. [*Economic and Philosophic Manuscripts*, 138–39 (translation modified).]
19. *Ökonomisch-philosophischen Manuskripte*, 121. [*Economic and Philosophic Manuscripts*, 142 (translation modified).]
20. *Ökonomisch-philosophischen Manuskripte*, 112. [*Economic and Philosophic Manuscripts*, 133.]
21. *Ökonomisch-philosophischen Manuskripte*, 111. [*Economic and Philosophic Manuscripts*, 132.]
22. *Ökonomisch-philosophischen Manuskripte*, 111–12. [*Economic and Philosophic Manuscripts*, 133.]
23. *Ökonomisch-philosophischen Manuskripte*, 82–83. [*Economic and Philosophic Manuscripts*, 107–8.]
24. *Ökonomisch-philosophischen Manuskripte*, 42. [*Economic and Philosophic Manuscripts*, 68.]
25. *Ökonomisch-philosophischen Manuskripte*, 44. [*Economic and Philosophic Manuscripts*, 70.]
26. *Ökonomisch-philosophischen Manuskripte*, 83. [*Economic and Philosophic Manuscripts*, 108.]
27. *Ökonomisch-philosophischen Manuskripte*, 41. [*Economic and Philosophic Manuscripts*, 67.]
28. *Ökonomisch-philosophischen Manuskripte*, 83. [*Economic and Philosophic Manuscripts*, 108.]
29. *Ökonomisch-philosophischen Manuskripte*, 83. [*Economic and Philosophic Manuscripts*, 108.]
30. "Reification" denotes the general condition of "human reality" resulting from the loss of the object of labor and the alienation of the worker that has found its "classical" expression in the capitalist world of money and commodities. There is thus a sharp distinction between reification and objectification (the latter will be discussed more fully below). Reification is a specific ("estranged," "untrue") *mode* of objectification.
31. *Ökonomisch-philosophischen Manuskripte*, 83–84. [*Economic and Philosophic Manuscripts*, 108–9.]
32. *Ökonomisch-philosophischen Manuskripte*, 91. [*Economic and Philosophic Manuscripts*, 117.]
33. *Ökonomisch-philosophischen Manuskripte*, 91. [*Economic and Philosophic Manuscripts*, 117.]
34. [See the glossary entry for *Ontologie*.]
35. *Ökonomisch-philosophischen Manuskripte*, 145, italics mine. [*Economic and Philosophic Manuscripts*, 165.] Compare the passage in Feuerbach that clearly underlies the sentence quoted: "Human feelings have no empirical or anthropological significance in the sense

of the old transcendent philosophy; they have ontological and metaphysical significance" (Ludwig Feuerbach, *Grundsätze der Philosophie der Zukunft*, in *Sämtliche Werke*, vol. 2 (Leipzig: Wigand, 1846), 324 (§33). [*Principles of the Philosophy of the Future*, trans. Manfred Vogel (Indianapolis IN: Hackett, 1986), 53 (§33).]

36. *Ökonomisch-philosophischen Manuskripte*, 157, 168, 87–88. [*Economic and Philosophic Manuscripts*, 177, 188, 113.]

37. Compare the following passages from Hegel: being-for-itself "comes into its own through labor." In labor the consciousness of the worker "is externalized and passes into the condition of permanence," "in working, consciousness, as the form of the thing formed, becomes an object for itself" (*Phänomenologie des Geistes* [Glockner], 148–50). [*Phenomenology of Spirit*, 117–19.]

38. For a more detailed discussion of these issues I must refer the reader to the extensive interpretation of Hegel's concept of labor in my book, *Hegels Ontologie und die Grundlegung einer Theorie der Geschichtlichkeit* (Frankfurt: Klostermann, 1932). [*Hegel's Ontology and the Theory of Historicity*.] See also Hegel's determination of labor in the new edition of the *Jenenser Realphilosophie* 2 (Leipzig: Meiner, 1931–32), especially pp. 213ff.

39. *Ökonomisch-philosophischen Manuskripte*, 88. [*Economic and Philosophic Manuscripts*, 113.]

40. *Ökonomisch-philosophischen Manuskripte*, 87–89; 159–63. [*Economic and Philosophic Manuscripts*, 112–14; 179–83.]

41. *Ökonomisch-philosophischen Manuskripte*, 114, 116, 160. [*Economic and Philosophic Manuscripts*, 135, 137, 181.]

42. [*Economic and Philosophic Manuscripts*, 236, n. 2 (Marcuse did not provide a cite for this quote).]

43. *Ökonomisch-philosophischen Manuskripte*, 34. [*Economic and Philosophic Manuscripts*, 64.]

44. *Ökonomisch-philosophischen Manuskripte*, 152. [*Economic and Philosophic Manuscripts*, 172.]

45. *Ökonomisch-philosophischen Manuskripte*, 87. [*Economic and Philosophic Manuscripts*, 112.]

46. [See glossary entry for *Sein/Seindes* ("being"/ "be-ing").]

47. *Ökonomisch-philosophischen Manuskripte*, 88. [*Economic and Philosophic Manuscripts*, 114.]

48. *Ökonomisch-philosophischen Manuskripte*, 87. [*Economic and Philosophic Manuscripts*, 112.]

49. *Ökonomisch-philosophischen Manuskripte*, 87. [*Economic and Philosophic Manuscripts*, 112.]

50. *Ökonomisch-philosophischen Manuskripte*, 88. [*Economic and Philosophic Manuscripts*, 113.]

51. *Ökonomisch-philosophischen Manuskripte*, 88. [*Economic and Philosophic Manuscripts*, 113.]

52. *Ökonomisch-philosophischen Manuskripte*, 88. [*Economic and Philosophic Manuscripts*, 114.]

53. See *Phänomenologie des Geistes* (Glockner), 136 [*Phenomenology of Spirit*, 107], the concept of "inorganic nature," and pp. 234ff. of my book *Hegels Ontologie*. [*Hegel's Ontology*, 207ff.]

54. *Ökonomisch-philosophischen Manuskripte*, 89. [*Economic and Philosophic Manuscripts*, 114.]

55. *Ökonomisch-philosophischen Manuskripte*, 114, 160. [*Economic and Philosophic Manuscripts*, 135, 181.]

56. *Ökonomisch-philosophischen Manuskripte*, 159. [*Economic and Philosophic Manuscripts*, 180.]

57. *Ökonomisch-philosophischen Manuskripte*, 160–61. [*Economic and Philosophic Manuscripts*, 181–82.]

58. *Ökonomisch-philosophischen Manuskripte*, 159. [*Economic and Philosophic Manuscripts*, 180.]

59. *Ökonomisch-philosophischen Manuskripte*, 160. [*Economic and Philosophic Manuscripts*, 180.]

60. *Ökonomisch-philosophischen Manuskripte*, 161. [*Economic and Philosophic Manuscripts*, 181.]

61. *Ökonomisch-philosophischen Manuskripte*, 123. [*Economic and Philosophic Manuscripts*, 143.]

62. [*Critique of Pure Reason*, 65 (§B 33).]

63. *Grundsätze der Philosophie der Zukunft*, 309. [*Principles of the Philosophy of the Future*, 40.]

64. *Grundsätze der Philosophie der Zukunft*, 321–22. [*Principles of the Philosophy of the Future*, 51.]

65. "Vorläufige Thesen zur Reform der Philosophie" [Prelimary Theses on the Reform of Philosophy], in *Sämtliche Werke*, vol. 2, 257.

66. "Vorläufige Thesen zur Reform der Philosophie" [Prelimary Theses on the Reform of Philosophy], 256–57.

67. *Ökonomisch-philosophischen Manuskripte*, 160. [*Economic and Philosophic Manuscripts*, 181.]

68. *Ökonomisch-philosophischen Manuskripte*, 161. [*Economic and Philosophic Manuscripts*, 182.]

69. *Ökonomisch-philosophischen Manuskripte*, 161. [*Economic and Philosophic Manuscripts*, 182.] The ontological concept of passion is found similarly in Feuerbach, *Grundsätze der Philosophie der Zukunft*, 323. [*Principles of the Philosophy of the Future*, 53.]

70. *Ökonomisch-philosophischen Manuskripte*, 123. [*Economic and Philosophic Manuscripts*, 144.]

71. *Economic and Philosophic Manuscripts*, 165 (Marcuse did not provide a cite for this quote).

72. *Ökonomisch-philosophischen Manuskripte*, 156. [*Economic and Philosophic Manuscripts*, 177.]

73. See, for example, "Vorläufige Thesen zur Reform der Philosophie" [Prelimary Theses on the Reform of Philosophy], 258, and *Grundsätze der Philosophie der Zukunft*, 337 [*Principles of the Philosophy of the Future*, 65.] The indications of a more profound determination, which doubtless exist in Feuerbach, are not followed through. Compare, for example, the concept of "resistance" (321ff.[51]), etc.

74. *Ökonomisch-philosophischen Manuskripte*, 160. [*Economic and Philosophic Manuscripts*, 181.]

75. [*Economic and Philosophic Manuscripts*, 144 (Marcuse did not provide a cite for this quote).]

76. *Ökonomisch-philosophischen Manuskripte*, 89. [*Economic and Philosophic Manuscripts*, 114.]

77. See the comprehensive formulation in *The Holy Family*: "that the object as being for man or as the objective being of man is at the same time the existence of man for other men, his human relation to other men, the social relation of man to man" (*Die Heilige Familie und Schriften von Marx von Anfang 1844 bis Anfang 1845*, in *Marx-Engels Gesamtausgabe*, half-vol. 3, sect. 1 (Berlin: Marx-Engels-Archiv, 1932), 213. [*The Holy Family*, 60.]

78. *Ökonomisch-philosophischen Manuskripte*, 115. [*Economic and Philosophic Manuscripts*, 136.]

79. *Ökonomisch-philosophischen Manuskripte*, 162, 125. [*Economic and Philosophic Manuscripts*, 182, 145.]

80. *Ökonomisch-philosophischen Manuskripte*, 125. [*Economic and Philosophic Manuscripts*, 145.]

81. [See glossary entry for *Geschehen*.]

82. Feuerbach: "Man is not a particular being, like the animals, but a universal being; he is not, then, a limited and restricted being, but rather an unlimited and free being, for universality, absoluteness, and freedom are inseparable. This freedom does not lie in a special faculty . . . [but] extend[s] . . . over man's total being" (*Grundsätze der Philosophie der Zukunft*, 342). [*Principles of the Philosophy of the Future*, 69.]

83. *Ökonomisch-philosophischen Manuskripte*, 171. [*Economic and Philosophic Manuscripts*, 192 (translation modified).]

84. [See glossary entry on *Verhalten/sich verhalten*.]

85. *Ökonomisch-philosophischen Manuskripte*, 88. [*Economic and Philosophic Manuscripts*, 113. See glossary entry for *Bestimmtheit* ("determinacy").]

86. *Ökonomisch-philosophischen Manuskripte*, 88, 115–16, 88. [*Economic and Philosophic Manuscripts*, 113, 136–37, 113. See glossary.]

87. [See glossary entry for *Bestimmung*.]

88. *Ökonomisch-philosophischen Manuskripte*, 118. [*Economic and Philosophic Manuscripts*, 139.]

89. *Ökonomisch-philosophischen Manuskripte*, 119. [*Economic and Philosophic Manuscripts*, 140.]

90. *Ökonomisch-philosophischen Manuskripte*, 86. [*Economic and Philosophic Manuscripts*, 111.]

91. *Ökonomisch-philosophischen Manuskripte*, 86. [*Economic and Philosophic Manuscripts*, 111.]

92. *Ökonomisch-philosophischen Manuskripte*, 118. [*Economic and Philosophic Manuscripts*, 139.]

93. [See glossary entry on *Geschichtlichkeit.*]

94. The *German Ideology* says of the critique in the *Deutsch-Französische Jahrbücher*: "Since at that time this was done in philosophical phraseology, the traditionally occurring philosophical expressions such as 'human essence,' 'species,' etc., gave the German theoreticians the desired excuse for . . . believing that here again it was a question merely of giving a new turn to their theoretical garments" (*Der Historische Materialismus* 2, 225. [*The German Ideology* (unabridged version), 259.]

95. *Ökonomisch-philosophischen Manuskripte*, 88. [*Economic and Philosophic Manuscripts*, 113.]

96. *Ökonomisch-philosophischen Manuskripte*, 90. [*Economic and Philosophic Manuscripts*, 115.]

97. [*Economic and Philosophic Manuscripts*, 117 (Marcuse did not provide a cite for this quote).]

98. *Ökonomisch-philosophischen Manuskripte*, 114. [*Economic and Philosophic Manuscripts*, 136.]

99. *Ökonomisch-philosophischen Manuskripte*, 114–15. [*Economic and Philosophic Manuscripts*, 136–37.]

100. *Ökonomisch-philosophischen Manuskripte*, 117–18. [*Economic and Philosophic Manuscripts*, 138–39.]

101. This turn from a state outside men to a human relation again illustrates the new problematic of Marx's theory: his penetration through the veil of abstract reification toward the comprehension of the objective world as the field of historical-social praxis. Marx emphasizes that this way of posing the question had already entered traditional political economy when Adam Smith recognized labor as the "principle" of economics, but its real sense was immediately completely concealed again since this kind of political economy "merely formulated the laws of *estranged* labor," italics mine (92 [117]).

102. *Ökonomisch-philosophischen Manuskripte*, 107. [*Economic and Philosophic Manuscripts*, 128.]

103. *Ökonomisch-philosophischen Manuskripte*, 93. [*Economic and Philosophic Manuscripts*, 119.] Marx directs his heaviest attacks in the *German Ideology* precisely against the concept of "truly human property" (particularly in his polemic against the "true socialists," *Deutsche Ideologie*, pp. 500–501 [516–17]); here, within Marx's foundation of the theory of revolution, this concept obviously has a significance quite different from that in Stirner and the "true socialist."

104. *Ökonomisch-philosophischen Manuskripte*, 93. [*Economic and Philosophic Manuscripts*, 118.]

105. *Ökonomisch-philosophischen Manuskripte*, 145. [*Economic and Philosophic Manuscripts*, 165.]

106. [*Economic and Philosophic Manuscripts*, 138–39 (Marcuse did not provide a cite for this quote).]

107. *Ökonomisch-philosophischen Manuskripte*, 118. [*Economic and Philosophic Manuscripts*, 138.]

108. *Ökonomisch-philosophischen Manuskripte*, 119. [*Economic and Philosophic Manuscripts*, 140.]

109. *Ökonomisch-philosophischen Manuskripte*, 117. [*Economic and Philosophic Manuscripts*, 137–38.]

110. *Ökonomisch-philosophischen Manuskripte*, 134. [*Economic and Philosophic Manuscripts*, 154.]

111. *Ökonomisch-philosophischen Manuskripte*, 93. [*Economic and Philosophic Manuscripts*, 118–19.]

112. *Ökonomisch-philosophischen Manuskripte*, 90–91. [*Economic and Philosophic Manuscripts*, 116–17.]

113. *Ökonomisch-philosophischen Manuskripte*, 156, italics mine. [*Economic and Philosophic Manuscripts*, 177.]

114. *Ökonomisch-philosophischen Manuskripte*, 91, italics mine. [*Economic and Philosophic Manuscripts*, 116.]

115. *Ökonomisch-philosophischen Manuskripte*, 90. [*Economic and Philosophic Manuscripts*, 115.]

116. *Ökonomisch-philosophischen Manuskripte*, 90–91. [*Economic and Philosophic Manuscripts*, 116–17.]

117. *Phänomenologie des Geistes* (Glockner), 145ff. [*Phenomenology of Spirit*, 115ff.] I also discuss this in my essay "On the Problem of the Dialectic." [Ch. 3 in this volume.]

118. *Ökonomisch-philosophischen Manuskripte*, 94. [*Economic and Philosophic Manuscripts*, 119.]

119. *Ökonomisch-philosophischen Manuskripte*, 121. [*Economic and Philosophic Manuscripts*, 141–42.]

120. *Ökonomisch-philosophischen Manuskripte*, 160. [*Economic and Philosophic Manuscripts*, 181.]

121. *Ökonomisch-philosophischen Manuskripte*, 150. [*Economic and Philosophic Manuscripts*, 170.]

122. *Ökonomisch-philosophischen Manuskripte*, 151. [*Economic and Philosophic Manuscripts*, 172.]

123. *Ökonomisch-philosophischen Manuskripte*, 151–52. [*Economic and Philosophic Manuscripts*, 172–73.]

124. *Ökonomisch-philosophischen Manuskripte*, 153. [*Economic and Philosophic Manuscripts*, 173.]

125. *Ökonomisch-philosophischen Manuskripte*, 153. [*Economic and Philosophic Manuscripts*, 173.]

126. *Ökonomisch-philosophischen Manuskripte*, 158. [*Economic and Philosophic Manuscripts*, 178 (translation modified).]

127. *Ökonomisch-philosophischen Manuskripte*, 162. [*Economic and Philosophic Manuscripts*, 182.]

128. *Ökonomisch-philosophischen Manuskripte*, 157. [*Economic and Philosophic Manuscripts*, 178.]

129. *Ökonomisch-philosophischen Manuskripte*, 157. [*Economic and Philosophic Manuscripts*, 178.]

130. *Ökonomisch-philosophischen Manuskripte*, 161 [*Economic and Philosophic Manuscripts*, 183.]

131. *Ökonomisch-philosophischen Manuskripte*, 161 [*Economic and Philosophic Manuscripts*, 182.]

132. *Ökonomisch-philosophischen Manuskripte*, 167. [*Economic and Philosophic Manuscripts*, 177(translation modified).]

133. *Ökonomisch-philosophischen Manuskripte*, 163–64. [*Economic and Philosophic Manuscripts*, 183–84.]

134. *Ökonomisch-philosophischen Manuskripte*, 166. [*Economic and Philosophic Manuscripts*, 186–87.]

135. *Ökonomisch-philosophischen Manuskripte*, 171 [*Economic and Philosophic Manuscripts*, 192.]

136. *Ökonomisch-philosophischen Manuskripte*, 168. [*Economic and Philosophic Manuscripts*, 188.]

137. *Ökonomisch-philosophischen Manuskripte*, 152–53. [*Economic and Philosophic Manuscripts*, 173 .]

138. *Ökonomisch-philosophischen Manuskripte*, 156. [*Economic and Philosophic Manuscripts*, 177 (translation modified).]

139. *Ökonomisch-philosophischen Manuskripte*, 153. [*Economic and Philosophic Manuscripts*, 173.]

140. *Ökonomisch-philosophischen Manuskripte*, 168. [*Economic and Philosophic Manuscripts*, 188.]

141. *Ökonomisch-philosophischen Manuskripte*, 159. [*Economic and Philosophic Manuscripts*, 180.]

142. *Ökonomisch-philosophischen Manuskripte*, 159. [*Economic and Philosophic Manuscripts*, 180.]

143. *Ökonomisch-philosophischen Manuskripte*, 156. [*Economic and Philosophic Manuscripts*, 177.]

144. *Ökonomisch-philosophischen Manuskripte*, 154. [*Economic and Philosophic Manuscripts*, 174.].

145. *Ökonomisch-philosophischen Manuskripte*, 167. [*Economic and Philosophic Manuscripts*, 187–88.]

146. *Ökonomisch-philosophischen Manuskripte*, 156. [*Economic and Philosophic Manuscripts*, 177.]

147. *Ökonomisch-philosophischen Manuskripte*, 167. [*Economic and Philosophic Manuscripts*, 188.]

148. *Ökonomisch-philosophischen Manuskripte*, 157. [*Economic and Philosophic Manuscripts*, 177.]

149. *Ökonomisch-philosophischen Manuskripte*, 157. [*Economic and Philosophic Manuscripts*, 177.]

150. *Ökonomisch-philosophischen Manuskripte*, 157. [*Economic and Philosophic Manuscripts*, 177.]

151. *Phänomenologie des Geistes* (Glockner), 146ff. [*Phenomenology of Spirit*, 115–19 (translation modified).]

152. *Ökonomisch-philosophischen Manuskripte*, 157. [*Economic and Philosophic Manuscripts*, 177.]

153. *Phänomenologie des Geistes* (Glockner), 141, 196, 346, 426, etc. [*Phenomenology of Spirit*, 111, 147, 281, 345 (translation modified).]

154. *Ökonomisch-philosophischen Manuskripte*, 152–53. [*Economic and Philosophic Manuscripts*, 173.]

155. *Ökonomisch-philosophischen Manuskripte*, 156. [*Economic and Philosophic Manuscripts*, 176.]

5. On the Concept of Labor in Economics

1. [See glossary entries on *Bestimmung/Bestimmtheit/Definition* ("determination"/ "determinacy" / "definition").]

2. Karl Elster, *Vom Strome der Wirtschaft* [Of the Flow of the Economy], vol. 1 (Jena: Fischer, 1931), 146ff.

3. H. Nowack, "Der Arbeitsbegriff der Wirtschaftswissenschaft" [The Concept of Work in Economic Science], *Jahrbücher für Nationalökonomie und Statistik* 131 (1929): 513.

4. Max Weber, *Wirtschaft und Gesellschaft: Grundriß der verstehenden Soziologie* (Tübingen: Mohr, 1929), 62. [*Economy and Society: An Outline of Interpretative Sociology*, ed. Guenther Roth and Claus Wittich, trans. Ephraim Fischoff et. al. (New York: Bedminster Press, 1968), 114.]

5. Friedrich von Gottl-Ottilienfeld, *Wirtschaft und Wissenschaft* [Economics and Science] (Jena: Fischer, 1931), 31 and 446.

6. Gottl-Ottilienfeld, "Arbeit als Tatbestand des Wirtschaftslebens" [Labor as a Constituent Fact of Economic Life], in *Archiv für Sozialwissenschaft und Sozialpolitik* 50 (1923): 293–94, 296–97, 307.

7. In the essay "Arbeit und Ethik" [Labor and Ethics] in *Schriften zur Soziologie und Weltanschauungslehre*, vol. 3 (Leipzig: Reinhold, 1923–24).

8. Fritz Giese, *Philosophie der Arbeit* [Philosophy of Labor] (Halle: Marhold, 1932), 24.

9. In *Jahrbücher für Nationalökonomie und Statistik* 112 (1919); also in *Vom Strome der Wirtschaft* [On the Flow of the Economy]. See also Nowack, "Der Arbeitsbegriff" [The Concept of Work].

10. [See glossary.]

11. *Phänomenologie des Geistes* (Glockner), 148ff. [G. W. F. Hegel, *The Phenomenology of Spirit*, 117ff.]

12. Lorenz von Stein, *Gesellschaftslehre* [Social Teachings] (Stuttgart: Cotta, 1856), 99.

13. *Marx-Engels-Gesamtausgabe*, half-vol. 3, sect. 1, 157. [Karl Marx, *Economic and Philosophic Manuscripts*, 177.]

14. *Marx-Engels-Gesamtausgabe*, half-vol. 3, sect. 1, 168. [*Economic and Philosophic Manuscripts*, 188. See glossary entries for *Entäußerung* ("alienation"), *Vergegenständlichung* ("objectification"), and *Mensch* ("man").]

15. *Das Kapital: Kritik der politischen Ökonomie*, vol. 1, ed. Karl Kautsky (Stuttgart: Dietz, 1928), 10. [Karl Marx, *Capital*, vol. 1, 133.]

16. *Das Kapital*, 133 and 136. [*Capital*, 283 and 287.] To be sure Marx determines labor also as "purposeful activity," but as such it is for him explicitly only a "moment of the process of labor" (134 [284]) and not the whole process of labor itself.

17. [See the glossary entry for *Geschehen* ("happening").]

18. Since play will be used a counterconcept to labor, the character of play cannot be based primarily on the play of *children*. It is still highly questionable whether in the life of children play does not fulfill a role similar or corresponding to labor in the life of adults. See H. Lufft, "Der Begriff der Arbeit" [The Concept of Labor], *Jahrbücher für Nationalökonomie und Statistik* 123 (1925).

19. [See glossary entry for *Vergegenständlichung/Verdinglichung/Gegenständlichkeit*.]

20. Karl Groos speaks of a "feeling of freedom" that dominates play, of the appearance of "ipse feci." *Die Spiele der Menschen* [The Games of Men] (Jena: Fischer, 1899), 502.

21. Karl Bücher, *Entstehung der Volkswirtschaft: Vorträge und Aufsätze* [The Emergence of the National Economy: Essays and Lectures], vol. 1, 17th edition (Tübingen: Laupp, 1926), 29.

22. *Nichomachean Ethics* 1176b and *Politics* 1339b.

23. The burdensome character of labor is almost always considered in economic theory—it even enters into many definitions of labor, e.g., in Roscher and Alfred Weber (compare Elster, *Vom Strome der Wirtschaft* [On the Flow of the Economy]). Just as frequent, however, are the attempts of economic theory to present the burdensome character of labor as inessential to it. As supporting evidence, reference is made to those laboring techniques that allow the transformation of apathy into interesting labor, or those types of labor that seem to lack any burdensome character. Both arguments are ultimately based on a complete misunderstanding of what this burdensome character really means.

The "science of labor" has likewise fallen prey to this misunderstanding insofar as it believes that it has found here a psychological condition that could be dealt with by psychological-technological methods. The burdensome character of labor is not identical with labor characterized by apathy or by "feelings of unhappiness," "inhibitions," "appearances of fatigue" associated with specific types of labor. To be sure, these things can be abolished through changes in the structure of the labor process, through changing the conditions of labor, and the like. But the burdensome character will not be affected by their removal because it is grounded in the structure of being of human Dasein itself. The following investigation should make this clear.

24. [See the glossary entry for *ursprünglich*.]

25. This essential difference between animal activity and human labor is dealt with in the introductory considerations of Erwin Wexberg, *Arbeit und Gemeinschaft* [Labor and Community](Leipzig: Hirzel, 1932): whereas animal activities are instinctively carried out and are thereby connected with the "want inherent in the function," labor is not "man's natural function" and never takes place "instinctually" (8–9).

26. Karl Diehl, *Theoretische Nationalökonomie* [Theoretical Political Economy], vol. 1 (Jena: Fischer, 1916), 2.

27. Gustav Cassel, *Theoretische Sozialökonomie* [Theoretical Social Economy](Leipzig: Scholl, 1921), 2.

28. Elster, *Vom Strome der Wirtschaft* [On the Flow of the Economy], 153.

29. As Franz Oppenheimer does in *System der Soziologie* [System of Sociology], half-vol. 3, pt. 1 (Jena: Fischer, 1923), 18ff, following the precedent of William MacDougall.

30. Theodor Brauer, *Produktionsfaktor Arbeit: Erwägungen zur modernen Arbeitslehre* [Labor as Fact of Production: Reflections on the Modern Theory of Labor] (Jena: Fischer, 1925), 1–2 and 10.

31. *Wirtschaft und Wissenschaft* [Economics and Science], 211–12.

32. *Wirtschaft und Wissenschaft* [Economics and Science], 441, italics mine.

33. *Wirtschaft und Wissenschaft* [Economics and Science], 754, italics mine.

34. *Wirtschaft und Wissenschaft* [Economics and Science], 442.

35. *Wirtschaft und Wissenschaft* [Economics and Science], 442.

36. [See glossary entry on *Ontologie*.]

37. [See glossary entry for *Sein/Seinde* ("being"/ "be-ing").]

38. This "autonomy" of the happening of the objective world as a historical world has been worked out clearly by Gottl: "Organization . . . does not refer back exclusively to human action. Rather more preponderant than this is a self-organization of all structures. All entities and processes occurring in common life press forward toward duration and constancy. For it only falls to human action to affirm what has been; the action adapts itself to it and seeks to maintain it." And: "Conscious action comes, however, already too late in regard to organization, because the economy is now already there, it or something similar to it in its effects must be there already, simply because it is the branch upon which we sit. Therefore, where action consciously intervenes, its value

lies only in transforming or realizing a form." *Arbeit als Tatbestand des Wirtschaftslebens* [Labor as a Constituent Fact of Economic Life], 291–92.

39. [See glossary entry for *Bewegtheit*.]

40. The broadest illustration of this historicity of the world of objects has been provided by Wilhelm Dilthey under the title of "Objektivationen des Lebens" ["The Objectifications of Life," pt. 2, ch. 3, *The Formation of Historical World in the Human Sciences*] (especially in vol. 3 of his *Gesammelten Schriften* [Collected Writings]). See also Felix Krueger, "Die Arbeit des Menschen als philosophisches Problem" [The Labor of Men as a Philosophical Problem] in *Blätter für Deutsche Philosophie* 3.2 (1929): 159: "Whatever man in his development designates as reality is a function of human labor." In order to define the historicity of labor, Bücher takes recourse to Freidrich List's "principle of the continuation of labor": it is "the universal historical principle of social development through which man distinguishes himself from the animal world. An equal existence begins with each new animal. . . . But every generation of men takes over the accomplishments of the culture of all previous generations in order to enlarge it and bequeath it to those that will follow" (*Entstehung der Volkswirtschaft* [The Emergence of the National Economy], 268).

41. [See the glossary entry for *Geschichtlichkeit* ("historicity").]

42. *Das Kapital*, 136 and 144. [Marx, *Capital*, 287 and 296].

43. The meaning for the social order of the general regulation of time has been particularly emphasized by Albert E. F. Schäffle, *Bau und Leben des sozialen Körpers* [Construction and Life of the Social Body], vol. 2 (Tübingen: Laupp, 1896), 101ff.

44. See section 8 below.

45. Bücher, *Entstehung der Volkswirtschaft*, 30ff.; Eliasberg, "Arbeit und Psychologie," in *Archiv für Sozialwissenschaft und Sozialpolitik* 50 (1922): 113; Ernst Grosse, *Die Formen der Familie und die Formen der Wirtschaft* (Jena: Fischer, 1896), 38ff.; Berka Gurewitsch, *Die Entwicklung der menschlichen Bedürfnisse und die Sociale Gliederung der Gesellschaft* (Leipzig: Duncker, 1901), 37ff.

46. The split does not indicate the social subdivision of vital space and time in the sense that both spheres are attributed to different groups, classes, etc. Rather, it is every single Dasein that is split within its own totality into the two spheres of the necessary and no-longer-necessary; every individual Dasein demands a becoming and a fulfillment in both spheres and the sundering of this totality through the just mentioned economic-social appropriation is only the result of a specific form of the "division of labor." We shall come back to this in the last section.

47. "That separation of functions according to which the economy—whose laws could be known in isolation and whose intensity would rise with time—leads its own existence has shown itself to be inadequate. . . . Human labor occupies so central a position in the spiritual-ethical world that no single empirical science is alone able to describe its phenomena in their real interconnections" (Krueger, "Die Arbeit des Menschen" [The Labor of Men], 164). See also Giese, *Philosophie der Arbeit* [Philosophy of Labor], 161ff.

48. This is shown very clearly by Marx. It is useless to reject his foundation of economic theory, especially as presented in the *Economic and Philosophic Manuscripts of 1844* and in the *German Ideology*, as philosophical sins of youth that were later overcome. Such a foundation is operative throughout *Capital* and is taken up explicitly in crucial places.

49. "Every activity is an element in the specialized process of production. The activity of every man is absolutely no longer his own occupation, but is rather only given insofar as it integrates itself into the framework of the specialized society" (Emile Lederer, *Grundzüge der ökonomischen Theorie* [Fundamentals of Economic Theory] [Tübingen: Mohr, 1923], 41).

49. In his disagreement with Franz W. Jerusalem, Max Scheler does not consider the distinction between "essential" and social-economic division of labor. See *Kölner Vierteljahrshefte für Sozialwissenschaft* 1.3 (1931): 36.

50. Compare, for example, Schäffle, *Bau und Leben des sozialen Körpers* [Construction and Life of the Social Body], vol. 1, 326ff.; Schmoller, "Das Wesen der Arbeitsteilung und der sozialen Klassenbildung" [The Nature of the Division of Labor and Social Class Formation] in *Jahrbuch für Gesetzgebung, Verwaltung und Volkwirtschaft im Deutschen Reich*, 14 (1890): 49 and 83; Herkner, "Arbeit and Arbeitsteilung" [Labor and the Division of Labor], in *Grundriß der Sozialökonomik* [Outline of Social Economy], vol. 2, pt. 1 (Tübingen: Mohr, 1923), 279; Ludwig Gumplowicz, *Grundriß der Soziologie* [Outline of Sociology](Innsbruck: Wagner, 1926), 103ff.; Oppenheimer, *System der Soziologie* [System of Sociology], vol. 1, pt. 1, 307–8 and 174ff.

51. "The coupling of the economic zone with labor leads to an ontological distortion" (Giese, *Philosophie der Arbeit* [Philosophy of Labor], 293).

52. Spending time in the truly "fulfilling" dimension beyond material production and reproduction is now for the laborer limited to a small "rest period": evenings, Sundays, etc. Through this suppression and degradation of the decisive happening of life to mere "free time," all that is accomplished is that this "rest period" is reified as well. Compare here Giese, *Philosophie der Arbeit* [Philosophy of Labor], 183–84.

53. *Das Kapital*, vol. 3, ed. Karl Kautsky (Berlin: Dietz, 1929), 316. [Karl Marx, *Capital*, vol. 3, in *The Marx-Engels Reader*], 441 (translation modified).]

6. German Philosophy, 1871–1933

1. [This Latin term was popularized by the eminent German physiologist Emil Du Bois-Reymond (1881–1896), who used it in a pathbreaking paper in delivered in August 1872 at an important annual conference for doctors and natural scientists in Leipzig. Du Bois-Reymond introduced the term in order to criticize the metaphysical materialism that dominated science and philosophy at the time, as represented by Ludwig Büchner, Karl Vogt, and Ernst Haeckel. Du Bois-Reymond argued against them that certain key phenomena, such as consciousness and desire, and problems, such as the relationship between matter and energy, could not be explained in exclusively physiological terms. He insisted that scientists recognize not only the limitations of the their current understanding of nature ("Ignoramus"), but also the fundamental limitations of scientific

knowledge ("Ignorabimus") in certain areas. Marcuse uses the term here to stress the limitations of positivist models in the social sciences.]

2. [The meaning of this neologism, which we have left untranslated, is not entirely clear. With the phrase, "the *ontonomie* of the physical sciences," Marcuse seems to be implying the absolute supremacy of the categories of the natural sciences, which the neo-Kantians were the first to question, if only in a modest way, by reintroducing philosophy as an independent discipline. See also his usage of the neologism "ontochronie" in his explication of Heidegger's philosophy below.

3. [*Die transszendentale und die pyschologie Methode* is the title of the *Habilitationsschrift* Scheler wrote under Eucken.]

4. ["Terrestre" is the French substantive form of the English adjective "terrestrial." We have been unable to determine the source of Marcuse's conceptual use of the term here.]

Glossary

1. See Herbert Marcuse, *Hegel's Ontology and the Theory of Historicity*, 335.

2. For Heidegger's polemic against Descartes' understanding of space, and his attempt to develop an alternative, see *Being and Time*, 114–48.

3. *Being and Time*, 473–74. Heidegger's concept of *Jetzt-Zeit* should not be confused with Walter Benjamin's concept of the same name. For a discussion of the differences, see Peter Osborne, *The Politics of Time: Modernity and Avant-garde* (London: Verso, 1995), 64.

4. See, for example, *History and Class Consciousness*, where Georg Lukács writes, "time sheds its qualitative, variable, flowing nature; it freezes into an exactly delimited, quantifiable continuum filled with quantifiable 'things' . . . : in short, it becomes space. In this environment where time is transformed into abstract, exactly measurable, physical space . . . the subjects of labor must likewise be rationally fragmented" (90). As he makes clear in several different places in these essays, Marcuse was familiar with *History and Class Consciousness*; however, he was critical of the vanguardist implications of Lukács's concept of "class consciousness" and believed that Heidegger's existential analytic of Dasein and his analysis of historicity more successfully addressed the central role of the concrete individual in the process of socio-historical change. For a comparison of Marcuse's attitudes toward Lukács and Heidegger during this time, see John Abromeit, "Herbert Marcuse's Critical Encounter with Martin Heidegger, 1927–33," 131–51.

5. See, for example, *Being and Time*, 86–90.

6. "On the Problem of the Dialectic," 64.

7. "On the Problem of the Dialectic," 58.

8. "Contributions to a Phenomenology of Historical Materialism," 9.

9. As Marcuse puts it, "As soon as *cognition* is defined as Life, history follows; as soon as Life is defined as *cognition*, however, historicity is pushed away from the history of Life. The truth of Life is then defined in relation to an absolute and thereby *un*historical mode of knowledge." *Hegel's Ontology and the Theory of Historicity*, 227. See also 153–70, 219–27, and 305–18.

10. Quoted by Marcuse in "New Sources on the Foundation of Historical Materialism," 87.

11. "Contributions to a Phenomenology of Historical Materialism," 1.

12. *Being and Time*, 427 (translation modified).

13. These passages are from a series of lectures Heidegger gave in Kassel, Germany, from April 16–18, 1925, entitled "Wilhelm Diltheys Forschungsarbeit und der gegenwärtige Kampf um eine historische Weltanschauung" [Wilhelm Dilthey's Research and the Present Struggle for a Historical Worldview]. When Heidegger gave these lectures he was working intensely on *Being and Time*; thus it is not surprising that they addressed many of the central concepts of *Being and Time*—such as the problems of *Geschichte*, *Geschehen*, and *Geschichtlichkeit*. These lectures have been published in the *Dilthey-Jahrbuch für Philosophie und Geschichte der Geisteswissenschaften* 8, ed. Frithjof Rudi (1993): 143–80. The passage quoted here is on page 174.

14. *Dilthey-Jahrbuch*, 174. For another example of Heidegger's attempt to demonstrate the derivative character of "Historie" see section 76 of *Being and Time*, "The Existential Source of *Historie* in Dasein's Historicity," 444–49 (translation modified).

15. *Being and Time*, 427 (translation modified).

16. For a discussion of the importance and of the concept of historicity with the larger scheme of *Being and Time* and its political implications, see Johannes Fritsche, *Historical Destiny and National Socialism in Heidegger's Being and Time* (Berkeley and Los Angeles: University of California Press, 1999).

17. For a discussion of the anthropological underpinnings of Marcuse's early and later work, see Stephan Bundschuh, "The Theoretical Place of Utopia: Some Remarks on Herbert Marcuse's Dual Anthropology," in *Herbert Marcuse: A Critical Reader*, 152–62.

18. For example, in his review of the *Habilitationsschrift* (a second dissertation) that Marcuse wrote under Heidegger's guidance, *Hegel's Ontology*, Theodor Adorno asked "why indeed should the 'ontological' question precede that of the interpretation of real, historical facts, since Marcuse himself would like to bridge the gap between ontology and facticity?" *Zeitschrift für Sozialforschung* 1 (1932): 410.

19. Robert Pippin has recognized that Marcuse is working with a nonconventional definition of ontology in his early writings; not, however, one that is without precedence in the philosophical tradition. Pippin points out that prior to modern times, in addition to the common understanding of ontology as the investigation of being qua being, there also existed a lesser known ontological tradition that sought to determine the basis of beings, the ultimate source on which being depended. Heidegger's and Marcuse's conception of ontology is more closely related to the latter than the former tradition. See "Marcuse on Hegel and Historicity," *The Philosophical Forum*, 16.3 (1985): 181–82.

20. On this point, see the introduction as well as the entries for "historicity" and "motility."

21. In this respect Heidegger moves decisively beyond the ahistorical epistemologies of neo-Kantians, such as Hermann Cohen's, or Husserl's early attempts to place philosophy on unshakeable, ahistorical logical foundations. Heidegger appreciates Kant's attempts

to inquire into the subjective dimensions of time, but he believes that Kant ultimately remained beholden to the inauthentic, Cartesian concept of abstract time, which he traced back to Aristotle. See, for example, *Being and Time*, 45.

22. See "On the Problem of the Dialectic," 67.

23. After 1933, Marcuse would realize that this was a mistake. As Adorno correctly recognized at the time, even before he broke with Heidegger in 1933 Marcuse was beginning to see concrete history rather than ontological "historicity" as the basis of his critical theory. See Adorno's review of *Hegel's Ontology* in *Zeitschrift für Sozialforschung*. For an analysis of the irreconcilable contradiction between Heideggerian historicity and Marx's understanding of history in Marcuse's writings during this time, see also Alfred Schmidt, "Existential-Ontologie und historischer Materialismus bei Herbert Marcuse," in Herbert Marcuse, *Existentialistische Marx-Interpretation* (Frankfurt: Europäische Verlagsanstalt, 1973), 111–42.

24. See the introduction to *Being and Time*, 21–64.

25. See, for example, "On the Problem of the Dialectic," 58ff.

26. "On the Philosophical Foundations of the Concept of Labor in Economics," 126–27.

27. Jürgen Habermas has defended the former interpretation most energetically. See, for example, *The Philosophical Discourse of Modernity*, trans. Frederick Lawrence (Cambridge MA: MIT Press), 75–82. Clearly displaying his penchant for hyberbole, Theodor Adorno made the latter statement in an interview near the end of his life. See Martin Jay, *The Dialectical Imagination: A History of the Frankfurt School and the Institute of Social Research, 1923–1950* (Boston: Little, Brown, 1973), 57.

Publication History

"Contributions to a Phenomenology of Historical Materialism" was first published in Germany as "Beiträge zu einer Phänomenologie des historischen Materialismus" in *Philosophische Hefte* 1 (1928): 45–68 and was subsequently republished in Marcuse's *Schriften* 1 (Frankfurt: Suhrkamp, 1978), 347–84. It first appeared in English in *Telos* 4 (1969): 3–34. It has been newly translated here by Eric Oberle.

"On Concrete Philosophy" originally appeared as "Über konkrete Philosophie" in *Archiv für Sozialwissenschaft und Sozialpolitik* 62 (1929): 111–20. It was subsequently republished in the *Schriften*, 385–406. It appears here in English for the first time in a translation by Matthew Erlin.

"On the Problem of the Dialectic" originally appeared as "Zum Problem der Dialektik." Part 1 was published in *Die Gesellschaft* 7 (1930): 15–30 and part 2 was published in *Die Gesellschaft* 8 (1931): 541–57. *Die Gesellschaft* was the main theoretical organ of the German Social Democratic Party (SPD) at the time and was edited by Rudolf Hilferding. The essay was subsequently republished in the *Schriften*, 423–44. It was first published in English translation (part 1 was translated by Morton Schoolman and part 2 by Duncan Smith) in *Telos* 27 (1976): 12–39. It has been retranslated here by John Abromeit.

"New Sources on the Foundation of Historical Materialism" was first published as "Neue Quellen zur Grundlegen des Historischen Materialismus" in *Die Gesellschaft* 9 (1932): 136–74 and was subsequently republished in the *Schriften*, 509–55. It was first published in English in a translation by Joris de Bres in *Studies in Critical Philosophy* (London: New Left Review Books, 1972), 1–48. De Bres's translation has been lightly revised by John Abromeit here to render it terminologically consistent with the other essays in the volume.

"On the Philosophical Foundations of the Concept of Labor in Economics" was first published as "Über die philosophischen Grundlagen des wirtschaftswissenschaftlichen Begriff der Arbeit" in *Archiv für Sozialwissenschaften und Sozialpolitik* 69 (1933): 257–92 and was republished in the *Schriften*, 556–94. It was first published in English, translated by Douglas Kellner, in *Telos* 16 (1973): 9–37. It has been retranslated here by John Abromeit.

Marcuse wrote one version of "German Philosophy, 1871–1933" ("Deutsche Philosophie im zwanzigsten Jahrhundert") in French in 1934 when he was living in Geneva, Switzerland, just prior to his joining the Institute for Social Research and departing for the United States in June 1934. It has never been published before in any language; the manuscript is located in the Marcuse Archives in Frankfurt, catalogue number 0030.01. Ron Haas has translated the text from French into English here.

"Heidegger's Politics: An Interview" first appeared in *Graduate Faculty Philosophy Journal* 6.1 (1977):28–40; the interview was conducted in English by Frederick A. Olafson, and it is reprinted here in its original form.

"Postscript: My Disillusionment with Heidegger" was first published as "Enttäuschung" in *Erinnerung an Martin Heidegger*, ed. Günther Neske (Pfullingen: Neske, 1977), 162. It has been translated into English here for the first time by Richard Wolin.

Index

CPSIA information can be obtained
at www.ICGtesting.com
Printed in the USA
LVHW041706300819
629534LV00002B/130/P